To Japan With Love

A Travel Guide for the Connoisseur

To Japan With Love
Edited & with contributions by Celeste Heiter
Photography by Robert George

To Asia With Love series created by Kim Fay
Cover and book design by Janet McKelpin/Dayspring Technologies, Inc.
Editing assistance provided by Robert Tompkins
Book production by Paul Tomanpos, Jr.

For information regarding permissions, write to:
ThingsAsian Press
3230 Scott Street
San Francisco, California 94123 USA
www.thingsasian.com
Printed in Singapore

ISBN-13: 978-1-934159-05-7
ISBN-10: 1-934159-05-0

Table of Contents

Introduction

Imagine that on the eve of your upcoming trip to Japan, you are invited to a party. At this party are dozens of guests, all of whom live in or have traveled extensively through the country. Among this eclectic and well-versed group of connoisseurs are contributors to acclaimed travel guides, popular newspaper writers, veteran gourmets, and pioneering adventurers. As the evening passes, they tell you tales from their lives in these exotic places. They whisper the names of their favorite shops and restaurants; they divulge the secret hideaways where they sneak off to for an afternoon or a weekend to unwind. Some make you laugh out loud, and others seduce you with their poetry. Some are intent on educating, while others just want to entertain. Their recommendations are as unique as their personalities, but they are united in one thing ... their love of Japan. If you can envision being welcomed at such a party, then you can envision the experience that *To Japan With Love* aspires to give you.

Kim Fay
Series Editor, *To Asia With Love*

Men bathing at Tokyo's Teppozu Inari Jinja shrine in mid-January

Japan is a nation in love with itself. It is a deep, abiding love that permeates its people to the very marrow, and holds reverent every aspect of its culture, from the lowliest yam to the pinnacle of Mt. Fuji. Japan is a nation so steeped in history, religion, and mythology that they are inextricably bound to every breath. And for reasons I cannot explain, Japan has always beckoned to me.

There is no logical explanation for why a girl who grew up in Mobile, Alabama, should have a near obsession for Japanese culture, unless I was Japanese in another lifetime. If there is anything even remotely Japanese within my sphere of perception, I am immediately drawn to it. As a child, I always gravitated toward the Japan entries in the encyclopedia. At five years old, I first saw a picture of the Daibutsu, the great statue of Buddha that stands in the city of Kamakura, and even at that young age, I had a feeling that someday I would go to Kamakura to see that great statue ... And one day, I did.

Even with full access to every word in the English language, Japan defies description. The beauty, the mystery, the irony: Subway trains so crowded at rush hour that people-pushers have to pack the passengers in ... Rare mushrooms and hothouse watermelons that cost more than one hundred dollars each ... A crime rate so low that policemen spend much of their time giving directions to lost tourists ... Ordinary women walking around the city streets in elaborate silk kimono ... Ancient temples and brilliant green rice paddies adjacent to modern office buildings ... Thriving family-owned businesses founded more than a thousand years ago ... Whale, horsemeat, and live fish served raw in neighborhood restaurants ... An ancient volcano that dominates every landscape for hundreds of miles ... A tectonic geology that causes thousands of earthquakes each year ... Cities so laden with smog that you can't see the stars at night ... Landscapes so beautiful that they leave you breathless ...

The time I spent living and working in Japan was the best two years of my life, not only because of the beauty of the Japanese landscape, the deep heritage of the Japanese culture, and the endearing nature of the Japanese people, but also because of the life-changing souvenir that I brought home with me: my son Will, who was born at Seibo Byoin in the Tokyo suburb of Mejiro.

Since my return to the United States, not a day goes by that I don't long to wake up in Japan, to see the flutter of cherry blossoms on the April breeze, to feel the resonant hum of humanity in downtown Tokyo, to taste the salty tang of *shoyu* and seaweed, to hear the dulcet melody of "Kimigayo"—the country's national anthem—amid the autumn foliage, or to catch a glimpse of Mt. Fuji at some unexpected turn.

Until I return, I have been given the gift of vicarious living through the words of my contributors to this book, to whom I am most grateful for their devotion of time and creativity. In the process, I have made many new friends who share my love for Japan, and I have called upon some cherished friends, and even my son, to share their memories as well. In this cultural mosaic, more than sixty writers have lovingly captured the beauty, the mystery, and the irony that is Japan. I hope their stories inspire you to go and see for yourself. To go to Japan with love.

Celeste Heiter
Editor, *To Japan With Love*

How This Book Works

A good traveler has no fixed plans, and is not intent on arriving.
~Lao Tzu

To Japan With Love is a unique guidebook with chapters organized by theme as opposed to destination. This is because it focuses foremost on the sharing of personal experiences, allowing each place to serve as the colorful canvas on which our writers overlay vivid, individual impressions. Within each themed chapter you will find the recommendations grouped by regions and then cities within each region. Geographically, the essays begin where most travelers start their journeys, in Tokyo and Central Honshu Island. From here the essays cover Southern Honshu Island (including Kyoto, Osaka, and Hiroshima) and then Northern Honshu Island, before moving south to Shikoku Island and Kyushu Island. Finally, chapters conclude in the farthest north, on Hokkaido Island.

Each recommendation consists of two parts: a personal essay and a fact file. Together, they are intended to inspire and inform. The essay tells a story while the fact file gives addresses, phone numbers, and other serviceable information. Because each contribution can stand alone, the book does not need to be read in order. As with an old-fashioned miscellany, you may open to any page and start reading. Thus every encounter with the book is turned into its own distinctive armchair journey.

To facilitate locating the recommendations in the essays, the index is organized by place. As well, additional information and updates can be found online at WWW.TOASIAWITHLOVE.COM/JAPAN. Keep in mind that *To Japan With Love* is selective and does not include all of the practical information you will need for daily travel. Instead, reading it is like having a conversation with a friend who just returned from a trip. You should supplement that friend's stories with a comprehensive guidebook, such as Lonely Planet or Frommer's.

Confucius said, "A journey of a thousand miles begins with a single step." We hope that this guide helps you put your best foot forward.

Key Terms and Important Information

Addresses: Addresses in Japan can be complicated. A written address might include the neighborhood, district, and other information, much of which can be identified with Japanese suffixes. If you have an address written down, you can take it to one of the police kiosks that are on the sidewalks every few blocks in metropolitan districts. Japanese cities are safe, so the police don't have much to do. The friendly officers will do their best to explain how to get to your destination.

Gaijin: Foreigner

Geography: Japan is comprised of four main islands—Honshu (home to Tokyo, Kyoto, and Osaka), Shikoku and Kyushu to the south, and Hokkaido to the north. Within each island are prefectures, which are similar to American states.

Metric system: Although we are an American publisher, we have used the metric system for all measurements. For easy conversion, go to www.metric-conversions.org.

Paying it Forward: Other volumes in the To Asia With Love guidebook series contain a chapter entitled "Paying it Forward," with essays about charities. Because Japan does not have the rampant level of poverty and homelessness that afflicts other

Asian countries, we were unable to gather essays on this topic, and the chapter has not been included in this book.

Phone numbers: We have provided phone numbers in the format you would use when making a call within Japan—for example: (01) 234-5678. The area/city code is in parentheses. To call a number from outside the country, drop the 0 at the beginning and add the country code, 81—for example: (81) 1-234-5678.

Shinkansen: Japan's high-speed "bullet train" system.

Suffixes: Many Japanese words use suffixes to define their meaning. Knowing these suffixes can be helpful when traveling. Among the most important are *tori*, *dori*, and *bori*, all of which indicate a street. For example, Kami-tori and Shinjuku Dori are Kami Street and Shinjuku Street. The suffix *ku* indicates a district; Shibuya-ku means Shibuya District. The suffixes *ji* and *in* indicate a Buddhist place of worship. For example, Engaku-ji is Engaku Temple, Zuigaku-in is a Buddhist Monastery, and Jakko-in is an ancient nunnery.

Yen: The yen is the currency of Japan. At the time of writing, the exchange rate fluctuated between ¥90 and ¥110 to the US dollar. We have used an average exchange rate of ¥100 for $1.

INTRODUCTION

Pleasure boats moored in a canal near Tokyo's Sumida River

Autumn in a park in Shinjuku District in Tokyo

Moveable Feasts

A tasting menu of exotic flavors

Food, glorious food! Nowhere on earth is it more alluring and attractively presented than in Japan. The spectrum of food experiences awaiting you runs the gamut from simple *bento* boxes of vinegared rice and pickled vegetables for sale on train station platforms, to swimmingly fresh sushi served at crowded counters on the fringes of Tsukiji Fish Market; from roasted yams wheeled through neighborhood streets in aromatic braziers, to seasonal *kaiseki* served in the elite elegance of Kyoto teahouses; from department store basements with bewildering arrays of food samples, to restaurant display windows filled with trompe l'oeil dishes that look almost as tasty as the real thing!

Sampling the local cuisine often provides the best travel experiences, and when it comes to trying the new and unusual, Japan offers a whole new world of opportunities. I had my favorite haunts when I lived in Tokyo, and the contributors to this chapter also did their share of exploring. In their essays, they generously reveal their discoveries.

Many focus on Japan's classic dishes. Alice Yamada takes you to a tempura bar, where she savors this crispy delight one bite at a time. With a passion for sensory detail, Helen Yee compares two irresistible places for golden *tonkatsu*, and Jacqueline Taylor's curiosity leads her to the joy of *okonomiyaki*, Osaka's tastiest dish. Like the characters in the must-see film *Tampopo*, both Steve Cooper and Nick Hall embark on quests for the perfect bowl of *ramen*. My own favorite find was Ganbi, a tiny restaurant on a narrow side street around the corner from my apartment. One taste of chef Ka-chan's tempura, and I became a Ganbi regular.

No culinary odyssey in Japan is complete without an evening spent in the convivial atmosphere of an *izakaya*, the Japanese version of a pub. Way out in Oji, Horanda was the first place I went for snacks and beer in Japan, and after many months of

Grilled chicken skewers in Tokyo's Ueno District

living in the city, it was still worth taking three trains to go out there for dinner. And Irohanihoheto, a fourth-floor *tatami*-mat pub overlooking Shinjuku Station, still offers a tasty menu of classic snacks. *Izakaya* are ubiquitous, so wherever you are, there is probably one nearby.

In one of the world's most expensive countries, a tight travel budget doesn't mean you have to forego its gastronomic pleasures. There was a *gyoza* place in Shinjuku where I could sit at the bar on polished sawn tree trunks and enjoy half a dozen of the best pot-stickers with chili dipping oil for about three dollars. And at the west exit of Ikebukuro Station, I discovered Komazushi, a sure bet for a quick bite of sushi that wouldn't bankrupt me for rest of the week. My friend Robert George, who lived in Tokyo for eighteen years, knows what it costs to dine at its famous restaurants, and offers a budget approach to the city's finest fare. If you can't afford to splurge on lavish meals, two of our writers introduce you to their secret indulgences. Renée Suen reveals the country's cult of the pastry, while Merry White takes you to meet a baker in Kyoto who serves artisan breads in his own living room.

In the mood for adventure? Follow Cobus van Staden all the way to Tsuki no Niwa for an out-of-this-world vegetarian feast. Or stare death in the face with Billy Applebaum as he braves the potentially deadly *fugu*. For the ultimate act of culinary bravado, join Helen Yee for the *natto* breakfast set. And if you still crave more, sample our Small Bites section for a few extra morsels.

Tokyo Prefecture

Helen Yee feasts on crispy, golden pork cutlets in Tokyo

I love fried food. What's not to love? Golden, easy to hold, and each bite accompanied by a shattering crunch.

Tonkatsu is perhaps the grandest celebration of deep-fried goodness in Japan. This pork filet, coated in spiky *panko* crumbs, demands center stage, and rightly so. It is not just finger food. It is a golden spectacular.

When craving *tonkatsu*, I make it my mission to take in two distinctive restaurant "performances." The first is at the smile-inducing Tonki, one of Tokyo's best-known pork cutlet restaurants. Queuing for dinner here is a rite of passage. Luckily, a row of chairs lines one wall; unluckily, these are generally occupied by hungry diners-in-waiting who have gotten there ahead of me. No matter though, as there's plenty to watch while I'm waiting.

The open kitchen offers a floor show that one might happily buy tickets for. Beneath the glow of four-dozen hanging lamps, a battalion of chefs can be seen, mid-attack, a flurry of arms, knives jabbing amid a soundtrack of hissing, crackling, bubbling oil. I watch one chef who is in charge of seasoning the meat, plump fresh filets of the best pork loin. The pork is bathed in a puddle of egg yolk, then patted all over with a generous coat of pale *panko* crumbs. There's another chef solely in charge of frying. He slides each piece gently into a pot of simmering oil. *Pink*! *Pock*! *Pink*! *Pock*! I smile with sadistic glee as the oil rushes up to greet its victims.

The cabbage chef does only as his title suggests: plating dish after dish, he dresses mounds of finely shredded cabbage with a drizzle of brown sauce, Worcestershire-like, but with a fruity tang. Another chef coordinates the dispatch of rice and soup. All this takes place behind a U-shaped, wooden counter made of smooth, shiny Japanese cypress, packed shoulder to shoulder with an assembly of *tonkatsu* pilgrims.

When I am finally seated, the efficiency of the kitchen means that it doesn't take long for my set meal, or *teishoku,* to arrive. Chunky slices of *tonkatsu* are surrounded by a mound of cabbage, a bowl of plain rice, miso soup, and a side of pickles. The pork is pristine white, moist and tender; the *panko* crumbs are crunchy and golden brown. The raw cabbage, thin ribbons of palate-cleansing sweetness, provides respite from the deep-fried excess. The miso soup clears my throat, and the acidity of the pickles refreshes my tongue. There's a boisterous mood in the air, the chefs verge upon rowdy, and the show is nonstop.

Maisen, my other *tonkatsu* favorite, has a completely different atmosphere. It is an oasis of quiet, bordering on austerity, in its former bathhouse location not far from the designer boutiques of Omotesando, a chic, tree-lined shopping boulevard. Maisen has the seriousness of an embassy, with parking valets and an imposing doorman guarding the entrance. Inside, ceiling fans turn overhead in lazy circles. There's an expectant hum from the dressed-up diners, and as I trail a perfumed beauty striding lithely on elegant heels, I feel a tad shabby in my jeans and rumpled T-shirt.

All discomfort is forgotten though, once my *tonkatsu* is served. I've chosen the *rosukatsu*, the extra fatty version. The crumb-coated pork cutlet is luscious and decadent, reclining seductively on a raised wire platform that resembles a stage. The flesh is succulent; the batter is heavenly. It's the Marilyn Monroe of *tonkatsu* ... hips are *goooood.*

A lacquered tray on the table holds an array of condiments. I lift the wooden lids to reveal three types of *tonkatsu* sauce, all varying in spiciness and sweetness. A pot of mustard packs a punch, alongside dry flakes of chili, a canister of salt, and a chef's assortment of herbs and spices.

The pork seems never ending, and I think perhaps I should have opted for the leaner *hirekatsu* version. Mouthfuls of snow-white cabbage, wafer-thin, crisp and clean, bring some oil-free relief, and my mountain of cabbage shrinks to a molehill before it's quietly replenished, my waiter smiling as he also provides extra rice.

There's no floor show in this kitchen. Such noise and commotion would be a distraction, and the silence allows me to focus instead on the sophistication and style of my *tonkatsu.* I reach for another slice of pickled *daikon*, chew thoughtfully, and watch helplessly as my chopsticks dive for another piece of pork. "Delicious, delicious!" my taste buds cheer.

Tonki

1-1-2 Shimo Meguro
Meguro District
Tokyo
(03) 3491-9928

Train: Meguro Station (west exit) on the Yamanote Line.

Maisen

4-8-5 Jingumae
Shibuya District
Tokyo
(03) 3470-0071

Subway: Omotesando Station (A2 exit) on the Chiyoda, Ginza, and Hanzomon Lines.

Robert George budgets his way through lunchtime in Tokyo

It's impossible to think about Japan without thinking about food, and if you're in Tokyo, which is often ranked as the world's most expensive city, dining out means money, and spending lots of it. For those in the know, there is an alternative to squandering your entire travel budget on a good meal. It's called "The Lunchtime Special," and it means that you can enjoy dining at some great restaurants that you might only dream of trying at much higher dinner menu prices.

Head for any major Tokyo district around lunchtime, and you'll witness fierce competitive pricing to lure you into the eateries. Best of all, menus cover the gamut of Japanese cuisine, including sushi, tempura, *soba*, *udon*, *ramen*, and *tonkatsu*, as well as all types of ethnic foods, with a new wave of French and Italian places popping up all over town.

If you're in the mood for sushi in Ginza or tempura in Shinjuku, throw caution to the wind and step inside. Competition for the businessman's dollar, or in this case yen, drives the machine, and *teishoku*, or set lunches, range in price from about five to fifteen dollars. And don't worry about your language skills. You can always just point to the plastic food display out front. A set lunch often includes a cup of coffee along with the food, and another plus—no tipping.

One venue that sums up the set lunch experience is Tsunahachi in the Shinjuku District. This popular tempura restaurant opened its doors in 1924, and has since launched a slew of branches in other Tokyo districts and beyond. Although deep-fried foods may put some people off the idea of tempura, here it is excellent, fresh and light. It is also a terrific deal at around ten dollars, depending on the exchange rate.

It's hard to imagine eating in Japan without sampling sushi. The scene has changed considerably over the past twenty-five years, but good sushi is still very expensive. Fortunately, many of the old-school sushi shops now offer great bargains on their lunch menus, and there are numerous choices in Ginza, an upscale shopping district near Tokyo and Ginza Stations, just a fifteen-minute walk from the famed Tsukiji Fish Market. These restaurants can be a little hard to find, but almost any sushi shop with an economical lunch menu has to be pretty good to stay open in this area. So take a chance.

Another option would be to try one of the *kaiten-zushi* shops, which are plentiful in Tokyo and beyond. *Kaiten* means "revolving," and *zushi,* of course, is sushi. The union of these words describes the conveyor belt serving method for counter seating. The plates that the sushi is served on are variously colored, with each color indicating a different price, beginning at around a buck a plate and rising as high as four dollars.

Kaiten-zushi shops offer a more pedestrian than upscale level of sushi, but their fare is quite tasty and the price is right. Just sit at the counter and grab a plate as it passes by. There is usually a sushi map on the wall with photos of the types of fish, labeled in both English and Japanese. If you can't find it on the conveyor belt, ask the sushi chef, and he will make it for you.

Tsunahachi

3-31-8 Shinjuku
Shinjuku District
Tokyo
(03) 3325-1012
http://210.143.110.172/

Train: Shinjuku Station on the Yamanote Line.

Directions: This restaurant is easily found east of Shinjuku Station behind Mitsukoshi department store.

Kaiten-zushi

There is a good *kaiten-zushi* on the east side of Shinjuku Station. Find the big, bright, gaudy Sakura Camera store near the main exit, *not* the south exit. Take the pedestrian walkway over Shinjuku Dori, keeping the store at your back. Turn left at the first corner, and the *kaiten-zush*i restaurant is in the basement one block farther, on your left.

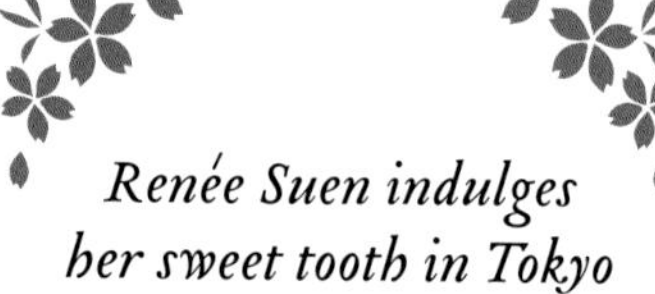

Renée Suen indulges her sweet tooth in Tokyo

Many believe that bread is the staff of life, and as a bread lover, I can't help but agree. So I was excited to discover the baked goods coming from Japanese ovens. Although Japan is relatively new to artisan breads, the superb *pan* in Japan can easily rival those of traditional France.

While traveling in Tokyo, I have noticed several locations showcasing breads and pastries of all shapes and sizes: there are several branches of Fauchon, the Parisian grocery store; the department store Seibu has a patisserie; and there are bakeries in the Anderson restaurant chain. Beautiful mixed nuts and dried fruit are blended into peasant loaves, perfect for breakfast or afternoon tea. Similarly, stellar Hokkaido milk loaves can be found at supermarkets and local bread shops. Fantastic when toasted, this melt-in-your-mouth bread is perfect to pair with a cup of English tea.

One of my favorite discoveries is the scrumptious melon bun. These round beauties reside in bake shops around town. Each palm-sized treat has a moist, fine-crumb bun base that is topped with a chewy, light, melon-scented sugar pastry. I can't recall how many of these I have eaten, but each one was divine.

Beside L'Atelier de Joël Robuchon in Tokyo's Roppongi Hills Hillside Mall is the posh restaurant's La Boutique—a patisserie and boulangerie. Patrons can purchase gorgeous *macarons*, breads, and petite cakes at the counter. I took my time to browse the shelves, noting how the colors of the desserts stood out so elegantly against their sleek, black background. Their contours and curves were so precise, each displayed as if it were a rare jewel.

I was overwhelmed by having to make a decision, and I wasn't alone, as I observed fashionable Tokyoites studying the displays before finally picking out their pastry of choice. Leaving with my own individually packaged selections, I noticed a large window facing the interior of the shopping complex, revealing busy bakers putting final touches on their creations. What a sweet temptation for passersby!

I also discovered upscale confections at La Boutique de Joël Robuchon, Ebisu. Located at the Chateau Restaurant Joël Robuchon in Yebisu Garden Place, this bakery offers delicate pastries and buns to tempt all palates. I remember being drawn into the little space by the sight of its many golden treasures piled on rustic wooden shelves. A few flaky pastries and a small baguette later, I was experiencing the ultimate carbohydrate high, wishing that every day could result in such fruitful discoveries.

For a taste of traditional flavors in the Ginza District, Kimuraya Bakery claims to be Tokyo's first Western-style bakery, founded in the 1860s. I recall walking into this packed bakery to find piles of delicious buns filled with pastes of *azuki* (red) bean, green pea, chestnut, white bean, and custard. I purchased a couple of these fluffy buns, and I even tried the *sakura*-filled version that was originally created at the request of the Emperor Meiji.

I had not tasted salted, preserved cherry blossom petals before, and I must say that I enjoyed the *azuki* bean and chestnut buns more. Cherry blossoms are one of those traditional flavors that take a little getting used to. Still, my sweet tooth was in heaven, nibbling on Kimuraya's delights, all of which were fit for an emperor.

Kimuraya Bakery

4-5-7 Ginza
Chuo District
Tokyo

Subway: Ginza Station on the Ginza Line. Ginza-Itchome and Yurakucho Stations on the Yurakucho Line.

La Boutique de Joël Robuchon, Ebisu

1-13-1 Yebisu Garden Place
Meguro District
Tokyo
(03) 5424-1345
http://robuchon.jp/ebisu/

Train: Ebisu Station on the Yamanote Line.

Subway: Ebisu Station on the Ebisu Line.

La Boutique de Joël Robuchon, Roppongi

Roppongi Hills Hillside Mall, 2F
6-10-1 Roppongi
Minato District
Tokyo
(03) 5772-7507
http://robuchon.jp/roppongi/boutique.html

Subway: Roppongi Station on the Hibiya Line.

Billy Applebaum braves deadly fugu in Tokyo

The raw fish shimmied and twitched in my chopsticks as I added it, piece by piece, to the hot stew. I felt as if I were killing it myself, which was ironic, since its slithery, still-living flesh had the power to kill me ...

It was a chilly Saturday night in December when my friends and I decided to venture out for this culinary escapade. We are foreigners living in Japan, so we try to take advantage of the cultural opportunities around us. For me, that definitely means eating things I might not find in the States.

My friends Mark and Gunter had stumbled upon Torafugu a few days earlier while exploring their new neighborhood of Shimokitazawa. They noticed a huge tank filled with ugly, beady-eyed fish staring back at them. They knew right away that this would be the spot for our next food adventure. We had heard about this scary Japanese delicacy from friends, we had read about its dangers in newspaper and magazine articles, and we had even seen it on an episode of *The Simpsons* ... now, we were about to eat one of the world's most dangerous meals: *fugu*.

Fugu is the highly toxic pufferfish, and while the meat is safe, the internal organs contain lethal amounts of the poison tetrodotoxin, which is up to twelve hundred times deadlier than cyanide. There is no known antidote, and if the poison is ingested, the victim remains fully conscious while the muscles become paralyzed, eventually causing asphyxiation.

Each year cases of *fugu* poisoning, including deaths, are reported, but many are fishermen who cook this deadly fish on their own. When prepared in a *fugu* restaurant by a trained expert, it's generally considered safe to eat. *Fugu* chefs must earn a special license to prepare and serve the fish, a rigorous process that takes many years to master.

Since two other friends had decided to join us at Torafugu, we were seated in a semi-private room, probably a good thing since we were a group of rowdy foreigners. Our waitress was a young Japanese woman who didn't speak English very well, but she was extremely patient with our horrible Japanese. She helped us decide on a multi-course meal that featured a classic array of *fugu* presentations.

I had been told that if the flesh of the fish is cut too close to the poisonous organs, I might experience a slight numbness on my lips and tongue. Fortunately for us, our *fugu* chef steered clear of the toxins. Dinner began with a small appetizer of *fugu* skin topped with green onions. The skin was virtually flavorless and a bit gummy, but nonetheless, an interesting way to start the meal. Next, the sashimi course arrived, beautifully arranged in a circle, with translucent slices so thin that we could see right through them to the plate. The *fugu* sashimi was very mild, with a much more pleasing consistency than the skin. Then came the crispy bits of fried *fugu*. If this tasty treat ever went mainstream, I could imagine it being called Fugu McNuggets.

When it was time for the main course, it included the fish that was still wriggling—a novel experience for all of us. This swimmingly fresh *fugu* was accompanied by onions, peppers, cabbage, and mushrooms, for a cook-it-yourself *nabe*, a hot pot stew steeped in a light, warming broth that was perfect for the cold winter night. When we had finished retrieving every bite of fish and vegetables from the stew pot, the waitress mixed an egg and some rice into the remaining broth and served us each a hearty portion. All the elements came together to produce a sweet aroma and a delicious flavor.

Not included in the multi-course meal was a drink called *fugu hire-zake*. My friend Gunter joined me in ordering a cup of this hot sake with *fugu* fins. The brew had a strong, fishy smell, and a slightly sour taste from the infusion of the fins, but it was an amazing experience nonetheless. We actually felt a rush of energy and a tingling sensation throughout our bodies. Red Bull's got nothing on *fugu hire-zake*.

Our meal ended as the waitress brought a round of ice cream to the table. We all wondered what *fugu* ice cream would taste like, and remarkably it tasted like ... vanilla. Sadly, there was no *fugu* in it.

Having braved the full *fugu* experience and lived to tell, I've come to the conclusion that *fugu* is a fish to be eaten more for the thrill than for the flavor. And like me, anyone with the courage to try it will have an unforgettable "near-death" culinary experience to talk about for years to come.

Torafugu

King Building, 1F
5-6 Maruyama-cho
Shibuya District
Tokyo
(03) 3462-7929
www.torafugu.co.jp (Japanese)

Train: Shibuya Station on the Yamanote Line.

The high cost of risking your life

While very good, our multiple course dinner came with few frills, and for that reason it was considered "cheap," even though it was about ¥6,500 (around $65) per person. In general, *fugu* is an expensive meal, with average prices starting around ¥10,000 (around $100).

Chiba Prefecture

Robert Carmack savors the emperor's soy sauce outside Tokyo

I have heard the Japanese say that *shoyu* is the undisputed emperor of the kitchen. This aphorism especially rules in Noda, a surprisingly charming industrial town located about thirty-two kilometers northeast of Tokyo, and home to the monolithic purveyor of soy sauce, the Kikkoman Corporation.

As a foodie, cookbook author, and leader of food tours and tastings around the world, I am as fascinated by an ingredient as I am by a recipe. When it comes to specialty products such as *shoyu* (Japanese soy sauce), my motto is, "Small is good; boutique is best." I strive to find foodstuffs of limited production ... and too often, stratospheric prices to match! So, when I was invited to visit the small, artisan facility where Kikkoman produces *shoyu* exclusively for the Imperial Household, I jumped at the chance.

Granted, Kikkoman is the world's largest soy sauce producer, but I don't hold that against it. After all, it was formed by a group of traditional, family-owned soy sauce companies in 1917. Who better to maintain the time-honored tradition of classic *shoyu* production, and to ensure that twenty-first century advancements don't take the condiment too far from its original formula?

Back in the seventeenth century, the city of Noda sprang to fame producing a unique *tamari-shoyu* sauce blended with fermented mash. Concurrently, in the small coastal town of Choshi (about an hour's journey east of Tokyo), locals experimented with the addition of roasted wheat. Through the merging of these independent discoveries, Japanese soy sauce evolved to its present state.

The traditional production of imperial *shoyu* takes place in an area of Kikkoman known as Goyogura—*goyo* means "official purveyor" and *gura* translates as "brewery" or "warehouse." Here, segregated from the industrialized buildings that churn out the ubiquitous brew known as soy sauce in the West, Goyogura looks more like a feudal castle than a manufacturing facility. More importantly, this is where the apotheosis of Japanese *shoyu* springs forth.

Goyogura offers an idyllic setting, surrounded by a moat, complete with swans, and a small arched bridge that leads to the entrance. To call it a "factory" is a disservice. From the time I entered this "temple of *shoyu*," I was in awe. Uniquely monochrome from afar, the white building and its gray roof and trim tones began to subtly change once I passed over a moat and into a garden of gravel that had been carefully raked to resemble waves.

Inside the walled compound, the interior of Goyogura is shockingly orange, symbolizing the shogunate—but for a reason: to differentiate between the common and the imperial. Vermillion (*shu*) was used in the early nineteenth century to distinguish the soy sauce made for the shogun from the soy sauce made for commoners. When Kikkoman built Goyogura, the practice was continued. From walls to vats, and even implements, *shu* is the prevailing color. Equally traditional are the workers. Garbed in loincloths and *happi* coats, they tend the huge vats, working to age-old specifications using huge paddles to stir the heady brew.

Unfortunately for the average tourist, Goyogura is not open to the public; entry is by invitation only, and the fact that the facilities are tucked behind a modern bottling plant makes even a glimpse nearly impossible. I consider myself privileged. It is possible, however, for visitors to take a tour of Kikkoman's main factory, as well as purchase Goyogura *shoyu* in the gift shop.

Kikkoman Factory

Along with tours, the factory also houses a soy sauce museum. The factory and local institute of history (below) make a nice day trip from Tokyo.

110 Noda
Noda
(0471) 23-5136

Kamihanawa Institute of History

There are other sites in Noda which are, not surprisingly, focused on either soy sauce production or the Mogi and Takanashi families. Once rivals, they eventually co-founded Kikkoman. I especially love the ancestral home of the Takanashi family, now run as the Kamihanawa Institute of History. Here, one can trace the history of the region, see original implements used to make soy sauce over the centuries, and view an early wooden mural detailing the production and sale of this famous brew. Nearby are the tranquil parklands of Shimizu, perfect for a contemplative bag lunch.

507 Kamihanawa
Noda
(0471) 22-2070

Directions: To reach the institute from Tokyo Station, take the Keihin Tohoku Line to Omiya Station. Transfer to the Tobu Noda Line and get off at Nodashi Station. From there, it is a fifteen-minute walk.

Defining shoyu

What makes Japanese *shoyu* distinct from its Asian cousins is the amount of wheat it contains. Typically, the wheat-soy ratio in Japanese soy sauce is around half and half, versus other countries' brews that are barely 10 percent wheat. Overseas, we tend to get a limited range of commercial sauces, but in Japan, myriad types are available.

Japanese soy sauce/shoyu varieties

Amakuchi: Sweetened soy sauce flavored with licorice, popular on the southern islands of Kyushu and Okinawa.

Gen-en: Low sodium.

Koikuchi: The ubiquitous soy sauce of Japan.

Marudaizu: Made from whole soybeans.

Saishikomi: Twice brewed, meaning distilled with previously brewed soy sauce instead of water.

Shiro Shoyu: White *shoyu*, made mostly of wheat, with little soy.

Tamari: Made mostly of soy, with little wheat.

Usukuchi: Lighter colored, saltier soy sauce, especially popular in Osaka and the surrounding Kansai region.

Yuki: Organic soy sauce

Food tours of Japan

To find out about Robert's next food tour of Japan (which may even include a visit to Goyogura), visit his websites.

www.globetrottinggourmet.com
www.asianfoodtours.com

Toyama Prefecture

Steve Cooper revels in ramen in Toyama

One of the best food movies I have ever seen is *Tampopo*, in which a widow, who has inherited her husband's *ramen* shop, sets off on a quest for the perfect *ramen* recipe. After two focused trips to Japan, no fewer than twenty-five bowls of *ramen*, a serious discussion on the philosophy of this dish with my friend Taro, and another viewing of *Tampopo*, I was finally ready to embark on my own *ramen* quest in Toyama. When it comes to food there are no half measures with the people of Toyama. For them, *ramen* is a religious experience, so I had to be prepared.

Marutakaya, the *ramen* shop that Taro and his father chose for my initiation, is located in the center of Toyama. This family establishment is run by the grandson of its founder, a young cook with an intimidating beard and uniform. The grandfather originally started his business as an *oden* stall outside the train station, but his *ramen* soup with noodles became his most popular dish. So he set up shop with his son, and the family has since specialized in *ramen*. Unlike the Tokyo places that I have been to, Marutakaya serves only one type of *ramen*: pork.

Upon entering, we were immediately welcomed with a round of "*Irasshaimase*!" from the staff. The place was surprisingly busy for a Sunday afternoon, which boded well. For appetizers, we ordered pork *kushi* (pork on a skewer) with a sweet sauce, and a side of English mustard—a house specialty. For beverages, we had *wari*, a cocktail made with *shochu* and red wine. Then came the *ramen*.

It arrived piping hot in generously sized bowls, and since I still hadn't developed a true understanding of the condiments for *ramen*, I followed the family's lead in adding a small spoonful of grated garlic and crushed tempura. The first spoonful was a revelation: this was the first time I had ever noticed the soup itself in a bowl of *ramen*. It was a light broth with a thick layer of clear fat on top—incredibly tasty. The noodles were yellow and curled, as compared to the straighter noodles I'd eaten in Tokyo. The entire experience was something to savor. Only when you have tasted the flavor of a truly good soup, or "the heart," as Taro's dad calls it, can you really begin comparing *ramen*.

I knocked my water back at one point, and something occurred that had never happened to me in Japan. The chef noticed that my glass was empty, and called for the waitress to refill it. This is what I like to call the *Tampopo* effect. In the movie, the widow learns that the secret to a successful restaurant isn't just the quality of the food, but also the attentiveness of the service. In Marutakaya, the chef was aware of each of his customers, anticipating their needs and reading their reactions at all times.

As a foreign tourist, I stood out, and therefore it was acceptable for us to talk to the chef, an act of bravery that the locals wouldn't dare. Taro explained to him that I had eaten *ramen* at many places in Tokyo, but this was by far the best. He thanked me, and at that point, we asked him the question that was foremost in our minds. What was the stock made of? Normally one would never ask this question, but given that I was a visitor, the chef obliged my ignorance and revealed that it was pork with a little bit of fish stock. While I'm certain that this was not the only thing that made his *ramen* special, I was grateful to know even a small part of the secret to the best *ramen* I had ever eaten.

Marutakaya

1-9-59 Shinjo
Toyama
(076) 442-6800
www.marutakaya.co.jp/ (Japanese)

Tampopo

To read a review of the movie *Tampopo*, go to page 244.

Aichi Prefecture

Alice Yamada eats unagi on memory lane in Nagoya

When you grow up eating something, you don't always appreciate how good it is, or what historical and cultural significance it has. For me, this summarizes my experience with the *unagi* at Horai.

Unagi is freshwater eel, and Horai is a prestigious, 160-year-old restaurant in my hometown of Nagoya, a city known for its strong and often unsophisticated flavors. Located near the Atsuta Shrine, Horai does not pretend to be a fancy-shmancy eatery. It is a classic, Nagoya-styled, Nagoya-flavored *unagi* joint, with dishes that have survived over time, and have been loved by locals for generations.

Revered as the keeper of one of the three holy relics associated with the origin of the Japanese people, the Atsuta Shrine plays an important role in Japan's Shinto religion. It is also intimately intertwined with Horai. The two places enjoy a symbiotic relationship. As pilgrims came, Horai grew, and as Horai grew, more diners stopped by the shrine. The aromas from the *unagi* grills at Horai are irresistible, offering an additional incentive to visit the shrine.

The dish most closely associated with Horai is *hitsumabushi*, which Nagoya boasts to the world. *Hitsumabushi* is a rice and *unagi* debauchery that will instill a love of eel in anyone. Assembled in a wooden container, it is made from alternating layers of rice, *unagi*, and *unagi* sauce, sort of like rice lasagna with eel filling. It is topped with a dense layer of *unagi* and served with chives, wasabi, and seaweed on the side.

Hitsumabushi has been served in this style of container for ages, and brings back so many childhood memories every time I eat it. Just thinking about it, I can feel the warmth of the wooden bowl, with its soft curves in my hands, as I look at the steaming hot rice and salty-sweet *unagi*, and inhale the smell of grilled oil, sugar, and soy sauce. For the record, no one eats *hitsumabushi* directly out of the wooden container. That would be considered scandalous! Diners are provided smaller porcelain eating bowls, which also have not changed in ages.

There are several ways to enjoy *hitsumabushi*, but many connoisseurs eat its three presentations in sequential order. First, as is. Next, topped with chives, wasabi, and *nori*. And finally, topped with chives, wasabi, and *nori*, and then soaked with *dashi* into a porridge-like state. My favorite is the last version, since I seem to gravitate toward soupy foods. Here, the richness of the *unagi* is tempered by the soup, and the combination of *dashi* and *unagi* sauce is simply delicious.

At the end of the meal, a cup of tea and a bowl of clear soup are served, and as with the *hitsumabushi*, everything about this soup—from the look of the bowls to what is in them—has not changed a bit since I was a little girl on my grandfather's lap. It really brings back my carefree childhood. I loved the yellow *yuba* (tofu-skin) roll served in the soup, and always begged everyone else at the table for theirs. My grandparents would ask that my soup be served with extra *yuba* rolls, making me feel so special when I saw that my bowl had more than one.

Although my grandparents are no longer with me, the love for food that they cultivated in me continues to grow with the passing years. And at Horai, the *hitsumabushi* allows me to travel back in time and reconnect with them in every bite.

Horai
2-10-26 Jingu
Atsuta District
Nagoya
(052) 682-5598

Atsuta Shrine
www.atsutajingu.or.jp/eng

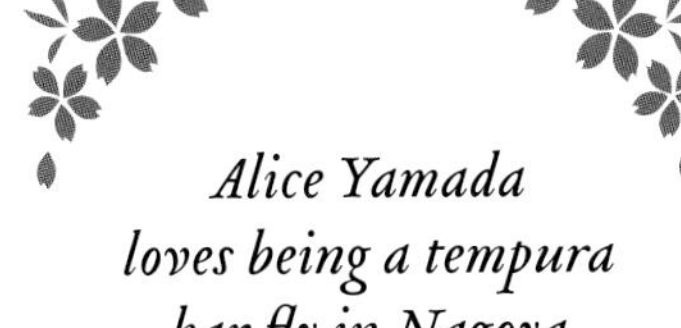

Alice Yamada loves being a tempura bar fly in Nagoya

For bar-side dining, Yaegaki is my favorite place in the world. Run by Chef Kunio-san, along with his friendly wife, it seats only about fifteen people, who all sit across the bar from him enjoying tempura one or two pieces at a time. While the style is similar to that of a sushi bar, this is even better. It is a concept I have not seen anywhere else. A tempura bar!

The tempura is fried in a secret blend of oils, a recipe Kunio-san inherited from his father-in-law, who ran the original Yaegaki, a restaurant so prestigious, rumor has it that getting a reservation required a recommendation from a regular patron. When his father-in-law retired, Kunio-san inherited both the name and the secret oil recipe, but he left the reservation restrictions behind. He built an entirely new Yaegaki, a warm and welcoming restaurant for anyone who wants to eat there.

Kunio-san's tempura is seasonal, with the menu changing depending on what he finds at the market. A typical meal consists of his special recommendations (*omakase*), and those with heartier appetites supplement the *omakase* course with à la carte items. My two favorites are shrimp wrapped in *shiso* leaf, and *anago* (saltwater eel). *Anago* is similar to the more commonly known freshwater eel, *unagi*, but it is meatier and less greasy. I prefer *anago* over *unagi*, but I've been told that *anago* is more difficult to prepare, and is less abundant because it is not farmed, as *unagi* is. Kunio-san's crispy batter is a perfect accompaniment to both the tender *anago* and the textured *shiso*-shrimp.

In fact, the batter complements everything Kunio-san selects, and the harmony of the crunch with the different textures inside is pure pleasure. The sweetness of an onion was brought to life by the tempura method of cooking, and the *kakiage* (mixed tempura), which can very well become a nightmare of a fried dough ball, was a delicious mesh of batter, shrimp, and greens. The squid tempura came with a *nori* belt, and the scent of the *nori* was highlighted by tempura cooking. The squid was meaty and strong, a perfect partner for the fragrant *nori*.

One of the best things about bar-side dining is the personal interaction. Wherever I eat, I have always preferred sitting at the bar over sitting at a table. The bar is where the action is. You get the best views of what the chef or bartender is doing, you can ask questions about the meal or beverage as you go along, and you can establish a relationship simply because of your proximity.

This kind of relationship is something I often feel is missing at fancy European and American restaurants, where the chef is put on an aloof pedestal, unavailable for questions from the common folk. Best of all, bar-side dining creates a communal feeling, as other diners join in the fun and conversation. New friendships are made around the bar, where a simple tempura meal can become a convivial experience shared by all.

Yaegaki

One note of caution: the restaurant does not take credit cards and meals cost around $40 to $100 (¥4,000-¥10,000).

3-1-1 Kikuzono-cho
Showa District
Nagoya
(052) 851-9105

Mie Prefecture

Cobus van Staden moons over a garden restaurant in Kameyama

In a country where an urban wasteland can be called Cherry Blossom Mountain, one's first surprise at entering Tsuki no Niwa restaurant is how well it fits its name—lush with silvery highlights, it actually does feel like the "Garden of the Moon." The second surprise is that such a haven can be found so close to Nagoya, the buckle of Japan's industrial belt.

From Nagoya Station, it takes about forty minutes to reach Kameyama. Don't be discouraged by its air of hamlet-turned-sprawl. The moment you cross the road in front of the station and find the hidden path up the hill, the air sweetens, and you're in another Japan.

At Tsuki no Niwa this Japan fuses ancient style with contemporary casualness. The garden is in a courtyard, complete with a teahouse that doubles as a stage, which frequently hosts performances of experimental and modern dance. The garden leads to a two-story farmhouse. On the bottom floor is a small dining room with tables, and a bar made from solid pieces of wood. Up a crazily steep staircase is a bigger, second-floor dining room in a huge attic, with low tables and cushions on the floor.

Run by a fresh-faced crew dressed in understated Japanese hippie chic, Tsuki no Niwa is an example of a renewed Japanese enthusiasm for stylish riffs on traditional dishes. It gives Japanese comfort classics an organic twist, and is deeply loyal to local farmers. Not only will you find the sources for all the ingredients on the menu, but also there is an adjacent shop where you can buy treasures such as artisan-dried *daikon* and shiny black beans.

Tsuki no Niwa is also that rarest of Japanese finds: a mostly vegetarian restaurant. For example, you can dine on marinated carrots fried uncannily like the shrimp a Japanese mom would put on the table. Another favorite is *konnyaku*, the jelly-like paste made from a tuber called "devil's tongue," fried in a crispy batter—the normally rubbery heft of the *konnyaku* melting and sensual after its hot oil embrace.

The organic and regional ethos also extends to sake. Tsuki no Niwa has an extensive range of organically produced sake, listed by region. If you still shudder at the memory of the chemical bite of cheap varieties, this selection will come as a pleasant surprise. The sake here is so delicate and pure, it's like drinking spirited spring water. You also get to choose a new thimble-sized cup from a tray each time you order a different kind. Just be careful descending that steep staircase on the way out. And when you're drunkenly running down the hill to catch the last train back to Nagoya, be grateful for stylish, vegetarian Japanese hippies. There just aren't enough of them in the world.

Finding Tsuki no Niwa

To reach Kameyama, take the Kansai Line from Nagoya Station. Trains on the Kansai Line usually leave from Platform 12 and 13. Kameyama is frequently the final stop on the line, but if it doesn't appear on the electronic signboard on the platform, ask a conductor—even if you don't speak Japanese, asking "Kameyama?" with an entreating expression will probably get you positioned on the correct side of the platform.

Kameyama is a small station with a single exit. Just outside the station, pass to the left of the giant orange *torii* gate and follow the curving path past the large chain restaurant set back a little from the road on your left (it's the only restaurant there) until you come to a large intersecting road. Almost directly across the road you'll see a path leading uphill through the trees. Follow this path. On your left, you'll see a stone embankment. Be careful, the path is steep and only sporadically lit. You'll pass one road to your right. Turn into the second road. You'll immediately see the bamboo fence surrounding the garden, and a sign on the left-hand side close to the corner.

You don't have to make a reservation, but it might be a good idea to call ahead and make sure that the restaurant is open because the owners sometimes travel to India. The staff members don't speak much English, but they are very friendly and willing to try. Keep in mind that the last train back to Nagoya leaves at ten.

Nishi-cho
Kameyama
(0595) 82-0252
www.za.ztv.ne.jp/tuki-niwa/top/top.html (Japanese)

Osaka Prefecture

Jacqueline Taylor chances upon okonomiyaki in Osaka

I have no idea what I'm doing here. Without rhyme or reason, cheap airline tickets and a split-second decision led me to Osaka. So it's just about perfect that I have ended up adrift on the sea of insanity called Dotonbori.

Dotonbori is not for the faint-hearted. In the Japanese "City of Merchants," it is a street where money changes hands at a bewildering rate. It is conspicuous consumption refined to an art form. As the sunlight fades and the neon glare intensifies, Dotonbori is a rushing river of random self-expression. Petite and perfect Japanese Paris Hiltons tiptoe on wedge sandals past Jon Bon Jovi rocker types, whose hair defies gravity. A girl whizzes by on a bicycle, pedaling impossibly in full kimono, complete with toe socks and flip-flops. Drunken foreign lads in carelessly half-laced boots amble into hundred-yen shops to buy shots of headache-inducing sake. It seems that all of Osaka will pass through this neon canyon tonight.

I cling to the shoreline, walking close to the edge as I trawl a thousand shop windows and restaurant displays. Plastic replicas of countless dishes gleam garishly under the lights, and I'm dangerously overstimulated. I stumble through a split half-curtain.

There is peace and quiet, along with bows and smiles, as I'm led to a table. The restaurant is filled mostly with men, eating alone or drinking beers together. In the evenings, Japan is a country of men forestalling the journey home. I wonder why, as I take my seat at a table with a hot plate set into its center.

The menu is a maze of Japanese. I notice a double date at the next table. The two couples are hacking relentlessly at the unidentifiable food on their hot plate. I point and tell the waiter I'll have what they're having. When he responds with a question in Japanese, I reply with "*Wakarimasen*" ("I don't understand"). He points to a list on the menu, and I realize I have to pick something. A flavor. A topping. I'm not exactly sure what, but something. I stab blindly at the menu, and soon enough, two unfamiliar piles of food are slipped expertly onto my own hot plate. In a land of raw fish, tofu, and rice, rice, rice, I have chanced upon something very special: *okonomiyaki.*

Okonomiyaki is a Japanese pancake—a traditional-style, pan-fried cake made of flour, grated yam, *dashi,* eggs, and shredded cabbage. Toppings range from pork, squid, prawns, beef, scallops, and other seafood, to scary ingredients like "devil's tongue," which you can avoid or eat for a dare. There is also *negiyaki,* a thinner spring onion pancake made of a similar batter and wrapped around a filling.

To me, *okonomiyaki* is Japanese comfort food. The name means "cooked as you like it," and to my immense relief, I appear to have picked toppings that I do, in fact, like. Small bits of perfect squid peek out at me atop the fluffy batter base, below lashings of tangy brown sauce and Japanese mayonnaise. Airy shavings of dried *bonito* fish top off the whole creation, waving lazily at me in the heat of the hot plate, beckoning me to tuck in. Feeling welcome and comfortable—and lucky given the random choices that got me here—I do just that.

Getting to Dotonbori

Dotonbori is in the Minami District, Osaka's main shopping area, and stretches more than two and a half kilometers. Take the Sennichimae Subway Line to Namba Station or Nipponbashi Station. Dotonbori is a short walk from either station, and offers a never-ending parade of people, oodles of restaurants, and plenty of sensory overload.

Dining on okonomiyaki

Although it is an Osaka specialty, *okonomiyaki* is popular all over Japan. You can identify *okonomiyaki* restaurants by the tempting photos or trompe l'oeil models of these tasty pancakes on display in the windows. The pancakes are huge, and are usually cut into wedges like pizza, and topped with a brown-and-white spiral of *okonomiyaki* sauce and mayonnaise. The best places to find *okonomiyaki* are in the food courts on the upper floors of large department stores, and in the labyrinth of tunnels surrounding many of the major train stations. Pubs called *izakaya* often feature it on their menus. Or you could just ask a kindly policeman or pedestrian, "*Okonomiyaki wa doko desu ka*?" ("Where is *okonomiyaki*?") and he will likely point you in the right direction—or even escort you to the nearest place himself.

Kyoto Prefecture

Merry White discovers the bread of life in Kyoto

Anabateki. It is the almost untranslatable Japanese word describing a place that no one else knows. A place where you experience the joy of discovery, a fierce sense of possessiveness, and even a bit of anticipation from all the bragging you long to do about it. There are many such experiences in Japan, those one-of-a-kind moments that make you feel rewarded and accomplished, and not just a tourist. For me, the best *anabateki* places have been—and are still—cafés.

I have been coming to Japan since 1963, when I got lost down dirt roads, among radish patches in what are now glamorous parts of Tokyo. It was a time when I could roam back alleys without risk of annihilation by cars or motorbikes, and houses were built low and open. Neighbors watched over each other easily as the *amado* (wooden doors) came down in the mornings and up in the evenings, and children and old people played and sat in the sun in the lanes. But the 1964 Olympics brought change, with new subway lines, everyone practicing English, and in the bootstrapping energy of that era, people running instead of walking in the streets.

Then, as now, my primary place of residence in Japan was a café. In those days it might have been a dark little neighborhood shop, or The Vienna, a four-story velvet extravaganza, where *kaffee mit schlag* was served with Mozart, amid gilt chairs and filigreed balconies. Now, I am in Kyoto, and down yet another hidden dirt road, my *anabateki* is all about the bread at Hachi Hachi Infinity Café. I admit that I did not "discover" this place. After all, Hachi Hachi Infinity even has a website. But I do own my experience there.

Down a rough, narrow path, at a house with the words "*Hachi Hachi*" and "Infinity Café," I knock on the door or slide it open, calling out "*Konnichi wa*" or "*Gomen kudasai*"—"Good day" or "Pardon me." The owner-baker greets me and beckons me to sit at the large table in his living room, which I do after leaving my shoes in the *genkan* at the entrance.

If it is winter, I will be covered with the *kotatsu* quilt that blankets the table, which is heated underneath. As I look out the glass doors at the quietly overgrown and untidy garden, I quickly forget the dusty, noisy city streets I've just left. I wait for the coffee and cheese, or the mixed open-face sandwich and soup I have ordered. And, of course, the bread.

Such densely textured, truly delicious bread I've never had before, even in a lifetime of making bread myself. Cardamom seed, walnut, fig, pumpkin, rye, and whole wheat. The baker takes his time. His breads are fine grained and chewy, quite the opposite of those soft, spongy loaves that most Japanese bakeries and markets carry. The yeasts are all natural, the flours and seeds organic. Flavor is the goal.

The first bite will give you a Proustian moment of nostalgia, even if there is no sentimental memory of bread in your past. This is love bread, a platonic ideal of bread, and yes, I admit, I lose control at moments like these. After all, if I'm the only one in the place, who is going to hear my moans of delight? Then, I realize, if I don't share this place, it probably cannot go on, just waiting for me to return, since the baker does not live by bread alone.

Hachi Hachi Infinity Café

Kamigo District
Kyoto
(075) 451-8792
http://hachihachi.org/

Directions: Take the Sagano Train Line or the Tozai Subway Line to Nijo Station. From the station, follow the directions on the Hachi Hachi Infinity Café website map. You will know you're getting close when you see a sign with "*Hachi Hachi*" and "Infinity Café" on it. Walk down the dirt road until you see another similar sign.

Fukuoka Prefecture

Nick Hall warms up on a winter night in Fukuoka

It was my first time in Fukuoka, and I was beginning to wish my three co-workers and I hadn't chosen a winter's weekend to visit. Unlike everyone else we passed, we'd forgotten our hats, scarves, and gloves, making the bitterly cold weather even harder to bear. On top of that, even though we'd remembered to bring a map, we nonetheless managed to get lost, and had been trudging the downtown streets for over an hour.

As darkness began to set in, my stomach was growling loudly, and I was beginning to lose the feeling in my fingertips and face, as well as the will to live. I'd almost given up hope of ever finding our destination, when we turned a corner and suddenly saw what we were looking for: the *yatai* that line the Naka River.

These small food stalls typically consist of a counter, some stools, and a set of portable kitchen equipment, all enclosed in a tarpaulin tent or shack. There were plenty to choose from, and although it was early evening, the *yatai* were packed with customers, drawn like moths to the light and warmth. After a few minutes, we found one with enough free seats for the four of us, and were greeted with a friendly "*Irasshaimase*!" as we entered through the transparent plastic flap that served as a door.

For such a small place, the *yatai* had a surprisingly large menu. However, we were only interested in one thing: *tonkotsu ramen*. The pork broth for this noodle dish was bubbling away in the rear of the tent, filling the enclosed space with steam and an intoxicating aroma. When the generous bowls of *ramen* were served, it tasted every bit as good as it smelled.

The thick, creamy broth and chewy noodles were complemented by a topping of seaweed, sesame seeds, and tender slices of roast pork. Attempting to slurp the noodles in the same loud manner as our fellow diners did, we soon began to warm up. The freezing temperatures we'd just endured made us even more appreciative of the steaming hot *tonkotsu ramen*, which passed our "good *ramen* test," meaning that we were unable to resist the urge to drink every last drop of the broth.

As we sat shoulder to shoulder with Japanese customers, it wasn't long before their curiosity got the better of them, and they struck up a conversation with us. We chatted over glasses of hot sake, before making our excuses to head off to Fukuoka's famous Oyafuko-dori nightlife area.

With our stomachs full, we left the *yatai*, hoping our questionable navigation skills would get us to our next destination. By then it had started to snow, but I couldn't have cared less. After the hearty, warming bowl of *tonkotsu ramen* I'd just eaten, I was ready for anything the elements could throw at me.

Tonkotsu ramen in Fukuoka

In true Japanese style, *tonkotsu ramen* is a local adaptation of an idea borrowed from another culture—in this case China. Although available in many *ramen* restaurants in other parts of the country, *tonkotsu* is a specialty of Kyushu, and Fukuoka in particular, where it is also known as *Hakata ramen*. In my opinion, it's undoubtedly the tastiest type of *ramen*, and it's one of my favorite foods in Japan.

Yatai can be found set up on sidewalks all over Fukuoka's central Tenjin and Nakasu areas. Take the Kuko Subway Line to Tenjin Station, then head west toward the Naka River. It's difficult to recommend specific stalls. Most serve very good quality *tonkotsu ramen,* but each has a different cooking and serving method, so the taste varies considerably. Eating at a *yatai* is as much about the experience of dining in a cheerful, intimate setting as it is about the food anyway, so chances are that any crowded *yatai* is a good choice. For more on Fukuoka in general, visit the following website.

www.welcome-fukuoka.or.jp

General Japan

Catherine Tully finds herself tongue-tied over yakiniku

I had lived in Japan for six months and was feeling quite confident about my knowledge of the language. Having completed two Japanese courses, I boldly declined the English menu that was graciously offered to me when I sat down to eat dinner with my Japanese friends in the city of Aomori.

We were at one of the *yakiniku* restaurants that feature tables with grills in the center for diners to cook their own meats and vegetables. As we slid into a comfortable seating area filled with cushions, the aroma of deliciously cooking food wafted over to greet us. As this was my first experience with a *yakiniku* restaurant, I looked around to get a feel for the place, and to see what the other patrons were doing. What struck me immediately was how much fun everyone was having. At each table, plates were being passed around, and the atmosphere was relaxed and convivial.

When the time came to order, I was ready to impress my friends with my command of their language. However, when I looked at the menu, I began to get a little worried. I suddenly realized that my reading skills were not on a par with my speaking ability. I could make out some of the Japanese characters, but not all of them. The waiter came over to our table, and everyone else placed an order in perfect Japanese. When my turn came, I pointed at an item on the menu that I thought was beef, attempted to pronounce it in Japanese, and hoped I was getting it right.

Once we'd ordered, I tried to make conversation in Japanese with my friends while we waited for the food to arrive. When it came, I felt a wave of relief. My plate looked a lot like everyone else's, and from what I could tell, it appeared to be beef. The only curious thing was that all of my slices were uniform in size and shape: long and rounded with one flat edge. I put a piece of meat on the grill and cooked it with newfound confidence, although it seemed as if I was getting an odd glance or two from my friends.

When I tasted my first bite, it was truly awful in both texture and taste. Not only was it tough and chewy, but I'd burnt it as well. Etiquette is very important in Japan, especially good table manners, so discreetly spitting it into my napkin was not an option. So I gulped it down quickly with my cup of green tea.

Upon seeing my discomfiture, my good friend Yuko-san made a comment that would humble me greatly. She grinned, and said loudly to everyone, "Eh, I don't think she likes tongue!"

Fortunately for me, it's customary for everyone to share at a *yakiniku* restaurant, so I was able to sample lots of other things that evening. As the food made the rounds, my generous friends offered me a taste of their dishes, and explained what each item was. The wafer-thin slices of perfectly cooked meat melted in my mouth, the grilled vegetables were bright and fresh, and the various sauces provided the perfect accompaniment.

We sat for hours, leisurely eating, talking, and sipping sake, never feeling rushed by the servers. Since that evening, going to *yakiniku* restaurants has become one of my favorite outings with friends. And once I learned not to let my meat cook too long on the grill, I discovered that I actually do like tongue.

Dining on yakiniku

Yakiniku means "grilled meat." Although various types of beef are the specially featured dishes, most *yakiniku* restaurants also offer chicken, seafood, and vegetables, as well as side dishes such as soup, salad, and rice. I actually like the chicken much better than the beef. *Rosu* (pork loin) and *karubi* (beef short ribs) are also very good. *Yakiniku* restaurants often have a set menu that offers a variety of dishes for a fixed price. This is a great way to experiment. You can try a little of everything so you will know what to order next time.

When the time comes to cook your meat, don't put too many pieces on the grill at once. It's rude to take up too much grill space, and it will make it hard to keep up with cooking them. Keep a close eye on your meat so it doesn't overcook. If your grill grate becomes overly charred, you can ask your server to change it for you.

Once your meat is done, try dipping it into one of the tasty *tare* sauces. Most are made of soy sauce flavored with ingredients such as sake, garlic, sesame, and sugar. Many *yakiniku* restaurants have their own special *tare* recipes.

Although the place where I first experienced *yakiniku* dining has long since closed, there are equally enjoyable *yakiniku* restaurants all over Japan. They're great places to eat out with family and friends, as the leisurely nature of a *yakiniku* meal encourages sharing and conversation.

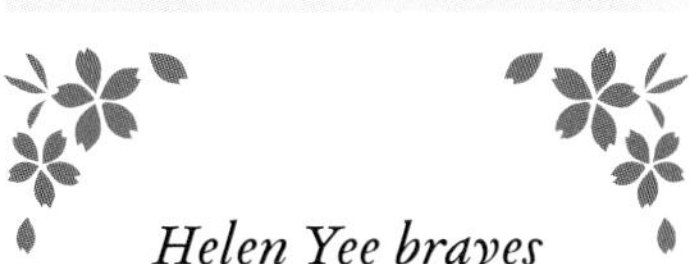

Helen Yee braves sticky, slimy, salty fermented soybeans

On my first trip to Japan, I knew that I had to try *natto*. This national dish of fermented soybeans, dear to the hearts of many Japanese, is an enigma of fiercely aromatic proportions. It's the kind of dish that baffles but intrigues visitors. Just as Malaysians have their durian fruit and Australians their Vegemite, the Japanese hold *natto* aloft as an iconic gustatory treasure.

As a globetrotting food lover, I have always enthusiastically sought out local delicacies, for what defines a culture more succinctly than its own cuisine? I've enjoyed haggis (sheep offal), *balut* (duck embryo), *tiet canh* (duck blood soup), and yes, even dog. A simple serving of *natto* seemed like a figurative piece of cake.

Natto is usually eaten at breakfast, so when the time to try it finally arrived, I found myself seated in a twenty-four-hour chain restaurant, still a little bleary-eyed at not quite 9 a.m. I'm not a morning person, and therefore, I was already starting to reconsider my boasts of gastronomic bravado.

It was a set breakfast meal, served on a white plastic tray. In one corner was a thin slice of pan-fried salmon, in the other, a bowl of fluffy white rice. A bowl of miso soup shimmered under the fluorescent lights, and a small plastic tub of *natto*, heat-sealed with a plastic sheath, seemed ominously protected.

With some trepidation, I removed the seal. The beans looked harmless enough, small and pale, a mass of legumes in a light shade of tan. Gingerly I poked a chopstick into the clumped mass. Suddenly, my chopstick was sinking into a squalid bog.

Scooping up a tiny bite, I caught a whiff of odd, fishy pungency as the chopsticks neared my mouth. The three pale beans seemed innocuous enough, but as they glistened, and the sticky tendrils surrounding them stretched back into the bowl below, I wasn't so sure that *natto* would be my cup of green tea.

A Japanese lady at the next table laughed at my reaction. She smiled warmly, and motioned for me to copy her.

First, a packet of mustard. "Hot, hot," she warned me. I cautiously tore it open and squeezed a tiny dollop into the container.

Next, a splash of soy sauce. "Mix, mix," said the woman, making rapid circling movements with her chopsticks. I grabbed the bowl with one hand, and mixed the contents vigorously with the other. As I stirred, web-like threads appeared and stretched threateningly. It was like a scene from *Alien*, and I tried not to shudder as a soundtrack of disconcerting squelches accompanied the elongating strands of goo.

My new Japanese friend leaned back in her chair and looked at me expectantly. The prep was done. It was time to eat.

Heart pounding, I plucked a small mound of *natto*, trying to ignore the strands of slime, and leaned in to receive it.

Reluctantly, my mouth closed around the sticky mass, and I closed my eyes as I chewed thoughtfully. It smelled and tasted of wet mushrooms, an earthy pungency that—*oh my God*! My nose and taste buds were overwhelmed. I felt as if I were eating something truly rotten, something from the back of the fridge that had gone both moldy and fizzy.

The beans themselves were firm but slightly mealy, a little nutty, but mostly just wrong-tasting to my unaccustomed palate. The sticky *natto* felt as if it were slowly expanding on my reluctant tongue. All I could think of were sweaty football socks abandoned in a gym bag during a heat wave. It took me forever to swallow.

"Do you like it?" the woman asked. She wrinkled her nose in empathy and giggled. "The taste ... it is, ah, special."

I smiled weakly. Special indeed.

She motioned me toward her and offered to show me a trick. First she poured a little saucer of soy sauce, and then she slid a sheet of seasoned seaweed lightly across the surface, just enough to moisten one side. She dropped a little glob of *natto* in her bowl of rice, and placing the seaweed sheet over it, sauce side down, she grasped a small amount of rice and *natto* beneath the sheet and enclosed the ends to form a miniature, cone-shaped *natto temaki* roll.

I followed suit, tasted the results, and was amazed at the difference. The flavors of the rice and the seaweed stood strong, while the potency of the *natto* was tempered. A definite improvement. Sure, it took a whole bowl of rice for me to finish the *natto*, but at least it finally felt safe to breathe. I heaved a sigh of relief as I finished my meal. The *natto* had not beaten me, but I was certain that I would never crave it again.

Braving natto

Most commonly served at breakfast, *natto* is usually part of a set meal that includes such items as rice, miso soup, pickles, raw egg, and salmon or tofu. If you're up for the adventure, it is most easily obtained from popular chain restaurants like Denny's, Meshiya, Yayoiken, and Yoshinoya. All of these chains have branches nationwide.

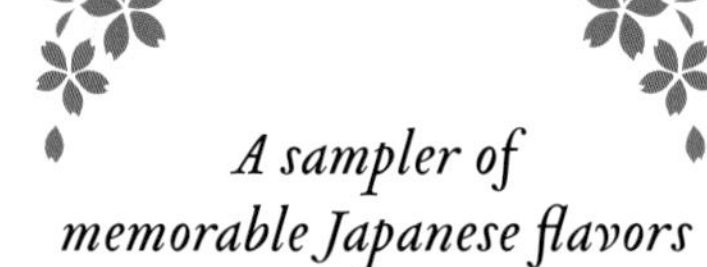

A sampler of memorable Japanese flavors

Our writers share more of their favorite restaurants and eating experiences around Japan.

Sachiko Asakawa

The town of Nakatosa has been well known for *bonito* fishing since ancient times. For its most famous local delicacy, *katsuo no tataki* (lightly grilled *bonito*), Kuroshio Koubou is the place to go. Located at the hot spring hotel called Kuroshio Honjin, this restaurant allows you not only to enjoy seared *bonito* dishes at a reasonable price, but from April to October, you can also have the unique experience of grilling your own *bonito* over a straw fire—a traditional method rarely used today. You can have your *bonito* vacuum-packed to take home, or you can eat it in the restaurant with a bowl of rice, miso soup, and a few small side dishes. For *bonito* making, reservations are necessary. Due to an emphasis on fresh, seasonal cuisine, *bonito* is not served from January to March.

Steve Cooper

Nutritious, protein-rich, and packed with calories, *chankonabe* is a traditional dish that is served to sumo wrestlers. A gas burner is placed on the table with a pot full of broth and an assortment of fish, meats, and vegetables. The ingredients are cooked for about twenty minutes, after which they are removed and eaten. You are then left with the broth, into which you put rice and an egg. Once these are cooked, you eat the broth and rice as a soup. I think it's fantastic, capturing the typical Japanese approach to food—very nourishing and nothing wasted. For *chankonabe*, I recommend Waka, even though it is quite expensive, since it is owned by a retired sumo wrestler. What better place to enjoy a traditional sumo meal?

Steve Cooper

In a country that prides itself on its intense enjoyment of food, one of the things that stands out for me is the fascination with curry rice, or as the Japanese call it, *karei raisu*. This dish was brought to Japan in the Meiji era, and it is a favorite at lunchtime, especially at Curry House CoCo Ichibanya, a chain with more than one thousand shops nationwide. This is not just simple curry and rice. This is an empire. The impressive aspect about the CoCo menu is the sheer variety. The curry is fantastic, and there are about fifty different types of ingredients on offer—basically, if you can grow it, raise it, or catch it, you will find it at the CoCo restaurants ... including a deep fried burger in curry.

Robert George

Another great curry recommendation is Moti. In the realm of ethnic restaurants in Tokyo, this popular restaurant led the trend. Now, with thirty years under its belt, and a few branches to boot, the original Moti, located in the Akasaka-Mitsuke neighborhood, is where I like to head at lunchtime for great Indian fare. For a little over ten dollars, one can sample a healthy portion of Indian curry with naan.

Nick Hall

Sitting shoulder to shoulder at a counter in a cramped bar or restaurant—eating, drinking, and chatting with staff and patrons—is a must-do on any trip to Japan. Some places are so small there's only room for a handful of people, and you can't help but wonder how these establishments make any money. This type of counter bar/restaurant may be found all over the country (often hidden away in large unassuming buildings), but two particularly good areas to find them are in the Shinjuku District in Tokyo. On the northwest side of Shinjuku Station, Shomben Yokocho (descriptively nicknamed Piss Alley) is lined with hole-in-the-wall restaurants, while the Golden Gai area off Yasukuni Dori features dozens of tiny bars.

Celeste Heiter

Japan is filled with enticing things to see and do, but many of these come with a steep price tag. Of course, there are exceptions, and one of my favorites is free of charge: food sampling in department store basements. In the larger cities, many of the busiest train and subway stations have huge multi-story department stores built above them, and on the basement levels of these stores, you can wander through in-house emporiums of food and beverage purveyors who offer samples to lure shoppers. My Sundays off work were my chosen days for food sampling, and without spending a single yen, I could go to Seibu or Odakyu and graze to my tummy's content on bite-sized bits of exotic fruit, roasted nuts, imported cheese, smoked fish, sausage, bread, cookies, pastries, and even Godiva chocolate. In one of my favorites, a wine shop, I sipped thimble-sized samples of half a dozen wines from vineyards all over the world. Of course I could never resist making a purchase or two. After all, isn't that the purpose of these complimentary smorgasbords?

Jennifer O'Bryan

In the summertime, as temperatures and humidity soar, residents of Japan escape to rooftops to enjoy liters of beer, bar-type foods, and a cool breeze. In Tokyo, just find a hotel, department store, or restaurant and look up. Chances are that ten stories above you there is an oasis of *yakitori* (grilled chicken) and all-you-can-drink beer for a reasonable set admission price. Some beer gardens are actually located amidst flowers and ponds, but most fit into the surrounding concrete jungle. These open-air restaurants offer a relief from the sweltering weather, with salary men, couples, families, and friends taking advantage of cheap grub and free-flowing drinks. While many beer gardens are still traditional in the food they serve—such as *edamame* (soybeans) and *yakiniku* (grilled beef)—themed beer gardens serving other Asian or European foods are becoming popular. Karaoke is a favorite pastime at beer gardens, but if you're lucky, you'll be treated to a lounge act singing disco classics.

Jennifer O'Bryan

When I traveled to Japan, the last thing I expected to come across was an Amish outpost in the middle of a town noted for its Buddhist temples and Shinto shrines. But this uniquely American subculture somehow found a home in the seaside city of Kamakura. Situated across from the Kotokuin Temple, which houses the famed Daibutsu Buddha statue, Café Amish reproduces the look and feel of a Pennsylvania Dutch country house. The set lunch or dinner menu is the best bargain; my friends and I ordered the ham loaf sandwich and hashed meat in mystery sauce meals, which came with distinctly non-Amish sides: salad with ginger dressing and sticky rice. While the cuisine is not completely authentic, the café makes for an interesting stop amidst the traditional noodle shops.

Sarah Skilton

One of my favorite restaurants in Kyoto is Asian Kitchen, a modern, crowded, spicy, Asian-fusion place. The translated American explanations on the menu crack me up, including "a plain soup." In reality, nothing about the place is plain. Strong cocktails flow freely and the sign above the bathroom reads "Used Beer Depot." You'll see men and women on first dates and boisterous groups of pals gathered in private booths. With loud, colorful decorations, it's like a slightly classier T.G.I. Friday's or Chili's in attitude and style. Try the mashed-up, breaded-and-fried pumpkin: delectable.

Renée Suen

Kaiseki is a traditional Japanese multi-course meal associated with the tea ceremonies that were developed in the sixteenth century. It uses the best ingredients of the season, combining flavor, texture, and color contrast to stimulate all the senses. I was fortunate to visit Shirogane restaurant in Tokyo's Ebisu District in the autumn, when chestnuts and sweet potatoes were the star ingredients. Surrounded by cool tones, a bamboo thatched ceiling, and a miniature Zen garden, I was blanketed in a sense of serenity as I ate the picture-perfect morsels of my superb, ten-course "Ladies' Lunch" (around $40). For another excellent *kaiseki* experience, I recommend Kakiden. Although it's located in the busy Shinjuku District, it offers a tranquil teahouse-like setting. I ordered the mini-*kaiseki* set lunch (around $60), which I found to be a great value because it included a succession of eighteen small dishes. The meal concluded with a tea ceremony performed by a kimono-clad waitress. You can also take classes here on proper *kaiseki* etiquette.

Renée Suen

In addition to the boutique food emporiums of the major department stores, tasty snacks and treats can be found in abundance along the streets of Tokyo. Follow your nose to find freshly roasted chestnuts sold by the pound from sidewalk pushcarts in busy shopping districts such as Shibuya and Shinjuku. Look to Ginza and Akihabara for Manneken Belgian waffles, thick and cake-like, with a crispy crust and a sugar-glazed crunch. Asakusa's Nakamise-dori is home to dozens of vendors selling traditional Japanese snacks. Especially tasty are the freshly grilled *sembei*, lighter-than-air rice crackers, at one hundred yen apiece.

Alice Yamada

Japan's Kobe beef has gotten quite a bit of attention from gourmets in the States. It is considered by many as *the* beef to try from Japan. I beg to differ. During my last trip back, my mama and I traveled to a resort near Biwa, Japan's largest lake. At Morishima restaurant, in the nearby town of Nagahama, we feasted on the regional *omi* beef, known for its juiciness and texture. I was told that Morishima is run by the great-grandson of one of the famous Takenaka brothers who popularized both *omi* beef and *gyunabe*, the dish assumed to be the origin of *sukiyaki*, in the late 1800s. Morishima's *sukiyaki* was top-notch. Perfectly balanced with the salty sweetness of the sugar broth, the beef was beyond tender while maintaining a lovely meaty aroma. The vegetables didn't leave much of an impression, but the beef ... *omi*, oh my!

Dining in Tokyo

Kakiden

Yasuyo Building, 6-9F
3-37-11 Shinjuku
Shinjuku District
Tokyo
(03) 3352-5121
www.kakiden.com

Train: Yamanote Line to Shinjuku Station.

Subway: Marunouchi Line Shinjuku Station.

Manneken

www.manneken.co.jp (Japanese)

Moti

3-8-8 Akasaka
Minato District
Tokyo
(03) 3582-3620

Subway: Ginza or Marunouchi Lines to Akasaka-Mitsuke Station.

Directions: The station is open on both ends and isn't very wide. Take the main exit, and at the top of the stairs, you'll see a busy boulevard on the right side of the station, and an alley-like street on the left. Take the alley street, walk about a minute, and you'll find Moti on your left.

Shirogane

6-16-28 Shirokane (above a Mercedes-Benz dealership)

Minato District
Tokyo
(03) 3449-0033

Train: Yamanote Line to Ebisu Station.

Subway: Hibiya Line to Ebisu Station.

Waka

Belza Roppongi, B1F
4-1-9 Roppongi

Minato District
Tokyo
(03) 3568-4507

Subway: Namboku Line to Roppongi-Itchome Station.

Dining on Honshu Island

Asian Kitchen

Kikusui Building, 5F
Teramachi-dori Shijo-agaru
Kyoto
Kyoto Prefecture
(075) 256-8840 (Japanese)

Subway: Tozai Line to Shi-yakusho-mae Station.

Café Amish

2-24-3 Yukinoshita
Kamakura
Kanagawa Prefecture
(0467) 25-2533

Directions: From Kamakura Station, walk along Komachi-dori to Yabusame Road. Café Amish is at the intersection on the left.

Morishima Omi Beef

Highway 8 (#50, see website below)
Nagahama
Shiga Prefecture
(0748) 37-4325
www.omi8.com/pdf/map_e.pdf

Dining on Shikoku Island

Kuroshio Koubou

8009-11 Kure
Nakatosa Town
Kochi Prefecture
(0889) 40-1160 (Japanese)
www.town.nakatosa.lg.jp/english/index.html

Dining all around Japan

Curry House CoCo Ichibanya

The following website includes a PDF of the massive menu and a list of restaurants around Japan.

www.ichibanya.co.jp/

Department store grazing

To get started, hop on the elevator at any large department store and press the B1 or B2 button for the basement levels. When the doors open, you'll have no problem figuring out when you're in the right place. You'll see shop after shop and stall after stall of tempting edibles. Don't be shy. It's all there for you to taste and enjoy. But do be a good sport and make a purchase or two.

Seeing the Sights

Fresh perspectives on exploring must-see attractions

What can I say about sightseeing in Japan, except that if your eyes are open, you're sightseeing. Everything about the country, its people, and their culture is worth looking at, whether for the aesthetic elegance, historical significance, cultural value, or simply the novelty. *"Mite! Mite!"* is one of the first Japanese phrases you should learn. It means "Look! Look!" and you will find yourself uttering it at every turn.

When I first arrived to live in Tokyo, everywhere I went in my daily routine, there was something new and wonderful to take in. Even months later, sights that had become familiar still held a certain mystique. Over time, at the advice of friends, co-workers, and students, I explored the city and beyond to see some of the most famous sights that Japan has to offer. Of course, I found a few favorites along the way. I especially love the view from the top of the Tokyo's Hotel Metropolitan in the Ikebukuro District.

Our contributors also have their own lists of personal favorites, which they reveal throughout this chapter. While Tokyo is well known for its transportation systems, one of the remarkable things about it is how pedestrian-friendly it is. In his essay on walking in Tokyo, Robert George recommends strolling from one train or subway station to the next for a close-up view of the neighborhoods in between. He even outlines his five favorite neighborhood walks. Rie Imanaka, on the other hand, believes that the best way to see Tokyo is from afar, on the deck of a *yakatabune* pleasure boat as it makes its way down the Sumida River, with the tasty bonus of a tempura dinner served onboard.

What I like about the essays in this chapter is the variety of perspectives from which the writers view sightseeing—the new and unique ways they experience popular tourist sites, and the out-of-the-way gems they discover in their travels. The temple mecca of Kamakura can be bewildering for a traveler. Philip

Rice paddy and farmhouses in Gunma Prefecture

Blazdell simplifies the prospect of choosing which monuments to visit by singling out his three favorites. In the ancient town of Nara, Landon Fry goes behind the scenes, ducking around the back of the Great Buddha to take on the challenge of wriggling through the Buddha's nose. Arin Greenwood spends an afternoon exploring a collection of old farmhouses in Osaka, and Ali Al Saeed not only tours Kyoto's Nijo Castle, he hears it sing!

Two of our contributors, Stefan Chiarantano and Josh Krist, take a thoughtful look at Japan's military controversies. Stefan pays a visit to the Yasukuni Shrine and Yushukan Memorial War Museum in an attempt to understand the politically charged issues behind the Prime Minister honoring Japan's fallen war heroes. And on a visit to Hiroshima's Peace Memorial Park, Josh engages in a conversation with a survivor of the nuclear holocaust, and walks away with a poignant understanding of war and peace.

Sometimes, sightseeing is about more than just a physical place. It is also about the feeling that a place evokes, as Tim Kaiser discovers when he unexpectedly glimpses the snow-capped peak of Mt. Fuji through his kitchen window. Kena Sosa recounts an unforgettable Elvis moment as she "can't help falling in love" with a natural amphitheater in Kumamoto. And as Sara Francis-Fujimura proves in her essay about Japan's roadside rest areas, the old maxim is true: seeing the sights is as much about the journey as the destination.

Tokyo Prefecture

Robert George walks the walk in Tokyo

I had lived in Tokyo for a couple of years before I realized that I was missing something. Like most people traveling around the city, I used trains and subways to get from point A to B. And why not? They took me most any place I would ever want to go. But as the equipment I used in my work as a sound engineer began to require me to navigate Tokyo by car, I came to understand the road system, and got to see a lot of Tokyo that I had never noticed before: the hundreds of colorful neighborhoods that exist between points A and B.

My views of these neighborhoods from the trains were often obscured by the utilitarian structures required to operate them, such as power stations, platforms, and protective fences. And when I rode the subways, I only popped up to ground level at my destination, and then returned to the tunnels to travel to the next stop, missing everything in between.

As I began to experience Tokyo from a driver's vantage point, I also got into the habit of walking between certain train or subway stations. The distance between most subway and train stops is about twenty minutes on foot. And although some of the long, busy boulevards aren't pedestrian friendly, there are still lots of nice strolls.

Once I discovered what a pleasure walking in Tokyo could be, it was only a matter of choosing a neighborhood I wanted to explore, and walking between the subway and train stations. At the very least, I always got some extra exercise, but it also gave me a chance to familiarize myself with neighborhoods that I would have never even noticed when traveling the rails. And I never knew when I might discover a specialty shop, a peaceful shrine, or an elegant temple along the way. In a city like Tokyo, the possibilities are endless.

Kasumigaseki to Ginza

One of my favorite walks is the neighborhood between the Kasumigaseki and Ginza Districts. This is a nice easy ramble, with lots to see and do. Kasumigaseki Station is served by the Hibiya, Marunouchi, and Chiyoda Subway Lines, so it's easy to get to. Once there, I take the Hibiya Koen exit to the large public park of the same name near many of Japan's government ministries.

I always try to arrive at lunchtime, to watch the hundreds of ministry workers pouring into the park to eat their *bento* lunches. Hibiya Koen features many floral gardens filled with cheery blossoms in the spring. I especially enjoy the tulips that bloom during April, but the paths through the park are pleasant at any time of year.

From the park I exit at the east side and head down Harumi Dori, past Yurakucho Station to the Ginza District, the city's lavishly upscale shopping area. I enjoy exploring its side streets, and from Ginza, I can go anywhere in the city from one of the dozens of subway stops accessible at every major intersection.

Ginza to the Sumida River

On another neighborhood walk, I start from Ginza's main intersection, Ginza 4-Chome, which is served by the nearby Ginza, Hibiya, and Marunouchi Subway Lines. At Ginza 4-Chome, I like to browse in the Mitsukoshi department store (the company dates back to 1673), and then I check out the latest installation at the famed Wako Building window display, which has been entertaining passersby since 1952.

From there, I head east along Harumi Dori toward the Kabukiza, the main theater for *Kabuki* performances. The building is always worth a look, and schedules are readily available for anyone interested in seeing a play. Continuing east to the banks of the Sumida River, I end my day with a leisurely stroll along the river walk, or I watch the world go by from a park bench along the way.

When it's time to head home, Tsukiji Station is conveniently nearby for a ride on the Hibiya or Yurakucho Subway Lines that connect with all of Tokyo's major train lines.

Shimbashi across the Rainbow Bridge to Odaiba

One of Tokyo's newer train lines is the Yurikamome, an unmanned train built to cross the Rainbow Bridge to Odaiba, a series of man-made islands that offer plenty to see and do. The automated Yurikamome departs from Shimbashi Station, and whenever I plan to spend the day at Odaiba, I buy an all-day pass for the train, which allows me to get on and off as many times as I like.

Four stops along the line from Shimbashi, at Shibaura-Futo Station, I hop off the train and walk across the Rainbow Bridge. Along the way, I stop at the two enclosed viewing platforms for fabulous vistas of Tokyo Bay and the city skyline. The walk along the bridge is about one and a half kilometers, and once in Odaiba, I can stroll the beaches, explore the shopping malls, enjoy a meal at one of many restaurants, and marvel at the architecture of the futuristic Fuji TV Building. One of my favorite Odaiba landmarks is a miniature replica of the Statue of Liberty.

Aoyama to Harajuku

For a more metropolitan Tokyo experience, I start out at Aoyama-1-Chome Station on the Ginza and Hanzomon Subway Lines, and walk along Aoyama Dori toward the Omotesando. Even with the traffic, it's a pleasant stroll along this busy boulevard, with its trendy boutiques, coffee shops, and restaurants.

A fifteen-minute walk takes me to Omotesando. This tree-lined boulevard features some of the hippest shops in Tokyo, and at the first big intersection, I can hop back on the subway, or I can continue walking toward Harajuku, where I enjoy people watching on the pedestrian-only Takeshita Dori, one of Tokyo's busiest shopping streets.

Harajuku equals youth, and the sea of teenagers flowing down Takeshita Dori is made even more dramatic by the fact that the street is only about three meters wide. When I've had enough of the slow parade, I head for Harajuku Station to catch the Yamanote Line that encircles the city and connects with all the major train and subway lines.

Nippori to Ueno

Yet another enjoyable walk begins at Nippori Station, on the Yamanote Line that circles the city. From Nippori, I head toward Uguisudani and Ueno Stations along the west side of the track. Along the way, I pass the Yanaka Cemetery, some of its old graveyards dating back to the Edo period. One of them has a small shrine, Suwa Myojin, and there is a unique view of the Tokyo skyline from a Nippori bluff, which is depicted in Hiroshige's woodblock series, "One Hundred Famous Views of Edo."

As I continue walking, I eventually come to Ueno Station, a huge hub for train travel out of Tokyo. This thriving area has a decidedly different atmosphere from Tokyo's trendier areas. Ueno feels more like old Tokyo to me. Colloquially, this neighborhood is known as Shitamachi, which roughly means "downtown," and while there I visit Ueno Koen, Ueno Zoo, the Tokyo National Museum, and the National Museum of Western Art.

One of my favorite spots within the vast expanse of Ueno Koen is Shinobazu Pond. The water is covered with thousands of lotus blossoms in the summer, and features a beautiful temple on an island in the center. The park is surrounded by a lively shopping district. Known for its bargains, it boasts a street called Ameyayokocho, where vendors sell fish and traditional Japanese foods, barking out the names of their wares in theatrical voices. It's worth the trip to Ueno just to hear these folks, each with his own showy style.

Getting your bearings

Before setting out on any of these walks, stop at the Japan National Tourist Organization, which has outlets at the Narita International Airport and Kansai International Airport, as well as a main location in the Tokyo International Forum Building near Yurakucho Station. Obtain a tourist map of Tokyo, which features a schematic of all the train lines in central Tokyo on one side, and a map of central Tokyo on the other. This map will help you get your bearings. I always use it on my walks in Tokyo.

Tokyo Kotsu Kaikan, 10F
2-10-1 Yurakucho
Chiyoda District
Tokyo
(03) 3201-3331 (English)

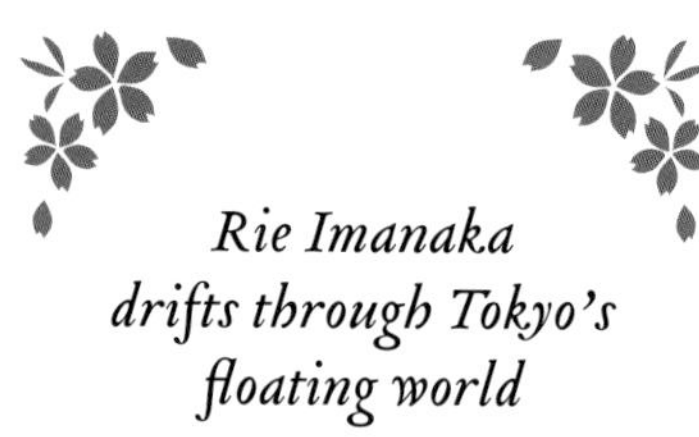

Rie Imanaka drifts through Tokyo's floating world

Picture this: beautiful geisha in kimono, sizzling tempura, an entertaining karaoke set, and a panorama of the Tokyo skyline.

On our two-and-a-half-hour *yakatabune* summer cruise down the Sumida River, we sailed out toward the kaleidoscopic lights of Odaiba Island, past the futuristic metal-and-glass Fuji TV Building, with views of Tokyo Tower and the Rainbow Bridge along the way. As we glided over gentle currents, the dark waters were illuminated by the reflection of the city lights in delicate shades of purple and gold. Our English-speaking host pointed out the sights, while crew members prepared tempura in the galley.

After dinner, under a starlit sky, we enjoyed the sea breeze from the deck. And although it seemed that we had the twinkling scenery all to ourselves, the distant strains of karaoke music drifting on the night air delivered a melodic message that ours was not the only *yakatabune* on the water that evening.

Yakatabune cruises are one of the best-kept sightseeing secrets in Japan. These narrow vessels are specially built for pleasure cruising on Japan's rivers, and although some are quite small, others may carry dozens of passengers. The best excursions are those along Tokyo's Sumida River, Kyoto's Kamo River, and Osaka's Yodo River.

It's easy to get hooked on *yakatabune* cruises. For those who do, it's fortunate that they may be enjoyed in any season, beginning with the New Year celebrations. You can cruise in the spring to view the cherry blossoms, throughout the summer for *hanabi* (fireworks) displays, and at the year's end for *bonenkai* ("forget-the-old-year") parties.

The tradition of *yakatabune* dates back to the ancient Heian period (AD 794-1185), when the cruises were aristocratic luxuries available only to the powerful *daimyo* and shogun. Centuries later, during the cultural flourish of the Edo period, *yakatabune* became accessible to commoners, and have since remained one of Japan's most pleasant traditions.

The printmaker's art of the Edo period even came to be known as *ukiyo-e* ("the floating world"), suggesting freedom from daily cares. On that summer evening so many centuries later, my *yakatabune* gently transported me from the drudgery of dry land, down the Sumida River aboard a floating world of music and magic.

Taking a yakatabune cruise

Many *yakatabune* companies specialize in chartered group tours. However, there are several that take individual passengers. In Tokyo, East Heaven schedules *yakatabune* cruises four times daily; for about $40 you can enjoy a two-hour, all-you-can-eat-and-drink excursion around Odaiba Island and the Rainbow Bridge.

(03) 3533-6699
www.4900yen.com

Yakatabune associations

For a *yakatabune* agency near your destination, contact the local Yakatabune Association.

Yakatabune Tokyo Association

(03) 3666-6811

Osaka Yakatabune

1-21-10 Tenma
Kita District
Osaka
(06) 6354-7011

Subway: Osaka Loop Line to Tenma Station.

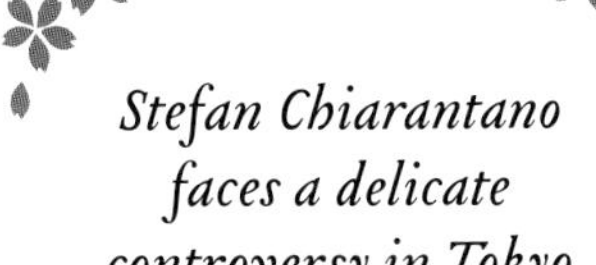

Stefan Chiarantano faces a delicate controversy in Tokyo

While teaching English in Japan, I wanted to learn as much as I could about the country's history, to better understand my students and the society in which I was living. Although I had already spent a year working at a junior high school in the rural town of Komagane, I hadn't had an opportunity to tour any of the country's cultural institutions. My move to Tokyo changed all that, and on a crisp April morning, I made my way to the Yasukuni Shrine.

I had read about Yasukuni in a newspaper article about Prime Minister Koizumi's controversial visit to the shrine. This visit provoked the ire of many countries, notably China and South Korea. Because there are fourteen convicted war criminals among the more than 2.4 million enshrined divinities—those who died for Japan—they voiced outrage that he was condoning Japan's dishonorable actions in World War II. I decided I needed to go to this source of international controversy myself, to understand what the Prime Minister had done, especially since it would hinder Japan's relations with its Asian neighbors.

The Yasukuni Shrine is enclosed within a walled complex, which was crowded when I arrived. I made my way toward the shrine, among the many cherry trees. Because of the ephemeral nature of both the cherry blossom and the life of a soldier, cherry blossoms have been used to decorate military armor and uniforms since the days of the samurai. People in a growing queue waited outside the shrine to pay their respects.

It was with surprise that I approached. I had expected something on the scale of the lavish Meiji Shrine, or comparable to the large-scale monuments to the war dead found in North America or Europe, but it wasn't so. While the *torii* gates leading up to the shrine were impressive, the shrine itself was a one-story structure made of weather-worn cedar planks. It seemed out of place, dwarfed by the beautifully designed war museum, which resembled a Japanese castle. Its traditional shape and size left me feeling humbled.

I even verified with the security guard that I had come to the right place. He assured me I had, and reminded me to observe the proper protocol. At the *chozuya* (purification) fountain, people washed their hands and mouths, and before they entered the shrine, they bowed, clapped, and bowed again. Some were teary eyed, and I felt out of place as they quickly walked past me to pay their respects. They moved with intent and purpose, while I inched my way along, taking in my surroundings and trying to understand this experience.

After paying my respects, I embarked upon a journey into Japan's military history at the Yushukan War Memorial Museum. I spent hours making my way through the two-story building. No one seemed to take notice of me, an inquisitive Western soul in a sea of Japanese, moving at a snail's pace, examining each exhibit in detail.

I learned that the Yasukuni Shrine dates from the Meiji era (1868-1912), and features a registry listing the names of those who died for Japan, some of whom were foreigners. According to the Shinto religion, the spirits of fallen heroes become guardian divinities called *kami,* who protect against evil. I found beauty in this magical thinking, imagining all the brave men who fought for Japan, continuing their protection of their nation and its people even after death.

Some of the Yushukan displays were on loan from the Imperial Family, and through them, I began to make the connection between the Emperor and the shrine. Dying for the Emperor, and thus for the nation, is an honor that renders a soldier worthy of being enshrined as a hero at Yasukuni.

The *kamikaze* exhibit was amazing, with hundreds of portraits of suicide pilots, along with English translations of their diaries and correspondence. Many knew they wouldn't be coming back, yet they saw their duties through. While viewing a video on Japan's military past, I became aware that many of the visitors around me were silently weeping.

My visit to Yasukuni Shrine and the war museum left me with a better understanding of the Japanese people. I came away with the realization that the symbolism of the ephemeral *sakura,* the sovereignty of the emperor, the soldiers who died honorably for their country, and the Yasukuni Shrine that commemorates them, are all institutions intertwined with the identity of the Japanese people. They form a powerful connection between the present and the past.

Afterward, I sat in the lounge, pondering my original question. Why would Japan's Prime Minister visit the shrine despite foreign condemnation? Because Yasukuni pays tribute to so much more than just a few dishonorable men; because it recognizes Japan's military as an integral part of Japanese history; and because the souls of the people who fought for Japan with bravery and loyalty, without question or protest, regardless of the circumstances or the flawed ideology of war, deserve to be honored there.

Yasukuni Shrine and Yushukan Memorial War Museum
3-1-1 Kudankita
Chiyoda District
Tokyo
(03) 3261-8326
www.yasukuni.or.jp/english

Train: Chuo Line to Ichigaya Station.

Subway: Tozai Line to Kudanshita Station.

Yamanashi Prefecture

Timothy Kaiser is honored by the serene presence of Mt. Fuji

I lived for a time on the outskirts of western Tokyo, along an incongruous strip of suburban concrete lined by peach orchards and cornfields. My employer rented an apartment for me on the first floor of a two-story walkup that took its architectural inspiration from a North American motel. Only the flashing "no vacancy" sign was missing.

I didn't have much of a view. The *tatami* room that functioned as my bedroom, living room, and dining room had a window that looked out on a dreary parking lot and highway. The landscape from my kitchen was better: a cornfield providing a lush canvas of green, speckled at night by darting fireflies. But what took me by utter surprise one particularly crisp and clear autumn morning when I was dumping out the dregs of my morning *o-cha* was the silvery cone of a majestic mountain that I could just make out above the corn tassels. There could be no mistaking what I was seeing. It had to be Mt. Fuji. I had no idea that where I lived was close enough to see it. Now here I was, tracing the outline of this legendary mountain through the condensation of my kitchen window.

After that morning of discovery, I hoped for Fuji-san to form a regular backdrop for my life in Japan, but no matter how hard I gazed through my window and wished the clouds and haze away, what followed were only occasional sightings. Nevertheless, on those rare occasions when that familiar snowy tip emerged, it felt like the return of a stoic and steadfast elderly neighbor—silver hair and all—just dropping in to see how things were.

Although my intention was always to climb Mt. Fuji, I never did. I flew over it, bullet-trained past it, slurped and spilled sake on a carpet of cherry blossoms at its feet, but I never scaled its heights. The closest I came was a gathering of friends, back-packs loaded with provisions, flash-lights, and maps, only to have our well-laid plans scuttled by a typhoon. At the time I was disappointed, but now I feel as Katsushika Hokusai may have felt when he created his famous *ukiyo-e* (woodblock prints), "Thirty-six Views of Mount Fuji." To reach the summit of Fuji-san is sublime, but to be in its serene presence is blessing and honor enough.

Viewing Mt. Fuji

In Hokusai's day, the mountain cast such a spiritual presence that very few but the most devout made their way along its forested foothills or dared its ascent. Now, especially from March to November, the Mt. Fuji region is abuzz with hikers, *onsen* enthusi-asts, sightseers, and day trippers of all ages deliriously snapping photos of the famed mountain. If you wish to recapture some of the solitude that marked the Mt. Fuji of bygone years, the best place to visit is the Fuji Five Lakes region of the northern foothills.

Perhaps the most tranquil of the five lakes is Saiko, particularly at the western end where the Koyo-dai Lookout offers a stunning view. Around Saiko is Iyashi-no-Sato, a restored village where traditional crafts such as silk weaving and paper making are demonstrated, and where *soba* and *konnyaku* ("devil's tongue") are prepared in the traditional way and available for sampling. For those needing a break from the above-ground pageantry, the nearby Fugaku Wind Cave and Narusawa Ice Cave offer a sub-terranean change of scenery.

www.jnto.go.jp/tourism/en/s041.html

Getting to Fuji Five Lakes region

The best way to visit Saiko or any of the other four lakes is to purchase the two-day pass for the Fuji Kawaguchiko Retro Bus that has hop-on/hop-off service around the Fuji Five Lakes region. For information about getting to the area from Tokyo, visit the following website.

www.japan-guide.com/e/e6905.html

Climbing Mt. Fuji

One of our writers almost man-aged to climb to the top of Mt. Fuji in a typhoon. To read his story, go to page 169.

Kanagawa Prefecture

Philip Blazdell chooses his favorite temples in Kamakura

Standing amongst the delicately scented flower gardens of Kamakura, soaking up the city's deep sense of history, it is hard to believe that you are only a short hop from metropolitan Tokyo. Kamakura is surrounded by forested mountains and Sagami Bay. It is one of the few places that live up to, if not surpass, the guidebook hyperbole often lavished on it. A sense of tranquility hangs in the air, even if you visit, as I did, during the middle of a national holiday.

With its dozens of temples and shrines, Kamakura is a challenge for even a diehard temple-goer. If, like myself, you don't fall into this category, you can focus on the three lovely temples I discovered during my stay: Engaku-ji, Tokei-ji, and Hase-dera.

A left turn out of Kita Kamakura Station takes you to Engaku-ji, one of the nicest temples in Kamakura, if not all of Japan. It is one of the city's five main Zen temples, originally built in 1282 to honor the fallen soldiers, both Japanese and Mongolian, who died in battle during the Mongol invasion of Japan by Kublai Khan. It was given the name Engaku, after the *Sutra of Perfect Enlightenment*, a copy of which is enshrined on the temple premises.

The San-mon Gate, adorned with a tablet inscribed by the Emperor Fushimi, is a fitting reminder of the antiquity and former magnificence of this peaceful temple. A climb higher, past flower gardens and sculpted willow trees, brings you to the Engaku-ji bell. Cast in 1301, this is the largest bell in Kamakura and represents both the style and accomplishment of the Kamakura period artists.

Opposite Engaku-ji is Tokei-ji, a wonderfully understated temple, quite different in character. The relaxing and well-planned grounds previously formed a refuge for abused women, who after spending three years here, could be officially recognized as divorced. I enjoyed a quiet hour soaking up the ambience.

Close to the city's well-known Great Buddha, and less crowded, is my third recommendation, the Hase-dera Temple. Near the entrance is a procession of statues dedicated to Jizo, the guardian of the souls of departed children. The figures are adorned with hats and aprons, brought by local women who have lost children to miscarriage or abortion, and who come to the statues to offer prayers for their departed loved ones.

Also on display at Hase-dera is an imposing statue of Kannon—Goddess of Mercy, Bodhisattva of Infinite Compassion—one of Japan's most enduring Buddhist deities. The nine-meter statue is carved of wood, dating back to the eighth century. Kannon has one large face, and ten lesser ones to represent the ten stages of enlightenment, and to allow Kannon to keep a watchful eye in all directions.

By narrowing your Kamakura temple tour down to Engaku-ji, Tokei-ji, and Hase-dera, you will discover three unique examples of the town's overwhelming number of historic attractions. Not only can you explore at a leisurely pace, but you won't feel burnt out at the end of the day, and you'll come away with more than just a blur of memories.

Getting to Kamakura

Kamakura is an easy day trip from Tokyo. From Tokyo's Shinagawa Station, take the Yokosuka Line. Both Tokei-ji and Engaku-ji are near Kita-Kamakura Station on the city's Yokosuka Line. To reach Hase-dera, take the little electric train line that runs from Kamakura Station.

Touring Kamakura

Within the city of Kamakura, there are thirty-seven official historic sites, including shrines, temples, gardens, and statues. The main attractions are close together and are best seen in a day of easy walking. These areas of interest are well signposted in both English and Japanese, but the Kamakura Tourist Information Center (0467-22-3350), just outside Kamakura Station, can provide detailed maps and guides, as well as help with booking accommodations. For more information, visit the city's official website.

www.city.kamakura.kanagawa.jp/foreign01_english/index.html

Gifu Prefecture

Sara Francis-Fujimura makes a pit stop in Kaizu

In a country with arguably the best train system in the world, why would people in their right mind decide to drive on one of Japan's congested highways at a fraction of the bullet train's speed? It has to be the *michi no eki.* These government-run, roadside rest areas are where truckers, tourists, and cross-country travelers can take a cat nap, snack on a local specialty, or chug a caffeinated beverage.

My favorite *michi no eki*, Tsukimi No Sato, is conveniently located five minutes by car from my in-laws' house in Kaizu on Highway 258. Every summer, my family makes an annual pilgrimage there. Tsukimi No Sato features a souvenir shop selling foods and crafts famous in the surrounding Gifu Prefecture, a small children's playground, various restaurants offering favorites such as *takoyaki* (fried octopus) and *taiyaki* (fried sea bream), and a long row of vending machines filled with sodas, coffee, tea, and cigarettes.

As soon as we get there, my kids usually start begging for ice cream. I never purchase it from the outside vendors. You can buy an identical cone of soft serve for a third of the price from the freezer chest inside the small grocery market. After the sugar kicks in, we follow a steep set of stairs at the back of the playground area for a mini-hike in the woods. This area is particularly beautiful in the summer when the hydrangeas are in bloom and swarms of brilliantly hued *tombo* (dragonflies) fill the air.

After picking up some reasonably priced, locally grown veggies from Tsukimi No Sato's farmers' market, my family always makes time for the free footbath. Outside, a large Jacuzzi-like tub is filled with hot, mineral-rich water piped in from the nearby natural hot spring. Having scalded delicate body parts in a Japanese bath previously, I find the footbath's 40 °C (about 104 °F) invigorating instead of painful. If you happen to forget your *tenugui* (the ubiquitous hand towel that should be on your person at all times while in Japan), one can be purchased for one hundred and fifty yen.

As much as I love shopping in train stations, the *michi no eki* have a certain charm all their own, and I never pass up an opportunity to stop at one. If you're traveling in Japan, I suggest you visit one at least once, to enjoy this uniquely Japanese experience.

Getting to Tsukimi No Sato

From Ogaki, in Gifu Prefecture, or Kuwana, in Mie Prefecture, take Highway 258 into the Nanno section of Kaizu City. The drive is a few hours from either starting point. The *michi no eki* is located on the west side of the highway by the Nanno Hot Springs. You may also walk there. It is a fifteen-minute walk from Komano Train Station on the Kintetsu Yoro Line. Many *michi no eki* are considered official tourist attractions and are even featured on websites, such as the following.

www.city.kaizu.lg.jp/english/spot-guide/tsukiminosato.jsp

Kyoto Prefecture

Ali Al Saeed hears the nightingale sing at a Kyoto castle

Fear of assassination attempts and treachery prompted some of Japan's feudal lords and military chiefs to create one of the most effective and musical security alarms. For centuries, nightingale floors were a valued architectural feature in temples, castles, and palaces. The moment I walked through the east gate of Nijo Castle, one of few places where one can find a nightingale floor in Kyoto, I was mesmerized.

I had read about the floors in tales of love and war in ancient Japan—stories that eulogized the haunting music they emitted. Their beautiful, bird-like sound is produced by the special design used in the joists. When the floorboards begin to warp after years of exposure to weather and everyday use, their clamps rub against holes in the boards, making a chirping noise. They were typically built into the hallways to prevent stealthy intruders from making surprise attacks.

Exploring Nijo Castle, I was impressed by the decorations of the structures, and the marvelous architecture spread across wide spaces. The garden pond, a marvel in its own right, was created in preparation for Emperor Gomizuno-o's visit in 1626. The Ninomaru Palace, which serves as a smaller secondary castle, was built in 1603, and is celebrated for its Momoyama architecture.

At the entrance of the palace, people huddled close, taking off their footwear before stepping onto the wooden platform. I removed my own shoes and ventured inside. Walking amidst the herd, I instantly recognized the squeaking as that of the nightingale floor, installed by the orders of Tokugawa Ieyasu, the shogun who built the castle.

My path wove around the various buildings on the palace grounds, including one of the shogun's rooms in which no other men were allowed, not even his guards. I was told that only the geisha who brought him tea could enter. The sliding doors and wall murals were extraordinary, with beautiful drawings that depicted the life of the household. I also stood at the entrance of the same room where Tokugawa Ieyasu held meetings with his court and military officers over four centuries ago.

No matter how carefully I stepped, how gently and softly I trod, the floorboards squeaked and creaked a song that could be heard throughout the palace. As I explored, I was transported to ancient Japan, and for a fleeting moment, imagined myself a samurai assassin, trying my best to make my way in silence across the nightingale floor.

Getting to Nijo Castle

451 Nijojo
Nakagyo District
Kyoto
(075) 841-0096

Directions: From Kyoto Station, take the Karasuma Subway Line to Karasuma Oike Station. Transfer to the Tozai Line and get off at Nijojo-mae Station.

Nightingale floors

These floors figure prominently in the book *Across the Nightingale Floor*, from Lian Hearn's Tales of the Otori series. To experience the real thing, a visit to Nijo Castle is a must. It is considered to have the most famous remaining example of a nightingale floor. For details about the castle, visit the following website.

www.yamasa.org/japan/english/destinations/Kyoto/nijo.html

Nara Prefecture

Landon Fry wriggles through the Buddha's nose in Nara

The dense Nara heat beat down on the members of the Kansai Gaidai History Club as we trudged to the gates of Todai-ji. Around us, families paused on the pathway for snapshots, junior high boys sweltered in their uniforms and threw friendly insults at each other, and visitors crowded around a brazier of burning incense for the ritual fanning of the smoke toward their faces and the places on their bodies that needed special blessing.

Inside the massive temple gate sat the Nara Daibutsu, a fifteen-meter-high bronze Buddha. Throngs of tourists hopped, crouched, and weaved their way toward the imposing statue, all vying for the perfect photo spot. The Daibutsu's bronze skin glimmered in the flash of their cameras. Once I'd taken my photos, I headed around to the back side of the statue, leaving an empty space behind for the crowd to fill.

Around back, a line of about sixty people, all under the age of fourteen, weaved toward an old support pillar with a hole cut in the middle near the ground. One by one, the kids crawled through the small opening, greeted by their families taking pictures as they emerged on the other side.

"That is the Buddha's nose," explained Aki, a senior member of the history club. "If you go through, it brings good luck."

Playing on my ego, Aki dared me to get in line with him, and being too proud to refuse, I did. Knowing that navigating the narrow passageway of the Buddha's nose might end in the humiliation of getting stuck in the process, with the eyes of all the spectators upon them, our other friends took note of our bravery, but failed to conjure similar boldness within themselves. Instead, they waited by the pillar with their cameras at the ready.

Aki and I exchanged small talk as we shuffled forward at rhythmic intervals, and I noticed that no one had yet failed to slip through the Buddha's nose. Apprehensively, I compared my own size to the diminutive statures of the students in line ahead of me, while Aki tried to bolster me with words of encouragement. When my turn came to face the hole, the confidence-building effects of Aki's pep talk vanished before the crowd around the pillar. But my ego, which had gotten me into this predicament in the first place, wouldn't allow me to renege. I was determined to try.

I raised my arms above my head to taper the width of my shoulders, and launched my body, head first, at the hole. In my initial attempt, I resorted to flailing, and soon came to a halt halfway through the passage. Anxiety emanated audibly from the crowd, fueling my panic.

Trapped inside the Buddha's nose, arms and legs thrashing, eyes focused on the tiny exit now visible in front of me, I imagined the feeling of a hundred hands gripping my ankles, yanking me toward freedom and humiliation. Before my worst fears materialized, I somehow gained backward momentum and squirmed out the way I'd gone in.

Disappointment and confusion filled the silence outside the hole. The crowd seemed unsure sure how to react. In all the time we'd been standing in line, watching one intrepid challenger after another, no one had failed to make it through. As if to show me how it's done, Aki squared his shoulders and aligned himself with the opening. I wasn't about to allow my failure to give him the satisfaction of teasing me for perpetuity, so I gathered my courage, and tilting my body at an angle between Aki and the pillar, I lunged toward the hole again.

As with most noses, the Buddha's is widest when measured diagonally, so I was able to gain a little extra wiggle room this time. At this angle, however, I could only reach the ground with one foot for traction. But with a few strong pushes, I finally managed to squeeze through, and tumbled clumsily out the other side. Flashes lit up the scene, exposing the intricate woodwork of the ceiling, and the applause of the crowd filled the temple. (Aki got through with no problem.)

Having successfully wriggled through the Buddha's nose, I still haven't decided whether my luck has increased, but I certainly entertained the tourists at Todai-ji that day. And, really, how many people can say they crawled through the Buddha's nose and lived to tell?

Getting to Todai-ji

In Nara, from Nara Station or Kintetsu Nara Station, it is about a twenty-minute walk east on either Sanjo Dori or Hanna Road respectively toward Nara Park. When you get to Nara Park, look for signposts pointing the way toward Nandaimon (Nandai Gate) and Todai-ji. Among the things to see in Nara are hundreds of deer that will walk right up to you in the park.

Osaka Prefecture

Arin Greenwood wanders among old farmhouses in Osaka

Well traveled and open to new experiences, my friend Dianne and I decided that we wanted to visit the Maishima Plant, where an average of 300,000 metric tons of Osaka's waste are crushed and incinerated each year. It was a surprisingly popular attraction, and it accepted only three hundred visitors per day.

Despite efforts worthy of his name, Hiro, our English-speaking volunteer guide, could not negotiate us into that group. So he arranged for us to visit another waste processing plant in the area, at which point Dianne and I were forced to confess that we were not actually interested in waste processing. We were interested in the playful, carnival-like exterior of the Maishima Plant, which was designed by the Austrian artist Friedensreich Hundertwasser.

As a consolation prize, Hiro picked us up at our hotel at nine on a sunny fall morning to take us to the Open Air Museum of Old Japanese Farmhouses. We rode the train to Ryokuchi Koen, the park where eleven traditional houses have been relocated from various places in Japan.

It was a beautiful day, with bright flowers everywhere, and the leaves changing colors. In the park, a group of older people practiced tai chi in a circle, while swarms of school kids in matching short-pant uniforms milled about carrying plastic bags. "They're collecting these nuts," said Hiro, picking up a little acorn-like object from the ground. He told us that the kids would bring them home and use them to make decorations.

Through a wooden gate, we walked along a path lined with tall rows of flowers and trees, their leaves a palette of autumn reds, yellows, and greens. We came to the first of the structures, a farmhouse from Kyushu with a thick, reed-thatched roof. Inside we breathed the old-house smell of time-mellowed *tatami* mats and hand-hewn wood. The floor of the main room had an inlaid hearth, and paper decorations from some long-forgotten holiday still hung from the rafters.

We meandered from house to house, enjoying the unique features of each one, and the peaceful setting of the natural surroundings. Along the way, near a grove of trees, Hiro translated a sign written in Japanese, the lyrics of "Aka Tombo," a popular children's song:

Dragonflies as red as sunset
Back when I was young.
In twilight skies,
there on her back I'd ride
When the day was done.

"The writer is saying that seeing the dragonfly makes him feel like a child again," Hiro explained.

Farther down the path, near an old *Kabuki* theater, stood a persimmon tree. Its summer leaves were still intact, and shiny orange persimmons hung heavy on its upper branches. Hiro told us that he had loved persimmons when he was a child, so Dianne and I set about trying to get some down for him. Although the branches of fruit grew very high, we jumped and tugged and finally managed to pick three. Hiro polished them with a cloth, and upon taking the first bite, his face lit up. "It is like I am a child again, eating persimmons in the fall." For Hiro, it was a trip down memory lane, but it was my first persimmon, and I had never tasted anything quite so delicious.

At the next house, a tiny woman who worked for the museum said that every day artists came to sketch the persimmon tree, and then when they came back the next day to finish their drawings, they wondered where the persimmons had gone. Oops ...

The next day, Dianne and I stayed at a *ryokan* just outside Osaka. That evening, we braved the chilly night air to sit in an outdoor hot pool beneath the boughs of a flowering tree. Perhaps being touched by the steam gave the tree its extra lease on life, while all the other trees were bare.

Sitting in the pool, looking up at the flowers, I thought of the children's story about the dragonflies, and of the persimmons of Hiro's childhood. I thought of Hiro, who had once traveled the world for his career, but returned home to volunteer as a guide. I too would soon be retiring from my travels, and Dianne would be moving to Saudi Arabia. As the steam rose around us, I knew that when I was older and had moved on with my life, there would come a time when I would be nostalgic for this.

Open Air Museum of Old Japanese Farmhouses

The museum is located on the outskirts of Osaka.

1-2 Hattori Ryokuchi
Toyonaka
(06) 6862-3137

Directions: Ryokuchi Koen is a short walk from Ryokuchi Station on the Midosuji Subway Line. At the station exit, there is a map with directions to the park.

Maishima Incineration Plant

To arrange for a free guided tour, call the number below ten days in advance.

2-2-7 Hokkoshiratsu
Konohana District
Osaka
(06) 6460-2830
www.osaka-info.jp/en/search/detail/sightseeing_6123.html

Directions: Take the Yumesaki Line to Sakurajima Station. From there, take the Maishima Sports Island bus to Konohana Ohashi Nishizume.

Volunteer guides

To contact a volunteer English-speaking guide in Osaka, visit the following website.

http://www18.ocn.ne.jp/~osakasgg/

Hiroshima Prefecture

Josh Krist meets a real Japanese girl in Hiroshima

While living in Japan, my girlfriend and I took the overnight bus from Kyoto to Hiroshima. Arriving in the early hours of a cold and still winter morning, we hoped a walk to the nearby Peace Memorial Park would warm us up.

A-Bomb Dome, once a government building, is the centerpiece of the park. To say that A-Bomb Dome survived is to say that the outer shell is recognizable, since whole walls are crumbled and you can see inside to an empty space.

We sat next to the dome and waited for sunrise. A drunken Japanese woman wearing a miniskirt and black schoolgirl socks stumbled up to us and told us in confusing Japanese that peace is something we should do, not something to come and look at.

Then she asked us to take a picture of her and smiled in front of the dome. "Real Japanese girl!" she told us.

As the sun rose we wandered over to the Children's Peace Monument, a memorial to Sadako Sasaki, who was two years old when Hiroshima was bombed. Ten years later, she fell ill on the track field. A once-healthy runner, she was soon dying from leukemia.

In Japan there is a belief that if you fold one thousand paper cranes, your wish will be granted. Hoping to live a long life, Sadako began folding cranes. Although she folded more than one thousand, she passed away at the age of twelve. That morning I visited the Peace Memorial Park, I saw what seemed like millions of paper cranes draping her memorial in thick curtains of colorful origami.

We stayed at a peace activist hostel, where members of various peace organizations volunteered, conducting tours and connecting visitors with survivors. The proprietors introduced us to Matsushimi-san, a survivor we met at the Peace Memorial Museum. He was sixteen years old when the bomb was dropped. His engineering school was right outside the main four-square-kilometer circle of destruction.

With a gentle smile and in good English, he explained that he had started school at eight in the morning, fifteen minutes before the bomb fell. If he had been late that day, as he had been a few times, he wouldn't have lived to be the kind old man he turned out to be.

When he saw the B-29s overhead, he didn't think much of it as there were always "*B-san*" flying reconnaissance for fire-bombing raids. "I thought they looked very nice, the silver American bombers. They were like ice flying across the sky," he told us.

He had no idea that the planes had dropped anything. There was a huge flash, like someone had turned on a tremendous orange-and-yellow light bulb. He instinctively crawled under his desk, but was still cut up by shattered window glass.

Like many in Hiroshima, he thought that a conventional bomb had landed near him. As he walked across town to get his things from the dormitory, he was shocked to see the whole city destroyed. He told us everything was flattened, and his sense of time was off. It looked like midnight because of the dust and smoke that blocked the sun.

"I didn't understand. People were black and their skin was falling off. They were walking like a procession of ghosts with their hands in front of them."

After the bomb, he ditched engineering to become an English teacher, and lived a few years in Chicago. After seeing what war could do, he wanted to build connections between people through language.

He told us that watching the people walking away in shock from New York City's World Trade Center on September 11, 2001, brought back unhappy memories. It reminded him of the procession of ghosts he had seen in Hiroshima.

This was the only time he was emotional. Everything else seemed very much in the past for him, even though he'd had a few operations on his stomach, and still had what he believed were radiation-related stomach problems.

I was prepared to break down at a shrine or have a heavy epiphany during my stay, but there was only once that I came close to tears. It was later on that night, when I thought about something my girlfriend Helene did.

As Matsushimi-san told us about the ghosts, he brought out a book and showed us a picture of a schoolgirl whose face had melted from her skull. Helene gasped in surprise and started crying.

In that moment, I realized that the drunken woman I'd seen that morning, Sadako and her paper cranes, and this little girl whose face had boiled away—each was the "real Japanese girl." And peace, or the lack of it, isn't something you learn from a building, but from real people.

Peace Memorial Park

The focal point of a visit to Hiroshima, this park contains most of the city's bomb-related sites, including A-Bomb Dome; the Flame of Peace, which will only be extinguished when nuclear weapons have been eradicated; and the Children's Peace Monument (Sadako's memorial), adorned with paper cranes.

www.pcf.city.hiroshima.jp

World Friendship Center

A fifteen-minute walk from A-Bomb Dome, this accommodation includes traditional *tatami*-mat rooms, enriching evening conversations with fellow guests, and a hearty breakfast. It was founded by an anti-nuclear peace activist, and the proprietors can arrange meetings with bomb survivors and guided tours of the Peace Memorial Park.

8-10 Higashi Kan-on
Nishi District
Hiroshima
(082) 503-3191
http://wfchiroshima.net/
wfchiroshima@nifty.com

KUMAMOTO PREFECTURE

Kena Sosa can't help falling in love with Kumamoto

I consider myself lucky to have been an exchange student in Kumamoto on the southern island of Kyushu. Kumamoto is known for its beauty, small town charm, and famous former residents, including Miyamoto Musashi, the samurai author of *The Book of Five Rings*; Natsume Soseki, the celebrated novelist; and Lafcadio Hearn, the cultural historian.

As you meander through downtown, your eye will catch the pointy edge of a rooftop on the near horizon, and as you approach, you will discover that, right in the middle of the city, is the wondrous Kumamoto Castle, with its strikingly dark hues. In every place I've lived, I've found one spot that was my refuge for people watching, writing, thinking, and drinking in the scenery. The grassy knoll that surrounds the castle gate on all sides was my Kumamoto sanctuary, a quiet retreat across the moat where I could be alone and observe from a distance.

For those who enjoy a lively city lifestyle, wander downtown to Kami-tori and Shimo-tori—Up Street and Down Street. Shimo-tori has commercial appeal, and is lined with large department stores, while Kami-tori is more edgy, with specialty shops and unique restaurants.

One of my favorite stores there was Bloomin' Brothers, a 1950s-inspired clothing store run by Jinn, one of Japan's "cool cats." Jinn is a big cheese in Kumamoto's rockabilly music scene. I first met Jinn and a few of his followers playing live along Shimo-tori late at night. They were one group among many artists filling the streets with sound, like a musical buffet.

On Kami-tori and Shimo-tori I witnessed Kumamoto dwellers at their busiest, bolting in and out of stores, darting through the crowds to catch taxis, and suddenly stopping and standing in front of my speeding bicycle for no reason. I felt like the poor frog in the video game *Frogger*, trying to ride my bike through the pedestrian streets. But there is so much to see and do that dodging businessmen and uniformed teenage girls seemed somehow worthwhile.

Kami-tori and Shimo-tori have the best restaurants, some of which even serve *basashi* (raw horsemeat), which is a local delicacy. Much like sashimi, it is served cold, with a special dipping sauce. *Basashi* is most popular in September, during the festival of the Fujisaki Hachimangu Shrine, which culminates in a parade in honor of war hero Kiyomasa Kato.

About an hour and a half away from Kumamoto is the region's volcano, Mt. Aso. I was shocked to be able to walk right up to its rim. I stood so close that the wind could have blown me in, and I was reminded of my mother's fears that living near a volcano would lead to her never hearing from me again. The smell emanating from the crater was strong, and since this was my first trip to an active volcano, I did not recognize it. A friend told me the stink was sulfur, which accounts for all the *onsen* (natural hot springs) in the area. Sulfur is also sold by the bag to bathe in at home. It is said to be great for the skin, although I can't say it's great for the nose.

Best of all my Kumamoto adventures was a visit to a natural amphitheater called Aspecta, in a deep mountain valley near Mt. Aso. One afternoon Aoki-san, my host mother, took a friend and me there. Aoki-san was a member of the Kumamoto chapter of the Elvis Presley Fan Club, and knowing that I also loved Elvis, she came prepared with her own CD. Leaving us to sunbathe in a sea of green grass, she disappeared for a short while.

Soon after she returned, we heard Elvis crooning across the basin. As if singing down from the heavens, his voice rang out for miles, seducing the wildlife ... and me. As he sang, "I can't help falling in love with you," it seemed that The King too had fallen for the great beauty of Kumamoto.

Getting to Kumamoto Castle

Located in the center of Kumamoto City, Kumamoto Castle is a ten-minute tram ride from Kumamoto Station. Get off at the Kumamotojo-mae tram stop.

Getting to Mt. Aso

Mt. Aso's Nakadake Crater is a thirty-minute bus ride from Aso Station. Buses leave about every two hours and stop at Aso-san Nishi Station, where the tram will take you to the crater. You can also walk to the crater from Aso-san Nishi Station in about thirty minutes, or you can drive all the way to the crater, where you will find parking. The Aspecta Amphitheater is located near Mt. Aso crater in Mt. Aso National Park.

Suizenji Koen

Another notable attraction in Kumamoto, this park includes a miniature reproduction of the fifty-three stations of the Tokaido Road, which connected Edo (now Tokyo) with Kyoto during the Edo period. Follow this path and you will even find a small Mt. Fuji. To get to the park, take the tram line that runs from Kumamoto Station to the Suizenji Koen tram stop or the Hohi Train Line to Shin-Suizenji Station. From both stations it is a short walk to the park.

www.suizenji.or.jp/E-index.htm

Higo jewelry

Keep your memories of Kumamoto alive with a piece of Higo inlay jewelry (damascene) made by local artisans. Higo is a centuries-old method of inlaying gold, silver, and copper into an iron base. Although Higo inlay was originally used to decorate scabbards, the craft is practiced today in jewelry and objects d'art that make great souvenirs. For purchasing Higo jewelry, Kami-tori, Shimo-tori, and Sunroad Shinshigai are our top choices.

Photographing cherry blossoms in Tokyo during ohanami *season*

Secret Gardens

Where to hide away from the touring masses

One of my favorite Japan-themed movies is the 1986 film *Gung Ho*, starring Michael Keaton and Gedde Watanabe. In a scene in which Watanabe is talking about how stressful and crowded life is for him back home in Japan, he says, "You put your pants on in the morning, and there's someone in them with you."

As humorous as it sounds, it is almost *that* crowded in Japan's metropolitan areas, with their kilometer upon dreary kilometer of urban sprawl. But for every square kilometer that is *sushizume*—packed like sushi— there are twenty-three square kilometers that are uninhabited. That's right, only a small percentage of Japan's land mass is occupied by urban development. So there are plenty of wide open spaces where you can get away from the grind and growl of the cities: vast national parks, lofty mountain peaks, and long stretches of empty beach.

Within the cities, every neighborhood has at least one haven—a hidden oasis you can escape to when the crowds bear down. Maybe it's a library, or a local *sento* (public bath). Even a typically busy place like the plaza outside Shinjuku Station or the statue of the beloved dog Hachiko in Tokyo's Shibuya District can be oddly quiet at a certain time of day.

When I lived in Tokyo, my secret garden was an actual garden—a tiny postage stamp of a garden that surrounded an equally tiny Buddhist temple called Higashi Nagasaki. It was only a few minutes by bicycle from my apartment, and was rarely visited by anyone but me on weekdays. It wasn't especially beautiful, and nothing of note ever happened while I was there, but I always felt better for having passed a few solitary moments in its quiet atmosphere, a feeling that I share with some of this chapter's contributors. In Kyoto, a hushed garden of raked pebble paths and still ponds inspires a chapter in Liza Dalby's new novel, which is excerpted here, and at a

Lotus blossom on Shinobazu Pond in Tokyo's Ueno Park

deserted public park in Toyokawa at dusk, Dwayne Lawler experiences his own creative inspiration.

Many of this chapter's contributors look to another classic setting for their peaceful reveries. *Onsen* (hot springs) are a popular custom, offering the perfect way to relax. Alice Yamada revels in being spoiled by her mama at an especially luxurious *onsen* inn outside Kyoto. And Johannes Schönherr travels all the way to the southern island of Yakushima, where he discovers a remote hot spring that emerges from the ocean at low tide.

Each season in Japan offers its own sanctuary, which Barbara Mori experiences on her daily ride between Kyoto and Ohara. When the snowdrifts of Hokkaido linger a little too long for Jessica Renslow, she escapes to the idyllic wilderness area of Hidaka, while Philip Blazdell shares his love of Nagano as he wanders its rustic streets in the off-season.

From a breezy beach in Tanihama to an art colony on Naoshima Island, you can follow in our writers' footsteps or seek your own escape. No matter how big a crowd you're in at the time, have faith that it's out there. You may find it when and where you least expect it, as Will Raus does as he travels through "the green that never ends" on a leisurely rail ride out of Tokyo, or like Scott Nesbitt, who ventures onto Kyushu's old rural trains and enters a strange and private world. Once you've discovered your own secret garden, only you can decide whether you want to tell the world about it. We're glad these writers did.

Tokyo Prefecture

Will Raus views the green that never ends on a train out of Tokyo

When I was in the second grade, some of the kids in my class used to sing the most annoying song. It went something like this:

It's the song that never ends
It just goes on and on my friends
Some people started singing it
Not knowing what it was
And they're gonna keep on singing it
forever just because
It's the song that never ends
It just goes on and on my friends ...

And so on, and so on. My classmates would sing it to the point of insanity. It would get stuck in my head for days. It kept me awake at night, and started up again before I even opened my eyes in the morning. Over time, though, I managed to free myself from the clutches of "The Song That Never Ends"—or so I thought.

On a visit to Japan with my dad, I was on a train headed for Matsumoto to see a famous Japanese castle. Outside the window of the train, I saw the greenest green I've ever seen—kilometer after kilometer of rice paddies, one after another, an emerald countryside dotted with out-of-the way temples and farmers' houses with brilliant blue-tiled roofs. At that moment, I realized that the only way to describe the Japanese countryside was "The Green That Never Ends."

And then it happened ...

Like a sequel to a bad movie, the song was back. But this time, I vanquished it before the melody from hell could spawn its evil mischief. I simply rewrote the lyrics into a song that I could stand to have ricocheting around in my brain, and that described Japan perfectly:

It's the green that never ends
It just grows on and on my friends
Some people started planting it
Not knowing what it was
And they're gonna keep on growing it
forever just because
It's the green that never ends
It just grows on and on my friends ...

Rice is so abundant and common in Japan that rows of suburban apartment buildings are sometimes separated by small fields of rice. But this green that never ends is made up not only of rice paddies. Where the land is too steep for rice, farmers cut terraces into the hillsides and plant ascending rows of jade-green tea plants. Higher up, the deep green forests grow so thick that only woodland creatures can inhabit them. And then there are the gardens ... vibrant green with stunningly beautiful plants and flowers. In those gardens, every centimeter that isn't used as a pathway is a botanical masterpiece.

Believe it or not, there is more farmland in Japan than urban sprawl, which is hard to imagine, since the cities are so huge, they sometimes seem impossible to escape. Statistically, however, urban development accounts for just over 10 percent of Japan's total area. As for the rest ...

It's the green that never ends
It just grows on and on my friends ...

I never thought "The Song That Never Ends" would serve any purpose other than driving me crazy. Little did I know that I would make my peace with it by adapting it to describe the most beautiful sight in the world: the abundant green spaces of Japan.

Tokyo to Matsumoto

You can take the local train from Tokyo's Shinjuku Station on the Chuo East Line, but this takes about five to seven hours and requires several transfers. More expensive (around $60 as opposed to $30) are the high-speed Azusa and Super Azusa limited stop express trains, which take just two to three hours from the same station along the same line. Express trains leave hourly. If you plan on traveling more than once on the Azusa Line, it's worthwhile to purchase a book of six tickets, sold at a discounted price. You may also take the bus, which takes about three hours from the Keio Highway Bus Terminal at Shinjuku Station.

www.city.matsumoto.nagano.jp

Discount travel

Long distance travel can be expensive in Japan. For the budget-conscious traveler, JR-East offers the Seishun 18 ticket, a specially discounted five-day limited travel pass that is available during the spring, summer and winter school vacation seasons. For detailed information, visit the East Japan Railway Company website.

www.jreast.co.jp/e/pass/seishun18.html

Nagano Prefecture

Philip Blazdell perches on the roof of Japan in Nagano

Sometimes, especially after another hectic week, when the meetings blend into one long procession of smiling suits and bowing figures, I have to escape. Tokyo is a fantastic place to live, and as I dart from meeting to meeting, it's hard not to be swept up in the city's infectious enthusiasm for life. But sometimes I need quiet. A place for contemplation, and most of all, a place to unwind.

For a year and a half, that place has been Zenko-ji, a temple in Nagano where the noble past of Japan is tantalizingly hidden just beneath the surface, where modern life cohabits with poignant reminders of the days of old. In autumn, the changing of the leaves brings hoards of camera-toting day trippers to the area; in winter the mountains wear their coats of snow with grim determination.

As my car hurtles along the expressway, I catch a glimpse of the Japanese Alps, soaring toward the sky. I am surrounded by jagged, tree-lined hills. A few hours outside Tokyo, and already the air is cleaner, the colors sharper.

The beauty of these lofty peaks has earned this region the title "Roof of Japan," and Nagano Prefecture is often compared to the alpine regions of Europe. Thousands converged on Nagano for the 1998 Winter Olympics, and although the crowds are nothing new, Nagano is more than just a winter resort. It escaped World War II mostly unscathed, and so retains much of the flair and flavor of an old Japanese city.

I wander its quiet streets in early autumn, too late for the summer tourists, too early for the changing of the leaves and the arrival of winter skiers. On each corner, an architectural incongruity: a small wooden temple nestled next to a convenience store, a delicately carved shrine tucked away in a back alley. All the while, the faint sound of Zenko-ji's temple bells teases my senses.

I follow the winding streets toward Zenko-ji. With its two-tiered roof, embellished with only a few bits of brass filigree, it's not the most architecturally appealing temple in Japan. Nor is it the most atmospheric, with its modest gardens and unpretentious surroundings. But I enjoy the colorful variety of visitors, and the friendly residents who always make me feel welcome. And far from the tumult that is my life in Tokyo, here at the Roof of Japan, I simply like to sit on the temple steps, breathing the pure mountain air, and watching the world go by.

Getting to Nagano

From Tokyo, Nagano would be a rushed day trip. It's best to make an overnight visit. Take the Hokuriku Shinkansen from Tokyo Station to Nagano Station. Zenko-ji is a short bus ride from the station.

Zenko-ji Temple

491 Motoyoshi-cho
Nagano

Zenko-ji Kyoju Youth Hostel

For centuries Japanese pilgrims have traveled the country's roads to scenic and religious places, and along these pilgrimage routes, they would stop to rest in tranquil temples. Part of the Japanese Youth Hostel Group, the lodging at Zenko-ji has achieved legendary status among backpackers. The charm of a room here is its simplicity: a futon on a *tatami* floor, and a floral arrangement in a small vase on a recessed shelf.

The last time I arrived, stressed from a hectic week in Tokyo, the *mama-san* guided me along dimly lit corridors. She had already laid out my futon, and no sooner had she bowed her way out of my room and silently slid the paper screen doors closed, I began to feel the tension and stress of Tokyo melting away. The sounds of monks at prayer floated through the still night air as sleep began to overtake me.

479 Motoyoshi-cho
Nagano
(026) 232-2768

Aichi Prefecture

Dwayne Lawler meets Macbeth at Toyokawa's torii gate

My first night in the town of Toyokawa was a lonely one. I was wandering the streets in search of a place to rest when I came upon Toyokawa Inari Shrine. It was dusk, that spooky time of day. As I entered the sacred space, I thought of the famous words from Shakespeare's "Scottish Play":

Now o'er the one half-world
Nature seems dead,
and wicked dreams abuse
The curtain'd sleep.

Macbeth had been on my mind, since I was preparing to produce it in Nagoya, and had been searching for a symbol, something to represent the spiritual conflict ever present in the script. These words followed me as I cautiously wandered the eerie grounds, guarded by its many fox idols, their frozen stares watching my every move.

For some strange reason I was uncomfortably aware of my foreign presence. At that late hour, there were only a few scattered visitors, and as they walked by, eying me with a look of what seemed to me suspicion (or was it even fear?), I bowed awkwardly, and received even more awkward bows in return. Half an hour of walking later, I had managed to achieve a shaky calm, and I arrived at the other end of the grounds and crossed the street. Turning back for one final look, I was struck by the magnificence of the *torii* gate, standing so erect, so proud, so knowing.

The gate, in all its glorious stature, had witnessed millions of guests passing beneath it, yet it seemed ever so slightly to nod. Not a bow, but a nod. Perhaps it was the fading light, or merely my eyes playing tricks, but I distinctly felt it nodding at me. Gazing up, it occurred to me that this was what I was looking for: a symbol that could cross cultures and capture the spirit of *Macbeth* onstage in Japan.

Toyokawa Inari Shrine

The name Toyokawa Inari is derived from that of Dakinishinten, the fox-riding god. According to legend, Dakinishinten was worshipped by famous samurai such as Oda Nobunaga, Toyotomi Hideyoshi, and Tokugawa Ieyasu as a deity of good fortune and well-being. The tradition continues to this day.

1 Toyokawa-cho
Toyokawa

Getting to Toyokawa

Toyokawa can be done as a day trip from Nagoya, although you might be a little rushed. From Nagoya Station, take the Meitetsu Line to Ko Station. Transfer to the Meitetsu Toyokawa Line for Toyokawa Inari Station. Toyokawa Inari Shrine is a short walk from the station. For more information about Toyokawa, visit the following website.

www.toyokawa-map.net/eng/index.html

Niigata Prefecture

Kimberly Fujioka shacks up on the sands of breezy Tanihama

Long stretches of black sand were all we could see outside our car. My husband Kazu slowed down and pulled off the road. I rolled down the window, as he stretched across the seat to get a look at the sign: "Tanihama Beach."

"We're here," he announced.

"I don't see anything." I said

He pulled into a dirt parking lot where a man in a straw hat greeted us and took our two hundred yen. "You'll see," Kazu said, as he walked around the back of our Honda Civic, opening up the hatchback to get our beach gear out.

Just then the baby woke up. "I need to find a place where I can nurse him," I told Kazu.

"Down there," he said, pointing to some falling-down, wooden shanties lined up on the black sand.

"What's that?" I asked, suspiciously.

"The beach houses." he said.

With the baby now screaming in my ear, we made our way down to the shacks, where an old woman invited us into one. The hut was shaded by a straw covering, open on three sides. Although there were other people sitting inside, we were given our own table and *tatami* mats. The breeze flowed through, and the *mama-san* served snacks and cool drinks as I nursed the baby and relaxed. Settled into our pleasant spot, with the baby fed, I was now able to look forward to a leisurely day.

What makes Tanihama so special are the beach houses that had horrified me on first sight. Once I saw them up close, they seemed like a perfect way to spend a day at the beach. These old-fashioned Japanese huts are loosely constructed of thrown-together boards, with thatched roofs and small, hidden kitchens at the back where food is prepared. Each is privately owned, and when you choose one, the *mama-san* will show you to an unoccupied area where you can sit for the day. Since the raised floor is made of *tatami*, you take your shoes off before entering, and make yourself at home at a low table, where your drinks and food will be served.

We paid for an entire day in our own private little area, where we could come and go while we swam and played in the sand. It's usually too hot to be out on the beach for any length of time, so we were grateful for the shade of the hut, cooled by the sea breeze. I took a shower while my husband ordered salted *edamame* (soybeans), *hiyayakko* (tofu topped with scallions, radish, and ginger), Yebisu beer, and *mugi-cha* (cold barley tea).

When I got back from showering, two boys were rolling an enormous watermelon onto the sand. "They're getting ready for *suikawari*, Kazu laughed.

"Huh?"

"A child is blindfolded and given a large stick, and he has to hit the watermelon."

"What are all the other children doing?" I asked.

"Just watch."

We observed as one small boy was blindfolded. The *mama-san* handed him a stick, and all of a sudden the children began shouting at him, instructing him where to turn. He whacked the side of the watermelon. It spun and went flying in the opposite direction. Ripping off the blindfold, he threw it down on the sand and walked away. Then another child stepped up to the center and was blindfolded. The watermelon was moved and the screaming began again.

The noise of the children woke the baby up, so we collected our things and made our way back to the car where it was quiet. The old man in the straw hat was propped up against a tree, asleep. We got in our car and turned on the air conditioning.

"What happens after all the children try to hit the watermelon?" I asked Kazu.

"They eat it. Do you want some? "

Once the baby quieted down, we went back down to the black sandy beach, where the children had finished their game, and we ended our day with the sweet taste of *suikawari* watermelon.

Getting to Tanihama Beach

Tanihama Beach is best done as an overnight trip or longer from Tokyo. From Tokyo Station, take the Joetsu Shinkansen to Echigo-Yuzawa Station. Transfer to the Hokuetsu Express on the Hokuhoku Line to Naoetsu Station. Transfer to the Hokuriku Main Line and get off at Tanihama Station. From here it's a few minutes to Tanihama Beach. This trip takes about three hours.

Where to stay

There are many accommodations near Tanihama Beach. The *minshuku* are the best deal. These small, privately owned hotels are similar to bed-and-breakfasts. They are old-fashioned and less expensive than a traditional *ryokan* (inn). Our favorite is Umi-no-yado Seaside Wakaba, with rates ranging from $42 (¥4,200) to $75 (¥7,500).

108-4 Nagahama
Joetsu Town
(025) 546-2123

Minshuku around Japan

For a list of *minshuku* around Japan, visit the following website.

ww.minshuku.jp/english/list.html

Kyoto Prefecture

Alice Yamada follows her bliss in Kyoto

When I was a child growing up in Japan, my family frequently vacationed at *onsen ryokan*, traditional inns with natural hot springs where the adults spent endless hours bathing and soaking, while the kids played in the arcades or at the ping-pong tables. As I grew up, I cared less for the arcades, and more for the quiet baths and terrific cuisine.

During a recent trip, my mama arranged for us to stay at a beautiful *onsen ryokan*, known for its sophisticated Kyoto *kaiseki*, traditional pre-tea-ceremony cuisine which also includes elegant seasonal meals. Arashiyama Benkei is located in Arashiyama, a district within the greater Kyoto region. Arashiyama is the spot where nobles living in Kyoto during the Heian period went to vacation, which sounds funny now, since today it is within the city limits.

The resort is famous for its cherry blossoms, and also has a hot spring source, with mildly alkaline water believed to clarify skin, soothe muscle aches, and relieve fatigue. This was high-end *onsen* vacationing, far removed from the holidays of my childhood. Benkei catered to my grown-up appreciation for quiet and calm, and I appreciated my mama's thoughtfulness for selecting a place that fit my state of mind so perfectly.

With only fifteen rooms, and five scenic bathing options, (two per sex and one "for rent" by couples/families/individuals), Benkei is relatively small. I prefer more intimate *ryokan* for many reasons. First, I don't really like to bathe with other people, and the spas at small *ryokan* during off hours are empty. Both times I went for a long soak, I was the only one in the ladies' outdoor bath. A giant tub all to myself is luxury at its best. I even practiced yoga between my soaks. Outside! Completely naked!! It was so liberating. These baths are very well protected, and no one can peek, much less sneak in, although I have seen footage of monkeys coming down from the mountains in the northern *onsen* for a dip alongside their human friends.

The other highlight was dinner. Meals at *ryokan* are served in your room, so you get to lounge around in your *yukata,* your hair wet from the *onsen* soak, and lie down in between courses. My mama also chose Benkei because the food was recommended as some of the best traditional *kaiseki* meals at any *ryokan.* I have to agree.

Our sashimi selection was plated on a bamboo mat resting on a bed of ice. The *amaebi* (sweet raw shrimp) was surprisingly good. And although the *tai shabu* was delicious, my favorite dish was the *unagi, sakuramochi*-style. Inside the fragrant cherry leaf was a ball of *mochigome,* the super-sticky rice known as "sweet rice." This was a warm, savory dish with a nourishing quality beyond description. There was a slice of *unagi* between the cherry leaf and the rice, with a thick, fish-based sauce that added a pleasant richness. The saltiness of the cherry leaf worked well with the warm, comforting broth. The final dish of the evening was a Japanese beef steak, cooked and kept warm by the same individual heaters that once held our *tai shabu* clay pot.

After we finished the meal with soup and rice, I think we had dessert, but I was so sleepy, I don't remember it. I rolled over and relaxed in the second room, while the *ryokan* ladies came and set up our futons in the other room. Within minutes of my epicurean debauchery, I was blissfully falling asleep, wondering how I managed to be so fortunate—resting so peacefully with a tummy full of fabulous food, surrounded by the wonderful scents of *tatami* and wood in a quiet *ryokan* with my mama taking care of me.

Arashiyama Benkei

Susukinobaba-cho Tenryuji, Saga
Ukyo District
Kyoto
(075) 872-3355
www.benkei.biz/~english

Train: Sagano Line to Saga-Arashiyama Station.

Staying at an onsen ryokan

The following website offers a good selection of *ryokan* around the country.

www.japaneseguesthouses.com

Liza Dalby fictionalizes her favorite garden in Kyoto

In this excerpt from my novel, Hidden Buddhas, *Nora, a young American woman, meets up with Koji, a Buddhist priest-in-training whom she had once taken around San Francisco.*

They were walking past the temple Myoshin-ji. A pale gray-striped wall enclosed the compound. Inside was a village of many smaller sub-temples. One of the first, on the west side as they entered, was the Taizo-in. Koji looked at a small sign posted at the entrance gate.

"There is a garden here," he said. "Have you seen it?"

Nora hadn't.

"They all have such poetic names," she said. "Ryoan-ji—'peaceful dragon'; 'the temple of the golden pavilion'; 'the moss temple.' What does Taizo-in mean?"

"*In* means 'temple,'" Koji began, "*taizo* means ..." he struggled to explain. "Like ... you have some special thing you don't want other people to know about. You hide it—make a secret place. That is *taizo* ..."

"So, maybe the garden here is the hidden treasure," said Nora.

And it was. Even Koji was amazed. He had seen temple gardens his whole life. He took them for granted. Ponds, paths, azaleas, maples, moss—it was a landscape vocabulary with which he was utterly familiar. But despite the fact that they lay practically at his feet, Koji had never in his adult life made a trip to a temple specifically in order to see a garden. They walked onto a pebbled path that meandered around to a pond fed by a brook.

"I suppose this is another garden that I should see in the spring," Nora said with a sigh. "That's what everybody is always telling me—or the fall."

Koji raised his hand to shade his eyes, looking toward the pond.

"No—this is a good time," he said. "I'll show you."

They approached the still water of the pond and Nora could see that it was full of lotuses. Not water lilies, but actual lotuses, in all stages—teardrop-shaped buds, dark pink partially opened flowers, and full blooms that had whitened as they opened, the pink tinge having retreated to the tips of the petals. A few green pods stood up on strong stems as well, their petals and stamens having fallen onto the round umbrella-like leaves floating on the surface. Water drops puddled into cabochons of crystal in the center of some of the leaves.

They followed the path to the side of the main hall. Here was an expanse of raked pebbles, the grooves of the pattern deep and well defined, ringing the rocks like ripples. Nora marveled at the dynamic feel of the still composition. You could almost hear the silent waves.

Koji looked at her. Being with Nora now reminded him of that brief period in California when he had been free of the expectations of the Buddhist priesthood he was expected to make his career. Since then he practiced English in his head largely by imaginary conversations with a phantom Nora. He had not expected to ever see her again. He was not prepared for the possibility that she would be even more appealing in person than she was in his fantasy.

"I think I could come back to this garden at any season," Nora turned to him. "This is the most wonderful garden I have seen yet."

Getting to Myoshin-ji and Taizo-in

From Kyoto Station, take the Sagano Train Line to Hanazono Station. The garden is a five-minute walk from the station. Several buses are also available; get off at Myoshin-ji-mae stop. While at the gardens, enjoy a bowl of matcha tea with Taizo-in's special catfish-and-gourd motif tea cakes.

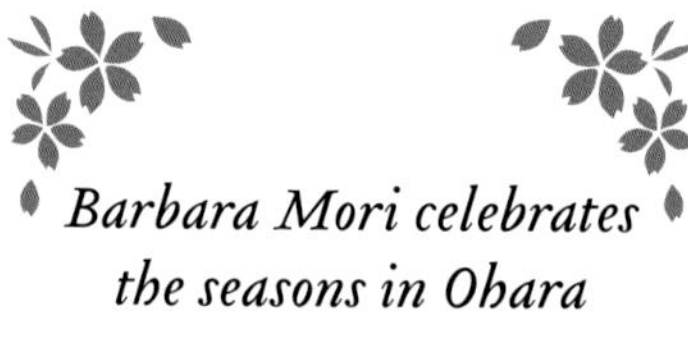

Barbara Mori celebrates the seasons in Ohara

You take the bus from Kyoto Station, and at first you are enveloped by the traffic of downtown. The bus weaves through the busy streets, past shops, department stores, theaters, people. It travels along the Kamo River, and then the Takano. You watch the white birds zoom and dive, resting in trees and walking regally along the banks. You pass the Iwashimizu Hachiman-gu Shrine, and you are now on your way toward Mt. Hiei.

In the summer everything is green, encroaching on the road, narrowing it. Branches scrape the roof of the bus. As you look into the water, you remember how it moves swiftly between its icy shawls in the winter. In some places, it has carved a deep valley, and in others it is broad and flat, spreading out and crowding the road.

Now the mountain is on your right, and the Ohara River on the left. In the spring you look for the delicate pink, white, and purple of the wild wisteria. In the autumn the russet, yellow, gold, and brown of the different trees make a patchwork cover to the hills.

You pass the cable car point where you can ride up to the Enryaku-ji, a mountain temple built to protect the city from evil, which is believed to come from the north and east. There are few people on the bus now, only those who live in the various villages. They are dressed in browns and blacks, not very fashionable clothes, and encumbered with shopping from the city.

Huge tourist buses vie for the road in the summer, and you marvel at the drivers' abilities to maneuver around the hills and not topple into the river or scrape another bus. Sometimes they engage in a delicate stop and go, edging around each other like snakes deciding whether or not to mate.

As you gaze out at the paddy fields, you remember how they are covered in snow in the winter, and only small white hills indicate the piles of rice straw beneath, contrasting with the shadows of snow on the roofs of black slate. The thatched houses of old are gone, and the antennas and dishes for televisions adorn the tops of the farmers' homes. The famed *Ohara-me*, the women who balanced large piles of wood on their heads to sell, are in evidence only in pictures sold in the tourist shops.

The hills bring to mind spring, when they are purple with the leaves of the *shiso* plants used to make pickles from radishes, cucumbers, and seaweed—a reason some visitors take the bus into the valley, even though the pickles are available in the downtown shops. It is also this time of year when the new school year begins, but there are fewer and fewer children to attend the rural classes. One school farther up the mountain only has ten students.

Getting off at the bus depot in Ohara, you can make a choice to go up the mountain or across the field. Choosing the field, you visit the lonely Tendai nunnery of Jakko-in, where the memory of Kenreimon-in still hovers as if in a Noh drama. It is small and quiet. A recording tells the story of the sad empress who lost all in the Battle of Dan-no-ura, including her child. She retreated to the nunnery, but was under constant surveillance lest she become the focus of a rebellion against the new rulers. The building overlooks a steep ravine, offering no access to escape. Despite the visitors roaming around, an air of sadness still remains.

Then travel back across the valley and up, up the mountain to Sanzen-in. In summer, the tourists swarm from the buses to the shops in front of the temple, taking pictures of each other at the stone gate. They make an important contribution to village families' incomes. With the coming of the tourists, like migratory birds, mothers disappear from homes, and children have their three o'clock snack alone or with grandma when they come home from school. Local stalls sell pickles and other mementos, and restaurants offer bowls of steaming noodles or cold noodles with ice.

First built in the tenth century, Sanzen-in is a large and active temple devoted to Amida. Surrounded by moss and tall stately trees, its *hondo*, or main hall, is protected by the other buildings in the complex and the wall that surrounds the grounds. Quite a contrast to the nunnery, it has many young men studying there and living in the dormitory.

On occasion, the head abbot will give a sermon to the visitors. He sits before the three main statues of the Buddha and tells of the love the Buddha has for people. Sometimes it is that of a mother who comforts and encourages, sometimes it is like a father who is strict and demanding. Confucius would be proud to hear the smooth blending of family values and compassion. The people listen quietly and then continue on to view the beautiful buildings, towering cedars, and moss garden, which are lovely in all seasons.

Getting to Ohara

A suburb of Kyoto, Ohara can be reached by taking the Number 17 bus from Kyoto Station. Ohara is ideal for walking, and you can easily explore the town and following temples on foot.

Jakko-in

676 Kusao-cho
Ohara
Sakyo District
Kyoto
(075) 744-2341
www.jakkoin.jp/ (Japanese)
www.taleofgenji.org/jakko-in.html

Sanzen-in

Famous for its cherries, Sanzen-in has a beautiful garden, so perfect that it's almost surreal. The *shoji* panels in the *tatami* viewing room open directly onto it.

540 Raigoin-cho
Ohara
Sakyo District
Kyoto
(075) 744-2531
www.taleofgenji.org/sanzen-in.html

Where to stay

Conveniently located just a five-minute walk from the Ohara bus stop, Ryoso Chatani is an economical home-style inn with traditional futon-and-*tatami*-mat rooms, shared toilets, communal bathing, and delicious dining. Ryoso Chatani is a ten-minute walk to the lovely, wooded, shop-lined path along the river that leads up to Sanzen-in.

160 Kusaocho
Ohara
Sakyo District
Kyoto
(075) 744-2952
www.r-chatani.com/ (Japanese)

Kagawa Prefecture

Alan Wiren immerses himself in the culture of Naoshima

At the end of the day, I slipped into the Cultural Melting Bath: a warm, bubbling Jacuzzi with the stars twinkling overhead. Surrounded by thirty-six tall, fluidly shaped stones, arranged in accordance with the ancient principles of *feng shui*, I could hear the surf lapping at the shores of Naoshima Island.

The stones were placed by the Chinese artist Cai Guo-Qiang, to channel the energy of the earth down from the mountains and out to Japan's Seto Inland Sea. What made it truly magical was that my day had been full of just this kind of experience. I had been participating in and becoming part of grand-scale artworks that were created as part of the Benesse Art Site, which integrates the landscape and culture of Naoshima Island.

The ferry that had brought me there in the morning was met by the courtesy shuttle bus that makes regular rounds throughout the day. I told the driver that I was staying at Benesse House and left my bags with him, so that I could start exploring right away. I began with a tour of Benesse's Art House Project. Once boasting nothing of greater interest than a copper refinery, Naoshima Island had become a graying community, with young people moving away to the cities to pursue their careers. Then Benesse came along, and several of the village's abandoned traditional houses were given over to different artists.

I found myself in a house containing the artwork *Sea of Time '98*, where one large room had been converted into a shallow pool with dim lighting and a catwalk around the edges. Just below the rippling surface of the water, dozens of light-emitting digital counters were arranged in an aesthetic pattern. Each one displayed, over and over, sequentially, the numbers one through nine.

Our guide explained that Tatsuo Miyajima, the artist, had lent each counter to a different village resident and asked that person to set the speed to his or her liking. A map was made so that each person's counter could be identified. Some of the participants were quite old when the work was created, so it is likely that a few have already died. The counters all ran at different speeds. Some raced so fast I could not read them. Others were slower than a heartbeat. The effect was dazzling.

Other houses in the project delve into equally impressive themes, and I regretted not having time to visit them all. In the afternoon I hopped onto the shuttle, passing by some of the works that are permanently placed out of doors. One was an enormous, bright yellow pumpkin covered with a pattern of large and small black dots, perched on the end of a narrow pier that juts into a bay; another work consisted of three huge, gray, metallic diamond shapes suspended over a grassy knoll overlooking the sea.

The shuttle brought me to the Chichu (Underground) Art Museum. Along with Benesse House, it was designed by the world-renowned architect Tadao Ando. The path toward the entrance of the museum runs beside a stream dotted with irises and lily pads, backed by a grove of bamboo, and I was overcome by a sense of familiarity. It felt like walking into a painting by Claude Monet.

True to its name, the museum is almost entirely underground, and it is hardly visible from the outside. Inside, it was like nothing I had ever seen. It contains permanent exhibitions by Walter De Maria as well as James Turrell, who specializes in optical illusions. The building does not simply house the artworks; it is part of them, and in the Turrell space the functions of your own eyes and brain are taken into account, to let you walk through a psychological terrain of color and dimension. The finale is the Monet space, where you are surrounded by four paintings from the Water Lilies series, commissioned for the L'Orangerie Museum in France.

As this special day drew on toward evening, I checked into Benesse House, a combination luxury hotel, modern art museum, and gourmet restaurant. I felt fortunate that, as a guest, I would have the run of it after it was closed to the general public. I had just enough time to enjoy an exquisitely aesthetic and delicious Japanese meal before picking up my towel and flashlight at the front desk and heading for my hour at one of the privileges of staying at the house: the Cultural Melting Bath.

Getting to Naoshima

While Naoshima can be done as a day trip from Osaka, the island is best enjoyed as an overnight trip or longer, so that you have time to experience all it has to offer. From Osaka take the Shinkansen Sanyo Line from Shin Osaka Station to Okayama Station. From Okayama Station, local trains and buses will take you to Uno Station, but it is a good idea to check ahead and keep both schedules with you, as there can sometimes be up to two hours between trains. From Uno Station, you can walk to Uno Port, where there are two ferry lines to take you to Naoshima, making multiple trips each day. One is a car ferry; the other is for passengers only. The ferry trip takes fifteen minutes.

Staying on Naoshima

Accommodation on the island, outside Benesse House, is limited. There are a few Japanese-style inns or boarding houses. The number of restaurants has increased, but there are still very few relative to the number of visitors to the island, and not one is open every day. If you plan to stay at Benesse House, visit the excellent Benesse Art Site website (noted below) to book accommodations, as well as tours and admission to sites that require reservations. This website also allows you to create a personal itinerary that you can log into and revise any time until your arrival date. It also suggests itineraries for one-, two-, and three-day visits. These are invaluable for a first-time visitor. The island is small, but the sites are spread out, and you should allow enough time to fully appreciate the ones you visit.

www.naoshima-is.co.jp/english

New artworks

Since my visit, Benesse added two new experiences. *Nirvana* is designed to lead you to an enlightened state; Mori Mariko, the artist, appears in this video work dressed as a goddess. The other is called *untitled 2008* (*hotel room for one*). It accommodates only one person at a time and is a three-day, meditative experience in a space designed by Rirkrit Tiravanija.

Nagasaki Prefecture

Scott Nesbitt rides Kyushu's friendly rails to Nagasaki

"Why do you want to go to Kyushu?" my Japanese friends asked.

Everyone seemed to be pushing me north toward Tokyo or Hokkaido, but neither place held any grip on my imagination. Kyushu, on the other hand, was different. I wanted to experience the famous hot springs, get close to a live volcano, and make the pilgrimage to Nagasaki.

So from Kobe I took the overnight ferry to Beppu, where I hung around for a few days. From there, I traveled to Kumamoto, where I boarded a ferry across Shimabara Bay and landed at Shimabara, the starting point for my journey to Nagasaki on Kyushu's old railway lines. At a weather-beaten Japan Railway station, I watched my train pull in. Its cars were faded white, with a liberal coating of grime just above the wheels. Not quite dilapidated, just old and growing rickety. "Kyushu," I muttered. "The place old JR trains go to die."

The cars came to a groaning stop, and I waited for the doors to open with their familiar pneumatic hiss. Nothing happened. Farther down the track, I noticed a man pulling a handle to open his door. When in Rome, I thought, and reached out.

The seats were like that old sofa in your parents' rec room, with the distinctive sponginess that comes from thousands of behinds straining springs beyond their limits. Perfect for the long journey ahead.

An avid rail traveler once told me that every train has a distinct personality. In Japan, the famous Shinkansen (bullet trains) exude a sleek, moneyed power. The intercity trains and subways are plain, prompt, and utilitarian. Both project an impersonality that can make you feel like an outsider. The old trains in Kyushu, on the other hand, are worn and scrappy, but also friendly and personable—a refreshing mix, and one so different from what I'd come to expect.

Sitting in that train was like sitting in a Canadian public school classroom in the middle of winter. Stuffy and overheated. It was so hot that perspiration began to glaze my forehead, and beads of sweat snaked down my back. After a few stops, the train began to fill up. Not quite *sushi-*

zume, "packed like sushi," but close quarters nonetheless. To my right, I noticed an elderly woman, standing with a cluster of shopping bags in one hand. I caught her eye and said, "*Oba-san, seki o yuzurimasho*"—"Ma'am, please take my seat."

What struck me was that the woman wasn't surprised that I could speak Japanese. She didn't pretend she couldn't understand me either, or refuse the offer. Instead, she sat down and started talking to me about the weather. We chatted about inconsequential things for awhile, then she got up and thanked me—for the seat or the conversation, I'm still not sure—and got off.

The train remained stationary for several minutes. An open door gave me the twin opportunities of enjoying a cooling breeze and taking a peek at the station. Beyond the barriers, blocking traffic with their flashing lights and annoying klaxon, there was nothing that I associated with a train stop. No ticket machines, no platform, no covered waiting area for passengers. The station house itself was nothing more than a small glassed-in shed at the edge of a beach.

Beyond the station was one of the nicest expanses of shoreline I'd seen in Japan—wide, flat, smooth, and empty. The sea rolled with an understated grace, and every so often, the waves assaulted a small breakwater. The shore hadn't yet been peppered with the monstrosities that the Japanese authorities put into place ostensibly to protect beaches. Here, the division between the beach and the nearby town was the railway itself. It bisected nature and civilization, like a line on a surveyor's map.

A couple of stops later, a group of five high school students boarded the train. My first instinct was to brace myself for the talk pointed in my direction. But it never came. The boys sat down and chatted with one another about their school's upcoming sports day.

In other parts of Japan, I was accustomed to stares, pointing, and shrieks of "*gaijin*!" Throughout my trip to Kyushu, no one seemed to notice me: no comments or gestures in my direction, and, blessedly, no one sidling up, speaking to me in what they thought was English. I drew no attention whatsoever.

Perhaps it had to do with history. Nagasaki was the first place in Japan to receive Western traders. Or perhaps it was because the residents of Kyushu were naturally more laid back than their stuffy northern cousins. The inhabitants reminded me of people in Atlantic Canada: friendly and easy-going.

On the last leg of the journey, from Isahaya to Nagasaki, I boarded a train of a slightly newer vintage than the one I'd just ridden. The cars were just as hot and stuffy, but there were fewer passengers, and I got a clear view of the landscape. Along the way, a long-unseen sight captured my attention: trees, lots of trees. Occasionally, a light shone through them, but the only other evidence of civilization was the stretch of rail I was on, and the stations along the way.

Reluctantly, I debarked at Nagasaki, and as I walked out of the station, I thought about the journey so far. I'd seen new facets of Japan, and a side of the Japanese people I didn't know existed. Near the station entrance, a clock caught my eye, and I smiled a silly little smile. It was reassuring to know that no matter how old the Japanese trains are, and no matter how run down their stations, there was one constant—they're always on time.

Riding the rails in Kyushu

The Kyushu Railway website provides information about traveling through Kyushu by train, including timetables, route maps, and information on fares and rail passes. For what to do when on Kyushu, the Kyushu Tourism Information website is a good place to start.

www.jrkyushu.co.jp/english/
www.welcomekyushu.com

Kagoshima Prefecture

Johannes Schönherr discovers Yakushima's hot spring by the sea

Having lived for a couple of years in Beppu, one of Japan's major hot spring towns, visiting the local hot springs was not exactly high on my to-do list when old friends, a couple from Europe, came to visit me. After a few good soaks in the town's *onsen*, I decided to take them to the southern island of Yakushima.

There we saw the fabled cedar forests, and swam in mountain rivers. But the best experience came on the day we decided to just drive the coastal road around the island. Along the way, I remembered something from an earlier visit to Yakushima, when I had hitchhiked around the island with a friend. We had been told that there was an ocean hot spring at the very south end of the island. Unfortunately, when we arrived, it was high tide and the rising sea had already flooded over the hot spring.

Sure that this was a hot spring to beat all the ones back in Beppu, I hoped I might get lucky this time. I drove around Yakushima with my European friends, and when we reached the southern coast, I slowed down at every little path that led toward the beach. I couldn't remember the exact location of the ocean hot spring, so I didn't tell my friends much about it. I didn't want to disappoint them in case we couldn't find it, or it was covered by the tide again.

Finally, I spotted a small wooden sign in English, directing us to the hot spring. I took a left turn that led down a tiny road, which ended at a teahouse with a large parking area, where a big sign read: "Don't park here for the Ocean Spring." It was back to the main road again. But along the way, we noticed there were cars parked in one section, and we saw someone folding a towel.

This must be the place, I thought. Fortunately, there was just enough space for my car to squeeze in.

Following a small path toward the sea, we arrived at a concrete walkway leading to a rock formation that had created several pools. Hirauchi Kaichu Onsen. We'd found it after all ... and the tide was low!

Signs in both English and Japanese offered instructions, although the rules were obvious from looking around. We should put one hundred yen per person into the metal collection box. We could keep our shoes on up to the white line on the concrete path, where we saw the shoes of the other bathers. We should get undressed among the rocks, and take one of the plastic bowls and rinse our bodies before entering the *onsen*.

Then, the instructions recommended carefully testing the water temperature in the various pools. A stone-faced, elderly Japanese man sitting in one of them doesn't necessarily mean that an *onsen* newbie can take the heat. Be careful. Those old guys are hard core. They have been going to these springs all their life. You could be boiled like a lobster at temperatures they might find a bit chilly.

The hot spring turned out to be a *konyoku onsen*, which means mixed bathing for both men and women. But at this time, there were only old men in the pools, and they all appeared to be in a Zen-like state. As we undressed, they made sure not to stare at the European girl in our group.

Some of the pools were rather hot, while others were cooler as they mixed with the sea water. The smell was unique—a blend of salty sea water and the sulfur-rich hot spring. We could easily have crawled over the rocks and swam into the sea, but instead, we settled into the hot water and listened to the waves crashing around us.

Every now and then, we stood up to cool off a bit and to look out toward the sea. Not an island in sight. This was the uninterrupted Pacific Ocean, and the rocks forming the pool where I stood, waist-deep in the steaming water, would soon be the sole property of the fish again.

I would love to have stayed, to see the baths slowly submerged into the ocean, but Seibu Rindo was still ahead of us, where the road gets narrow and curvy high above the coast. There were plenty of monkeys on the road there too. I wanted my friends to experience that drive in the daytime and, of course, save myself the danger of driving that stretch in darkness.

So we left, looking back many times while walking up the concrete path toward the car. I had to admit, even after living for years in the midst of mud *onsen*, sand baths, and remote forest hot springs, the Hirauchi Kaichu Onsen was something really special.

Getting to Hirauchi Kaichu Onsen

There is hourly daytime bus service from Miyanoura (in the north, where ferries arrive and where most tourists stay) and Anbo (in the east, where ferries also arrive) around the island up to the Oko-no-taki Waterfall near Kurio village. Tell the driver that you want to get off at the Hirauchi Kaichu Onsen stop. Note that there is a break in bus service between the waterfall and Nagata, which means you cannot travel by bus completely around the island. For this stretch you will need your own car, or you can try hitchhiking, which is generally easy on Yakushima. Be aware that there is not much traffic passing through the northwest Seibu Rindo area. The Japan National Tourist Organization has a good map and bus details on its website.

www.jnto.go.jp/eng

Timing your visit

There is a *minshuku* (inexpensive, family-run inn) called Hirauchi Kaichu Onsen-So next to the Ocean Hot Spring. Staff here will be able to tell you the times of the tide.

(0997) 47-2403 (Japanese)

Hokkaido Prefecture

Jessica Renslow gets back to her roots in Hidaka

I'm tired of the Siberian cold and the fishbowl life of the lone *gaijin* in the town of Pippu-cho. Its location in the deep Taisetsu Valley keeps the surrounding Kamikawa-gun snowbelt frozen well into spring. As I dig myself out of my dreary apartment yet again, I look out at the Taisetsu Mountain Range. Taisetsu-san himself has decided to make an appearance. He squats before my tiny village like a protective *oji-chan* guarding his grandchildren. No concealing cloud kimono for him this morn. It's an unseasonable sight.

While excavating my Toyota and preparing to get away, my mind travels to memories of the American south, to summer camping and silly sing-alongs slung out in my cousins' slow drawls. It's early June, after all. I want to see some daylight, a little scenery. So I head for Hidaka ...

As I glide through the southern, sun-dappled mountain range of Hidaka Subprefecture, I smile at the steady decrease in snow and increase in greenery. The seaside hugs the cliffs as the last of the *sakura* bloom before me. Wildlife emerges. Sleepy snow foxes and chubby Shetland ponies examine me from afar. I wave to them like a fool. They dismiss me and go back to whatever it is that foxes and ponies do. In this sweet setting, my cynical winter mindset slips away.

When I reach the town of Urakawa, I could almost swear I'm in rural Kentucky—if Kentucky had a seascape, that is. Even the aggressive advertisements exploding from the roadsides can't kill my spring buzz. White-fenced horse country gives way to a consuming forest.

In the foothills the trees are thick. I almost miss my turn. Birches yield to evergreens. The shaded sun reminds me of my girlhood haunts. These were the secret places I went to escape homework and humidity, spots that could only be found on foot.

Coming back to my favorite campsite in Hidaka's Ikanti Forest Park has become a ritual these past three years. It's a way to take a break from the eyes of my village, and a way to remember who I am and where I come from. I climb up the hill and pay my entry fee. The site is rustic, even for Hokkaido Island.

I claim a spot for my tent that's close to the communal sink, but not too close. This is the most grass I've seen in nine months. I want to take off my shoes and run barefoot. But three years living in a group-oriented society has left a mark ... or has it? Rebelliously I decide to forget about being a "good" *gaijin*. I shuck off my sweaty socks and toss my shoes aside. The campsite attendant gawks and smiles at me. I shrug back and let out a loud laugh. He chuckles as he goes back to his work.

I slip into some sandals and follow a trail. Deep in the woods I head toward the cliff. Though it is no longer the peak of *ohanami* season, I am pleased to see that the coastline is still adorned in an explosion of pink. I have missed the cherry blossom seekers by a week, and the view is all mine.

Getting to Ikanti Forest Park

Plan to spend at least a few days when visiting Hokkaido. A car ferry with sleeping accommodations travels from the port of Oarai near Tokyo to the port of Tomakomai on the southern coast of Hokkaido. From Tomakomai, the Hidaka Railway Line serves the town of Urakawa, which is located in Hidaka Subprefecture. Ikanti Forest Park, with hiking and camping, features forest trails and beautiful coastal views. The Urakawa Town Hall information center listed below can provide general information and directions.

www.sunflower.co.jp/ferry/english_guide.pdf (Ferry guide)

Urakawa Town Hall

1-3-1 Tsukiji
Urakawa
(01462) 22-5000 (English spoken)
www.town.urakawa.hokkaido.jp/english/
urakawa@lilac.co.jp

Horsing around

On January 2, the town of Urakawa celebrates the Horse Festival in which a dozen horses are ridden down the main street and up the steps to the Urakawa Shrine. This ninety-year-old tradition is celebrated to pray for the fertility of the horses and the success of area ranches in the coming year. The city's biggest festival, which also celebrates horses, is held the first weekend in August, with a horseback parade, musical entertainment, an abundance of food, and the wedding of two specially chosen couples.

Tulips in Tokyo's Hibiya Park

Spiritual Japan

Discovering Buddhism and beyond

There's something about Japan that seems to evoke the spirituality in everything and everyone. It is inherent in the Japanese people, and upon witnessing the country's natural beauty, it's not hard to see why they believe in the *kami*, sacred spirits that reside in every natural thing. Spirituality is in the air, it's in the water, it's in the earth.

Even the simplest and most humble daily tasks are carried out with mindful devotion. Store clerks wrap purchases with origami-like precision, taxi drivers in their crisp uniforms and white gloves lovingly detail their cabs with feather dusters, and even the unremarkable act of making a bowl of tea has been elevated to an art form. People spend their days off at Shinto shrines and Buddhist temples to pray for health and good fortune. And not a season goes by that they don't stop to appreciate its beauty and its gifts.

It is impossible to spend any length of time in Japan without being imbued with this essence. My stay there instilled in me a lasting reverence, not only toward the country, but toward life itself, regardless of where I have lived since then. And the days I spent observing the rituals of the Japanese people, visiting shrines and temples, and witnessing the astonishing beauty of the land, have inspired a lifelong career of writing about Japan.

The contributors in this chapter were equally inspired, as they reveal in their essays. So dedicated is Stefan Chiarantano to Zen Buddhism that he hikes all the way to the top of Mt. Takigo to have tea with a renowned priest, and Mary Cook returns to Japan time and again to make the pilgrimage to Taiseki-ji in the foothills of Mt. Fuji. On a lighter note, during an evening spent meditating with Buddhist monks in Kyoto, Frank Lev allows us to eavesdrop on his amusing inner dialogue, as he tries to resist a persistent ant and finds himself overcome by inappropriate thoughts.

Incense brazier at Tokyo's Asakusa Kannon Temple

Shrines and temples are often the settings for spiritual epiphanies, which Shane Cowlishaw discovers while following a pilgrim through an eerie cemetery to a temple atop Mt. Koyasan. One of my own occurred in a Zen garden in search of *satori* (enlightenment) at Japan's most famous Zen garden in Kyoto, and another upon walking away from a temple in Kanazawa, an experience that led me to write my very first essay about Japan.

Outside the religious world, opportunities for transcendence await in many settings. Karryn Miller finds spiritual fulfillment in her daily work as a yoga instructor in Tokyo, and Leza Lowitz experiences hers in the silence of a bamboo forest in Kamakura. Unexpectedly, Kimberly Fujioka becomes one with a glassblower as he guides her through the process of turning a lump of molten glass into a vase in the artisan village of Tsuchi-to-Hi-no-Sato.

By sharing some of their most private moments, our writers invite you to discover the spiritual side of Japan. They also capture the quality that gives Japan such a special place in so many travelers' hearts.

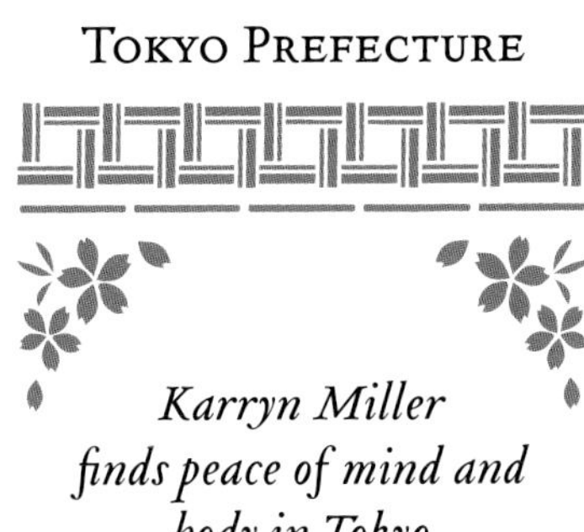

Karryn Miller finds peace of mind and body in Tokyo

As I open the security shutter, the metal screeches. I reach for the familiar lock and sweep the *noren* curtains to the side. Looking around in the dim morning light, I savor what has become my second home in Tokyo—my place of solitude when the city's noise starts to devour my thoughts. I am a teacher at Sun & Moon Yoga and among the lucky few people whose jobs are their passion, who feel a sense of calm when they arrive at work rather than just when they leave.

The long lines of the polished wooden floor planks draw my eyes to the end of the room, where sunlight trickles in, filtered by paper *shoji* doors. The air retains the faint scent of sandalwood from incense long since extinguished. I feel myself welcome the lingering warmth from the active bodies that filled this space the night before. I walk toward the altar adorned with a jagged mass of amethyst, and reach out for a stick of fresh incense. Once it is lit, the smoke starts to rise, layering itself upon the traces of the last.

Soon the door opens and students trickle in, locals and foreigners coming together. Some enter cautiously, testing the waters to see if they are in the right place; others bound in swinging their bags—and worries—onto the long counter before unfurling their mats and finding their usual places. There is friendly chatter with familiar faces, and then the lesson begins.

Coming onto the mat and into the present moment, bodies extend into *Utthita Trikonasana*, the triangle pose. As the hour unfolds, the students open their hearts in the wheel pose of *Urdhva Dhanurasana*, and they melt tension away with the child's pose of *Balasana*. Finally, each returns to his or her center in *Savasana*, the corpse pose of complete and utter relaxation.

When class comes to an end, the students float gracefully out the door, rejoining the masses. I gaze toward the back of the room, where four bamboo poles extend from floor to ceiling, uneven in size and the space separating them. They remind me that this studio never has, nor ever will be, about striving for perfection. Their flaws and lack of symmetry are what make them beautiful. Aligning with the Japanese concept of *wabi sabi*, finding beauty in natural imperfection, the posts represent self-acceptance, rather than self-criticism, both in life and in the yoga practice.

Immersed in the calm that follows each class I teach, my eyes drift back to the altar, where a painting towers above it. The simple design—one black rectangle resting above a white rectangle of equal size—symbolizes our studio's name, as well as the Hatha Yoga we practice here. *Ha* stands for "sun," while *tha* means "moon." Just like yin and yang, the masculine and the feminine, Sun & Moon represents finding balance between two opposing forces. Even the schedule reflects the search for equilibrium with both restorative yoga and active practices like Ashtanga.

While this fifty-three-square-meter space in a characterless office block may seem restricted in size, it is always overflowing with warmth and character. Students from around the world pass through its doors daily. Some are stopping by on a hasty business trip, looking for comfort in what can be an overwhelming city; others frequent the studio, deepening their understanding of the ancient practice. The reasons why each student parts the *noren* and chooses to enter may be varied, but one thing is often shared. The sign above the entrance reads: "Find what you love. Love what you find." Whether it is friendship, confidence, understanding, or just a little slice of calm, Sun & Moon fulfills many desires.

For me, I first went to Sun & Moon in search of solitude, to find stillness in my mind. Instead, I encountered something that, at the time, I didn't even know I was craving—a community, a support network of caring students, inspirational teachers, and friends that I will cherish long after I leave Japan.

Sun & Moon Yoga
Meguro Eki Mae Mansion
Higashi Guchi Building
3-1-5 Kami Osaki, Suite 204
Shinagawa District
Tokyo
(03) 3280-6383
http://sunandmoon.jp/

Train: Yamanote Line to Meguro Station.

Yamanashi Prefecture

Mary Cook makes a pilgrimage to her spiritual home near Mt. Fuji

Once is not enough to tread the holy ground of Taiseki-ji, the Head Temple of Nichiren Shoshu Buddhism. It tugs at my heart, calling me back year after year, for this serene plot in the foothills of Mt. Fuji is my spiritual home.

Joyfully, my husband Nick and I make the tiring journey from the UK to repay our debt of gratitude to Nichiren Daishonin, our sect's founder. Having passed through the San-mon Gate, we take the path that leads upwards between the rows of small local temples. As always, we feel a need to walk on the pairs of irregularly shaped stones in the middle, for they mark the route taken by the earliest believers, who carried with them the building materials with which they would construct the Mutsubo, the original building on which the Head Temple was founded.

Walking on paths lined with cherry trees, punctuated by stone lanterns, we can imagine ourselves to be members of a structured feudal society in medieval Japan. Everywhere, we hear priests and believers chanting "*Nam-Myoho-Renge-Kyo*." The sacred, all-powerful phrase resounds in the stream that cascades downward, icy cold, from the melting snows of the mountain. Gray-robed priests, sandals slapping, flit here and there like doves of peace. Smiling broadly, they return our reverent bows.

The air, sharp with the scent of pine needles, echoes to the metallic sound of cicadas. Dragonflies buzz past us, and tiny green frogs, like jeweled brooches, cling to the volcanic stone walls that surround the smaller temples. Each of these temples has its own secluded garden. Together they form a hidden sanctuary of spiritual healing and tranquility. Opposite the Ever-Chanting Temple, a white crane speculatively eyes the carp in the Bright Mirror Pond from the safety of a tree.

In the early hours of each morning during our stay, we attend Ushitora Gongyo, called to prayer by a massive gong sounding through the blanketing darkness. In this daily ceremony, our High Priest prays for world peace, and our chanting is accompanied by two young priests on the *taiko* drums.

At Taiseki-ji there are times when Mt. Fuji is felt only as a hidden presence. On other days, it's so clear I feel as if I can reach out and scrape the snow from its peak with my fingernail. It was on just such a day that Nick and I caught our first glimpse of the Hoando, the magnificent building raised in 2002 to celebrate the seven hundred and fiftieth anniversary of the birth of True Buddhism.

The Hoando was built to enshrine and protect our object of worship, the Dai-Gohonzon, the Great Mandala inscribed by Nichiren Daishonin in 1279. The single-story structure stands fifty-five meters at its highest point, and we always marvel at its size and the refined simplicity of its design. It's as if the Hoando has always stood there, and will continue to stand for centuries to come. As for Nick and I, we will return to Taiseki-ji for as many years as we are able, to follow in the footsteps of the early pilgrims of Nichiren Shoshu Buddhism.

Getting to Taiseki-ji

Taiseki-ji is an easy day trip from Tokyo. From Tokyo Station, take the Tokaido Shinkansen to the town of Shin Fuji. You can take a cab from Shin-Fuji Station to Taiseki-ji.

Nichiren Shoshu Buddhism

The practice of Nichiren Shoshu Buddhism, known by its practitioners as True Buddhism, is open to all. Nichiren Daishonin's teachings have been handed down from one High Priest to another in an unbroken line for more than seven hundred and fifty years. To learn more about this school of Buddhism, visit the official website.

www.nichirenshoshu.or.jp

Stefan Chiarantano seeks enlightenment atop Mt. Takigo

One of the things that drew me to Asia was a desire to deepen my faith in and understanding of Buddhism. Imagine my excitement when on a temporary teaching assignment in Uenohara, I discovered that Zuigaku-in, a Zen Buddhist monastery where foreigners are welcome to study and practice, was located in the neighboring town of Hatsukari.

Early on a misty Saturday morning, I set out. An invigorating walk brought me to the train station, followed by a thirty-minute ride to Hatsukari. My school's principal had scribbled a map on a piece of paper with the most basic instructions. I approached the station attendant and asked for directions. He gave me a quizzical look, pointed straight up, and told me that the temple was perched seven hundred meters atop Mt. Takigo. No matter. I was on a mission, undaunted by the challenge of a trek up the mountain.

A kindly Japanese couple gave me a lift to the base of the trail, where a garage mechanic started me in the right direction. There were no taxis and no public transportation, so I had to rely on trail markers and people I met on the mountain path to guide me. As I walked, I felt a certain measure of trepidation, since I had no phone number for the temple and so couldn't make an appointment. Japan is a formal culture, where everything is planned down to the minute, and the Japanese do not like surprises.

The landscape was quiet, and the air was crisp and fresh. I could hear the rush of water from a river that followed the road. By now, I was sweating profusely, and flies were buzzing over my head, but the excitement of visiting the Zen temple kept me focused.

At a fork in the road, I met an elderly Japanese woman, who flashed me a warm smile, and gently pointed out the way. A half hour later, I came to a marker that read: "Zuigaku-in 2 kilometers." My excitement reached its peak when I came upon the two tall, marble gateposts that mark the entrance to the temple grounds.

Just then, I heard the sound of a car approaching, and stepped aside to let it pass. The driver stopped and rolled down the passenger window. In a combination of both English and Japanese, I said, "Hello. I'm visiting the temple, but don't have an appointment. I hope it's okay." The man got out of the car, extended a handshake, and introduced himself. It was Moriyama Roshi, the Zen Master himself! He asked if I wanted a ride up. Although I was thrilled at meeting him in such a personal way, I felt embarrassed that I was drenched in sweat and out of breath. But my aching feet screamed "*Yes*!" and I jumped in.

Within minutes, we reached Zuigaku-in in a rustic wooded setting. The fresh mountain air was filled with the sounds of buzzing insects and chirping birds. Moriyama Roshi escorted me into the temple and invited me to rest in a *tatami* room overlooking a quiet courtyard. The walls were hung with photographs of Moriyama Roshi and his disciples, and a shelf of literature included some of his own published works. He asked me how much time I had, and, not wanting to intrude on his daily routine, I said, "Only a little."

We talked in English, which was a relief since my Japanese was very poor. He gave me a personal tour of the center, first through the spacious *zendo* (meditation hall), which was sparsely furnished with a row of blue-cushioned wooden benches along the wall. A drum stood at the entrance, a beautiful carved clapper in the shape of a fish hung from the ceiling, and a statue of Monju, the Buddha of Wisdom, was centered in the section reserved for ordained monks and nuns. Next, we visited the *hondo* (main hall), a vast *tatami* room where chanting takes place. Another statue of Buddha stood near the altar, flanked on both sides with bodhisattvas.

Created in 1978, Zuigaku-in welcomes novices, lay practitioners, and guests who want to study the ancient tenets of Buddhism, and I regretted that my teaching obligations would not allow me time to join them. At least I got to see the kitchen and living quarters, which, along with the *hondo*, are located in a two-hundred-year-old farmhouse. The building has no electricity, and water is drawn from a neighboring stream. Water for bathing is heated in a steel drum outside in the garden, and gas burners are used to cook simple, vegetarian fare.

Moriyama Roshi made me tea, and during our conversation, he explained that his lineage goes back many centuries, all the way to Dogen Zenji, who introduced Zen Buddhism to Japan. Moriyama is a kind and gentle soul, and his thoughtfulness and interest in my own quest filled me with a sense of peace and purpose. I imagined all the people who had come there to meditate and seek enlightenment, and I felt honored that he devoted so much of his time to my visit. Before leaving, I returned to the *hondo* to offer a donation of appreciation, and when I left Zuigaku-in, I knew that I had met an enlightened being whose presence I will carry with me always.

Getting to Zuigaku-in

Hatsukari is about a two-hour train ride from Tokyo's Shinjuku Station on the Chuo Line. Before departing, check your train ticket and double check with the attendant, as you may need to change trains at Mt. Takao or the Hachioji Station, depending on the time of day and the train's schedule. Zuigaku-in is at least a one-hour trek from Hatsukari Station.

To find the road to take you up to Zuigaku-in, ask a Hatsukari Station attendant, who can point you in the right direction or draw you a map. Japan Rail (JR) attendants are famous for the kind assistance they provide to foreigners. As I discovered from my experience, many residents of Hatsukari also know of Zuigaku-in and have become familiar with seeing foreigners trekking up Mt. Takigo. Should you find yourself lost, you can approach them for assistance as well. Also, there are markers along the path to help you find your way. If you don't feel up to trekking, you can make arrangements with the monastery in advance to be picked up at the station.

Zuigaku-in International Zen Monastery
Hatsukari District
Otsuki
(0554) 25-6282
www.geocities.com/tokyo/towers/3169/

Kanagawa Prefecture

Leza Lowitz seeks silence among the bamboo of Kamakura

If jostling with the hoards of gawkers at the Great Buddha of Kamakura isn't your preferred way of seeking enlightenment, I would like to offer an alluring alternative. The Moso Bamboo Garden at the city's Hokoku-ji is a small oasis of peace and calm.

I first discovered this temple garden twenty years ago, through my friend Eric, then a speechwriter for the Prime Minister of Japan. He took me there one day when I needed to blow off steam from my Tokyo life. I have been returning ever since.

Passing through the temple grounds, I seek out a small enclosed garden where hundreds of huge evergreen bamboo have been planted in dense, off-kilter rows. Streams of sunlight filter in among the shadows, creating an ethereal outdoor cathedral. Upon entering, I feel that I can finally breathe, and I fill my lungs with deep inhalations of fresh forest air.

What seems at first to be silence envelops me, but as I venture into the surrounding bamboo forest, the subtle sounds of nature emerge:

trunks gently creaking in the breeze, wind softly rustling through the leaves, a waterfall in the distance.

The tall bamboo trees offer just the right amount of breathing room without a feeling of claustrophobia. Hokoku-ji is sometimes called "The Bamboo Temple," and it's easy to see why. Who needs a meditation hall and a *zafu* cushion when you can find peace and solace under a canopy of bamboo? And if that isn't serene enough, there is a teahouse, where kimono-clad women will gracefully prepare a frothy bowl of *matcha* green tea for you, using a traditional bamboo whisk.

As I sit on a wooden bench in the teahouse, cupping the bowl in my hands and breathing in its grassy fragrance, a gentle rain might fall outside. Soothed by the warmth of the tea, and protected by the bamboo, the city and its stresses seem light-years away.

I can spend hours in the garden, and yet feel as if no time has gone by at all. Always, I am reluctant to leave. So upon my departure from this little-known sanctuary, I allow my path to wind back through the bamboo grove, enjoying a much-needed stroll amidst its stillness before returning to the real world.

Hokoku-ji and Bamboo Garden

Built in 1334 and devoted to the Rinzai sect of Buddhism, Hokoku-ji houses many cultural treasures including a rare manuscript of Chinese poems. Visitors can also practice *zazen* meditation on Sundays in the main temple hall. But the Bamboo Garden is the real reason to visit.

2-7-4 Jomyo-ji
Kamakura
(0467) 22-0762
www.kamakuratoday.com/e/sightseeing/hokokuji.html

Directions: Walk from Kamakura Station (about twenty-five minutes) or go by bus or taxi (about ten minutes) to Kaido Street. Cross over a footbridge to the right and you'll find the temple.

Healthy dining in Kamakura

If you want food that goes along with a Zen lifestyle, your wish can easily be fulfilled by one of the many young people in Kamakura who are promoting healthy lifestyles at various venues around town.

Magokoro

This small shop is billed as "An Organic Hemp Style Café & Bar." Watch the waves from the large picture window as you feast on health food lunch sets including spicy curries with brown rice and organic coffees, teas, and desserts.

2-8-11 Hase, 2F
Kamakura
(0467) 25-1414
www.magokoroworld.jp

Café Life Force

A bit closer to Kamakura Station, this café has an excellent selection of fresh juices and foods such as pasta, falafel, and pilaf.

2-5-19 Yuigahama
Kamakura
(0467) 25-5359

Kibiya

For a healthy take-out treat, visit this fabulous little organic bakery tucked away in an alley near the station. You will find whole grain breads, pastries filled with red beans, and a variety of delectable cookies and scones. Closed Wednesdays.

5-34 Onari-machi
Kamakura
(0467) 22-1862
www.kcn-net.org/senior/tsushin/tgourmet/y06/0612hiro/index.html

More vegetarian dining

Keep an eye out for the vegetarian dining map guide to Kamakura, distributed at the train station and in local cafés and shops. The guide has a complementary blog.

http://vegemapkamakura.blogspot.com/ (Japanese)

Gunma Prefecture

Kimberly Fujioka puts her faith in the process outside Fujioka

There is a mountain village north of Fujioka in central Japan, where traditional glass blowers raise long, hollow metal rods to their lips and blow. The other ends of the rods are immersed in fire.

Tsuchi-to-Hi-no-Sato is where I am heading with my friends Betty and Mariko, up a long mountain pass. Mariko is behind the wheel, Betty is asleep, and I am already there in my mind, captivated by the possibility of creation.

In the glass-blowing studio that we have come to visit, it is so noisy that nobody can be heard over the roar of the fire. We stand around the glass blower who delicately twirls the hot metal rod between his gloved fingers. We cannot see the glass formation that we have been told is in the furnace's belly, but we trust that it is there.

We are watching and waiting for his masterpiece to emerge from the oven when he taps me on the shoulder. He leans down to grease my lips and then lifts the rod up to my mouth.

Surprised, I suck as much air into my lungs as they will hold, but he steps back, pulling the rod away from me.

I look into his eyes and understand what he wants me to do. Breathe naturally. He returns the metal rod to my mouth, and I try again. He turns the rod in my hands, then moves toward the furnace, to peer through the small window. Looking over his shoulder at me, he gives me the okay sign. I let my breath out slowly and steadily until he cuts his hand through the air, telling me to stop. Then he makes the signal for me to start blowing again. He turns the metal rod ever so slightly from where he is standing by the oven. I relax my hands and let him take control.

I know that there are others around me, but I don't see them. It is only the glass blower and me, and my desire to keep going, to keep my breath moving out at a steady pace, knowing that at the other end of the rod, growing in size and shape, is a creation that I can call my own.

I look over at the glass blower peering into the small window of the immense furnace where my vase is coming to life. He uses sign language to tell me when to let up, when to blow, and when to twirl the rod. Our work is a collaborative effort: I trust his long experience working with glass, and he trusts my intuition, my ability to rest in the moment. I understand that knowing the elements of fire and glass are important, but having faith in the process is critical.

Finally the vase is finished. We pull it out of the oven, hanging off the end of the long metal rod, dripping in violet and cobalt blue. He immerses it into the cold water bath. The others huddle around to see what we have created, while the glass blower and I collapse against the cool cement wall of the studio to rest.

Creative escape

Tsuchi-to-Hi-no-Sato is an artists' village in Gunma Prefecture. It is located in the midst of the Hino Valley, nestled in the mountains with the Ayu River running through it. The village is comprised of a semicircular formation of huts covered with traditional straw roofs, each housing a different traditional art. If you plan to try pottery making, go early so your teacher will have time to fire your pot for you to pick up later in the day. And if you plan to try the indigo dyeing, bring your own cotton items (T-shirt, dress, scarf, tablecloth, etc.) The vats that hold the dye are large and the classes are small, so there is plenty of room for your own item, and the teacher can give you individual attention. Teachers may not speak English, but it doesn't matter, since these are hands-on learning experiences, and there is literature in English.

Getting to Tsuchi-to-Hi-no-Sato

Given travel time, and the time needed for the activities offered, Tsuchi-to-Hi-no-Sato is best done as an overnight trip or longer from

Tokyo. If you are staying in Fujioka, it is an easy day trip. By train from Tokyo, take the Hachiko Line from Hachioji Station to Gunma Fujioka Station. From there, take the Ayugawa-go bus to Tsuchi-to-Hi-no-Sato Koen bus stop.

Ishikawa Prefecture

Celeste Heiter walks away from a Buddhist temple in Kanazawa

It was the pinnacle of summer, and we'd been on the road for several days when we reached Kanazawa. In the western prefecture of Ishikawa on the Sea of Japan, it is a city famed for its seafood, its lacquerware, and its gardens. For reasons I can no longer remember, perhaps from too many uninterrupted hours together, or perhaps from something more significant, the day that we visited Kenrokuen Garden, my then husband Mark and I were angry at each other.

By the time we arrived at the famed garden, the tension between us was palpable, yet we paid our entrance fees and went in anyway. But there was no hope of reconciliation between us that day, and after walking the manicured paths for most of an hour, we erupted into an argument at the site of one of the garden's most idyllic views. Overhead, in the growing heat and humidity of the day, the cicadas droned and buzzed, heightening the drama of our impasse. That's when I knew I had to be alone for a while.

As a peace offering, Mark pointed me in the direction of a kimono factory, where the bolts of silk used to make the garments are hand painted on the premises. Since I have both art and tailoring in my blood (my father was an artist and my mother was a seamstress), watching the serene silk painters behind a glass display window, precisely and patiently creating opulent floral patterns on meter after meter of silk, was the perfect antidote for the morning's anger and frustration. After watching them paint for more than an hour, I toured the factory and, as a souvenir, bought a tiny silk coin purse made from the scraps of a hand-sewn kimono.

The locale of the kimono factory offered no other attractions, and its utilitarian streets were bereft of other shops and storefronts, so I turned back to Kenrokuen. After all, this would be my only chance to enjoy its beauty, and perhaps I could appreciate it now that I was on my own. I returned to the garden, but instead of going in through the main entrance, I entered somehow through a smaller gate in a remote corner of the grounds. Just inside, I found a small, humble, very old Buddhist temple.

With the discord of the day still thrashing around in my head, I sat down on the low stone wall that surrounded the temple, to study it in detail and bask in its tranquility. It was so old that almost all of the original paint had been worn away, down to the bare wood. As I sat there on the steps, somehow, in those few moments, I was able to put my feelings into perspective, to realize that they were insignificant and meaningless in the grand scheme of things. A hundred years from now, who would be around to care? Not even me. All at once, I felt a sense of relief and resolve. I was ready to move on. So I rose and headed off to enjoy the beauty of the garden that I had traveled so far to see.

A Japanese garden is evaluated according to six attributes: The vastness of its size, the tranquility of its location, the abundance of moving water, the beauty of its views, the artfulness of its design, and its endurance over time. Rivaled only by Korakuen and Kairakuen, the garden of Kenrokuen in Kanazawa is regarded among the three most beautiful in Japan. Even knowing this in advance, Kenrokuen exceeded all promises and expectations. An exquisite marriage of man and nature, a divine consummation of heaven and earth.

Afterward, when I went back to our lodgings, Mark still had not returned. I was glad, because I was in the mood to write something about the day. So, after a soothing soak in the *furo*, I donned a fresh *yukata* and settled down on the *tatami* mat at a low table to begin writing "Upon Walking Away From a Buddhist Temple."

Getting to Kenrokuen

1-4 Kenrokumachi
Kanazawa

www.pref.ishikawa.jp/siro-niwa/kenrokuen/e/

Directions: Kanazawa makes a leisurely few-day trip from Tokyo. Once in Kanazawa, a bus ride from Kanazawa Station to Kenrokuen takes about fifteen minutes. The garden is near Kenrokuenshita and Dewa-machi bus stops.

Silk kimono factory

Kaga Yuzen Traditional Industry Center
8-8 Kosyo-machi
Kanazawa
(076) 224-5511
www.kagayuzen.or.jp/english_kaikan.html
info@kagayuzen.or.jp

Kyoto Prefecture

Frank Lev takes a whack at Zen meditation in Kyoto

While living in Kyoto, I worked for a wonderful group of people who ran a children's school. About once a month, we'd skip our Friday meeting and go somewhere special. Once, we visited Daisen-in, an ancient Zen temple, unusual in that the resident monks welcome foreigners and beginners to practice with them. I had practiced meditation off and on for years, but had never tried Zen.

Returning to the temple for a meditation session, I arrived a few minutes before five, and was ushered to a raised platform in front of a gravel garden. Kyoto is famous for these types of gardens, meticulously kept by monks who sweep and rake the gravel into designs intended to induce feelings of peace and aid meditation. The garden at Daisen-in is dominated by two large gravel cones a little more than a meter apart, and the rest of the gravel is raked into rows of undulating lines around them.

The other students, all Japanese, were already seated. An assistant set out some mosquito coils. I imagine there's nothing worse than being bothered by mosquitoes when you are trying to attain enlightenment. Soon the master came out, a monk with a shaved head, wearing loose-fitting robes. There was an intensity about him as he gave instructions to the group.

He rambled off a long string of words in Japanese, and then looked in my direction, pointed to his head, and said, "Empty." Then came more Japanese, before he pantomimed breathing to me and said, "One to ten." I took this to mean, count your breaths from one to ten. Following yet another Japanese instruction, he looked at me, pointed to his eyes, and then to a point midway between the two cones. "Look there."

After giving directions, he showed us how to sit perfectly still in the lotus posture, legs crossed, feet resting on opposite thighs. When you do it properly, you look a little like a pretzel. There was no way I could get my body into that position and sit still for an hour, so I just sat cross-legged.

I'd heard that in Zen meditation, the master walks around with a stick, and if you feel your mind wandering, you can request a hit to help keep you focused. The master now demonstrated "the hit." Holding a narrow paddle that looked a little like a child's cricket bat, he approached the man sitting next to me. The student put his palms together, and the master and student bowed. Then the student placed both palms on the floor, exposing his back to the teacher, who patted the student with the bat, twice on the left, twice on the right. That didn't look so bad.

Finally, we were ready to begin. The master walked over to the left side of the porch and rang a small bell. *Bong-ggggg* ... The meditation began.

One ... *two* ... *three* ... I counted my breaths as I listened to the ring of the bell fade away. *Four* ... *five* ... *six* ... The master paced in front of us with the bat slung on his shoulder. I was afraid to look at him because he would know that I was not focusing on my breath. *Seven* ... *eight* ... *nine* ...

After a few minutes, the man sitting next to me put his palms together to summon the master. The master walked over and bowed. The man assumed the position. Then I heard it. *Whack, whack ... whack, whack.* These hits were different from the ones in the demonstration. The master was really bearing down. *Ten ... one ... two ...*

The master descended the platform risers to ground level. As he did, I thought, *I should ask for a hit, just to see what it feels like. After all it may be my only chance to experience it.* But the master had just gotten off the platform. Maybe he would be mad if I made him climb up again unnecessarily, so I waited. *Three ... four ... five ...*

As I continued to stare at the garden, something strange happened. The two cones began to look like breasts. The more I looked, the more my vision blurred, and I couldn't shake the thought that I was meditating on breasts, and large ones at that. It felt like some kind of joke. I did my best to return my focus to my breath. *Six ... seven ... eight ...* But the more I tried not to think about it, the more it seemed that I was looking at breasts.

It was time, I decided, to brave the paddle. When the master walked by again, I put my palms together, bowed to him, and placed my hands on the wooden floor. He reared back with the paddle, and ... *whack, whack! ...* right over the shoulder blade. Ouch! It stung. He switched to the other side. *Ouchhhhh*!!! We bowed again, and he stepped off the porch and continued his walk. My back stung for a few seconds, but in a good way. My mind was certainly clearer. I got back to counting my breaths, and focused my eyes on the garden. *Nine ... ten ... one ...*

Again, I tried hard to follow my breath. *Two ... three ... four ...* But now I felt a tingle. A large black ant was crawling up my leg. *Please turn around ant. You don't want to go there.* To my relief, it turned around. Then I felt another one on my chin, and despite my best efforts, my mind took off with "The Bug Song," a little ditty I had composed a few weeks ago for the school.

There's a bug on my chin, and he's walking to my ear. Oh no! Not my ear. There's a bug on my ear ... Please don't go in.

I saw the master turn the corner and walk toward me. *Five ... six ... seven ...* Just then I felt a terrific pain. The ant *bit* me! My hand shot up, slapped the ant, and sent it flying onto the wooden porch. Mortified, I sneaked a peek at the master, who gave me a terrible scowl. I had violated two rules at the same time. You're not supposed to move during meditation practice, and Buddhists are not supposed to kill any living thing. My mind was racing wildly, but after the withering look I'd gotten from the master, I thought it best not to ask him for any more whacks. I'd just have to manage the last few minutes of meditation on my own ... *eight ... nine ... ten ...*

Daisen-in Temple

Daisen-in offers sessions where visitors can join a Zen meditation class with the master. Contact the temple for days, times, and admission fee.

54-1 Daitokuji-cho Murasakino
Kita District
Kyoto
(075) 491-8346
www.kyoto.travel/place_to_go/daisenin_temple.html

Directions: The temple is a five-minute walk from the Daitokuji-mae bus stop and a fifteen-minute walk from the Kitaoji Subway Station.

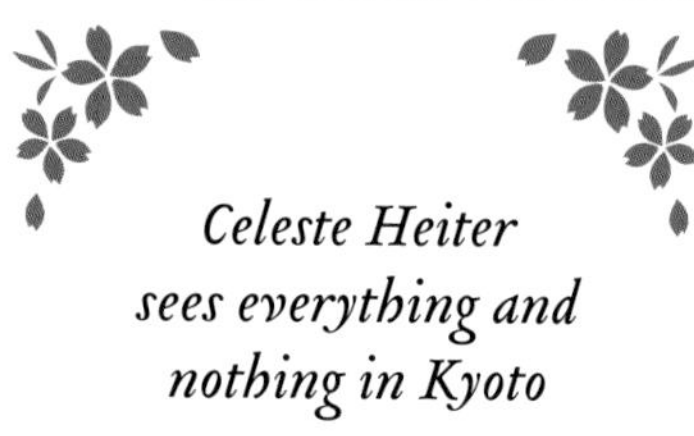

Celeste Heiter sees everything and nothing in Kyoto

Although I am not a daily practitioner of Zen Buddhism, I have always been drawn to its ideology, and try to incorporate its precepts into my daily life. So when the chance presented itself for a visit to Ryoan-ji, Japan's most famous Zen garden, I was ecstatic. For me, it was tantamount to a visit to Mecca or the Vatican.

Ryoan-ji is a magnet for tourists year round, and the day I visited was no exception. There were already hundreds of people when I arrived, many of whom were seated on the viewing pavilion. Nevertheless, I found an empty spot and sat down to ponder the mystery of the garden.

The name Ryoan-ji means "Temple of the Peaceful Dragon," and the site where it stands was established in 1450. Ryoan-ji measures thirty meters long by ten meters wide, and is comprised of fifteen natural stones of various sizes placed on a bed of pure white gravel, raked into meticulous patterns around the stones. A low, earthen wall surrounds the remaining three sides of the garden, with cedar, pine, and cherry trees beyond.

I had read a few things in advance about Ryoan-ji, most notably that from any point in the garden it is impossible to view all fifteen stones at once. One always remains hidden from view. A fifteenth stone can only be seen in the mind's eye when spiritual enlightenment has been attained. As well, by staring at the stains on the weathered earthen wall, one might experience mystical visions.

As I sat on the viewing pavilion with great expectations, my first feeling was something akin to "The Emperor's New Clothes." I imagined that everyone else was seeing or experiencing something that I did not. So there I was, hoping for some kind of *satori*—a moment of enlightenment—as I gazed at the hypnotic patterns of the gravel, raked in long, straight rows that, when met with the stones, detour from their linear path to perfectly encircle them.

I was more than a little surprised and disturbed when the next feeling I experienced was an overwhelming urge to run wildly into the garden and wreak havoc on its austere perfection. For the next few moments, I contemplated the consequences of such lunacy, and prayed for a distraction that would curb my impulses. As an antidote to my unbridled thoughts of vandalizing that sacred place, I began to count the stones. Almost like a three dimensional haiku, they are arranged in groups of five, two, three, two, and three, and I soon discovered that what I'd heard was true: all I could see from my position on the pavilion were fourteen. This set me to wondering where the fifteenth stone was hidden.

I occupied my mind with that conundrum for the next few minutes, and being unable to solve it without getting up and wandering around, obstructing the view of the other visitors, I turned my attention to the wall. It had once been painted or plastered in pure white, but over the years, its surface had become yellowed and weathered by exposure to the elements. Pigmentation from the composition of the natural building materials had been leached to the surface by moisture. The effect is a group of sepia-toned images that resemble an ancient parchment map or an ethereal watercolor. I searched the images for a glimpse of the fabled visions, and although I am given to prophetic dreams from time to time, Ryoan-ji offered none that day.

So that was it. I'd exhausted every avenue of contemplation Ryoan-ji had to offer and had found nothing. No enlightenment ... no transcendence ... not even a small *satori* ... only stones and gravel. But just as I was about to rise and walk away, it happened. Sitting on the steps of the viewing pavilion, I came to the realization that there was nothing mystical in the garden. Never was. Never would be.

I would only find there what I had brought with me. When I asked myself what that was, I saw the culmination of my life. All my joy, my pain, my accomplishments, my disappointments, my fears, and my dreams. In that moment, something changed. A wave of peace and fulfillment washed over me. All is as it is. The garden of Ryoan-ji was perfectly empty and still, like a Zen meditation. When I looked again, I saw everything ... and nothing.

Getting to Ryoan-ji Zen Garden

From Kyoto's Shijo-Omiya Station, take the Keifuku Kitano Line, which travels through the scenic district where Ryoan-ji is located. From Ryoan-ji-michi Station, it's a five-minute walk to the temple.

Wakayama Prefecture

Shane Cowlishaw follows a pilgrim to a tranquil Koyasan temple

An almost frightening sense of silence fell upon me. *Calm, beautiful, serene*—all these words could be used to describe the place I had just entered. But you could also add *eerie, unsettling,* and *peculiar* to that list.

I had been trailing a white-robed pilgrim for the last thirty minutes through the mountain town of Koyasan, keeping my distance, observing his slow yet steady pace toward some unknown goal as his wooden staff beat a regular rhythm on the cobblestoned roadway. However, as the *tap, tap, tap* of his staff faded into the distance, I soon forgot about the man, and began to notice that each step was taking me not only farther from town, but seemingly back in time.

Towering cypress trees suddenly loomed all around me, and everything in sight was covered with ancient moss. In the dim light of the forest, I began to notice tombstones, varying in style and size, from the most simple and basic, to immense structures that rivaled the imposing stature of the trees. Effigies of people, animals, symbols, and deities emerged all around me, some cracked and broken, others barely visible where the dark forest had devoured them.

Walking for twenty minutes brought me no closer to a visible destination, and I had long since lost sight of my pious escort. But I wasn't worried. Despite the spooky surroundings, my earlier apprehension had been replaced by a sense of inner calm that was unique to itself.

Finally, I arrived at a sign explaining that Gobyo Mausoleum, a few paces ahead, is the eternal resting place of Kobo Daishi, founder of Shingon Buddhism in Japan, and the vastly populated cemetery I had just passed through is called Okunoin. I read that the graveyard had grown in size since the founder's death in the ninth century, as so many people—from corporate CEOs to some of Japan's most powerful feudal lords—wanted to be buried near the beloved priest.

Reading this, I mulled over my final resting place. Where would it be? Although at the moment, I had no answer, the thought did occur to me that this would be a perfectly fine place to spend eternity, and certainly to spend a few hours of my waking life.

The temples of Koyasan

The center of Shingon Buddhism in Japan, the small town of Koyasan has more than one hundred temples. Not to be missed are Okunoin, the massive forest and cemetery, and Daito, a huge pagoda built as a symbol of Shingon Buddhism. To learn more about Shingon Buddhism and area attractions, visit the following website.

www.koyasan.or.jp/english/

Getting to Koyasan

Koyasan can be done as a day trip from Osaka, but your time will be rushed. It's best done as an overnight trip or longer. From the Namba Train Station in Osaka, take the Nankai Koya Line to Gokurakubashi Station at the foot of Mt. Koya. From there, a cable car runs up the mountain. Recommended is the purchase of a two-day Koyasan Free Sabic ticket, which includes a round-trip train ticket from Osaka, unlimited cable car and bus travel within Mt. Koyasan, and admission to select attractions. You can buy this ticket at any major Nankai railway station and travel agencies in the Osaka area. For details, visit the following website.

www.nankaikoya.jp/en/iku/04.html

Where to Stay

About fifty of the town's temples offer lodging for the night. Such temples are called *shukubo* and overnight stays usually include a delicious vegetarian dinner and breakfast, served by the monks themselves. For more about temple lodging, as well as pilgrimage routes and general Koyasan information, visit the following website.

www.shukubo.jp/eng

Torii *gates at Tokyo's Hie Shrine*

Cultural Encounters

A celebration of traditions and festivals

It seems the Japanese people are always celebrating something, from the Emperor's birthday to the rice harvest, and everything in between. Festivals and rituals start on the first day of January with Oshogatsu, the New Year celebration, and continue throughout the year. Most are based upon ancient traditions, and follow the course of nature throughout the seasons. But the people of Japan also gather together in huge crowds to enjoy sporting events, cultural performances, fireworks, and the pleasures each season has to offer.

Just a few weeks after I arrived in Japan, I visited Asukayama Park in the suburb of Oji for *ohanami*—cherry blossom viewing. I couldn't have asked for a more perfect spring day; the blossoms were at their blushing best. I never imagined that the park, which had been so barren just weeks before, could become so transcendent. During my two years in Japan, I watched a thousand fireworks explode over the Sumida River; I witnessed monstrous *taiko* drummers repel imaginary invaders on the beach at Wajima; and I went to the Meiji Shrine to see hundreds of adorable children in brilliant kimono getting blessed on Shichi-Go-San Day.

One summer evening, on my way home from work, my shortcut through Nishi-Guchi Park landed me right in the middle of a *bon odori* dance, commemorating the return of departed ancestors. And on a Sunday afternoon, I unwittingly wandered into a *mikoshi* parade, where I witnessed two dozen heaving, sweating, nearly naked young men, carrying a portable Shinto shrine on their shoulders. Hauquan Chao learns firsthand the excitement of such a parade, as he is offered the rare opportunity to add his muscles to a *mikoshi* crew in Wajima. And Landon Fry has a similar experience when he is invited to help navigate a huge wooden float through the streets in Kishiwada's *danjiri* parade.

Paper lanterns in Tokyo's Ginza District

Although Japan's major festivals are ubiquitous and easily accessible, there are certain esoteric celebrations held in out-of-the-way places, attended only by those in the know. Tim Patterson tells how he traveled all the way to the remote island of Teuri to feast on freshly shucked seafood at the Sea Urchin Festival. Geoff Reid lets you in on everything you need to know to witness the pounding rhythms of Sado Island's Earth Celebration. And Jasmin Young invites you to catch a wave at Taito Beach during the Surf Town Fiesta.

Sporting events also offer perfect venues for immersing yourself in the culture. Join Frank Lev as he takes you out to a baseball game in Nagoya, and gives you an intimidating up-close look at a sumo wrestler in Osaka. Then travel to Kofu with my son Will Raus, who attends a week-long training camp, where he is trussed up in a *mawashi* belt and learns the finer points of sumo wrestling.

There are also the cultural immersions that can be found any day of the week and give you a better understanding of the Japanese. Throughout their explorations, Chris Carlier discovers the perfect watering hole in the Shibuya entertainment district, Kena Sosa belts out The Supremes over cocktails at a karaoke bar, and Jennifer Huber ventures into Shinjuku Ni-Chome for a glimpse into Tokyo's gay community.

Whether you plan your experience to the last detail, or serendipitously find yourself in the middle of one, a Japanese cultural encounter is sure to be the highlight of your trip.

Tokyo Prefecture

Celeste Heiter is dazzled by fire flowers in Tokyo

When translated literally, *hanabi*—the Japanese word for fireworks—means "flower-fire," and on warm evenings throughout the summer season, along the banks of Japan's rivers, the night sky explodes in bursts of fiery color. On the day that I was fortunate enough to attend my first fireworks display, my companion and I headed for the Sumida River after work, and arrived with little time to spare.

As it winds its way through rural Japan and the suburbs of Tokyo, this river is crossed by many bridges, some of which are quite close together. The Sumidagawa *Hanabi Taikai*—Sumida River Fireworks Displays—are launched over two such bridges, creating a doubly dazzling spectacle. When I arrived, the river was already dotted with sailboats, motorboats, and rowboats, all vying for the best location from which to view the show. Rooftops were a popular spot for those lucky spectators with access to a perch above the crowd. Mostly, though, the streets were jam-packed with us common folk.

Having been offered no invitation to one of the private rooftop parties, we were clueless as to where to view the display, and therefore, had to rely on our intuition. We followed the migration toward what we guessed were the banks of the river. Block by block, the crowds became progressively thicker, moving more and more slowly, until we finally reached a standstill, packed like proverbial sardines, unable to move in any direction.

Ordinarily, I would have worked myself into a state of panic over the closeness of so many people, but at that moment, there was a deafening boom. The world around me disappeared as I turned my gaze heavenward, and to my surprise, the fireworks began to burst directly overhead. It appeared that, as we were propelled along by the crowds, we had somehow managed to land in the epicenter of the event.

For the next ninety minutes, the sky lit up in explosions of fiery red, brilliant green, cobalt blue, dazzling gold, and shimmering silver. Supernovas of light and color shot up in alternating salvos from the two bridges, with nary a moment's lapse between them, and our ears rang with their thundering resonance. Each burst was like the biggest, grandest finale of a fireworks show I'd ever seen, multiplied by an hour and a half of nonstop, state-of-the-art pyrotechnics. When the very last *hanabi* had been set ablaze, and the show was over, I felt as if I'd witnessed a lifetime's worth of fireworks in a single evening.

Sumida River Fireworks

Sumidagawa *Hanabi Taikai* are held annually on the last Saturday in July in Sumida Park.

Taito District (Asakusa/Mukojima neighborhood)
Tokyo
(03) 5246-1111
http://sumidagawa-hanabi.com/index_eg.html

Subway: Ginza Line to Asakusa Station.

Viewing the fireworks

Good spots for viewing the fireworks are along the section of the Sumida River which flows through the eastern part of Tokyo and empties into Tokyo Bay. In particular, the neighborhood around Asakusa Station fills with spectators. Venue No.1 covers the area from downstream of Sakurabashi Bridge to upstream of Kototoibashi Bridge, while Venue No.2 is located from downstream of Komagatabashi Bridge to upstream of Umayabashi Bridge.

Fireworks around Japan

To learn where you can view fireworks displays around the country, check out the calendar section of the Japanese Fireworks website.

www.japan-fireworks.com/eindex.html

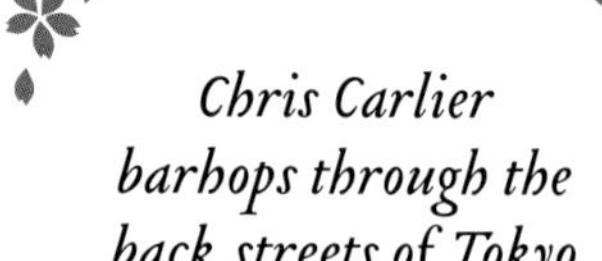

Chris Carlier barhops through the back streets of Tokyo

Japan is a boozehound's paradise. Alcohol is available twenty-four hours a day, from bars, convenience stores, and even vending machines. You can wander drunkenly down the darkest back streets without running into any trouble, and you're more likely to end up playing *Jenga* or *Pop-up Pirate* with middle-aged businessmen than getting into a fist fight. Best of all, you're always within stumbling distance of one or two unique little late night bars.

There are thousands of delightfully quirky watering holes all over the country that have been lovingly conceived and decorated to reflect their owners' idiosyncratic tastes. I've been to '80s bars, jazz bars, country rock bars, a short-lived bar themed on the Bay City Rollers, and even a bar dedicated to Diego Maradonna, the hell-raising Argentinean soccer legend. I've visited bars with delirious names like Bar Sushi and Men, White Lover, or Piggietail Connection.

One of my favorites is Garage Land in the Shibuya District, which is themed around the Punk and New Wave music scenes of the 1970s and '80s. I discovered it one day while roaming the neighborhood. I spotted the garish yellow-and-pink sign, which was unmistakably modeled on the Sex Pistols' iconic record sleeve for *Never Mind the Bollocks*.

Inside, I was overjoyed to find the faces of Johnny Ramone and Joe Strummer scowling down from posters on the walls, and their music booming from the speakers. The place was plastered in punk-rock paraphernalia, and oozing individuality.

Wow! I thought. *A bar just for me*!

The barman wasn't aggressive or intimidating, as one might imagine a punk publican to be. Instead, he was convivial, and had the endearing habit of digging out any song I mentioned in conversation and playing it with childlike enthusiasm. The regulars were happy to chat with me, and my language limitations were rendered irrelevant when it was discovered that I could communicate through song and band names. They told me Garage Land is a popular hangout for touring rock musicians who want somewhere discreet to drink when they are in town. Their autographs are drunkenly scrawled all over the walls and ceiling.

I'm fond of Garage Land because it's near my house, and I love the music they play. But wherever you choose to go in Japan, you can find your own little Friday night haven. All tastes are catered to in this densely populated country. Even if you're obsessed with polka music and table tennis, you can bet there's a bar out there just for you.

My advice is to go to any large or mid-sized transit station and wander down some nearby alleyways. You will easily find a few friendly bars. Don't make the mistake of searching for bars on the ground floor, as I did when I first arrived. The best ones are usually in the basement, or on the fourth or fifth floors, and are posted with brightly colored, wall-mounted signs on the face of the building.

I find that you're better off sticking to places with *bar* in the name, and avoid joints with the words *pub* or *snacks*, which are generally less welcoming to outsiders, and often employ grinning hostesses that you pay through the nose for the privilege of talking to. They tend to be frequented by elderly men who sing old folk songs and stare in shock when you walk into the room. Then again, finding out the hard way is all part of the fun.

Happy hunting!

Garage Land

Monday through Wednesday are "Happy Days" and beer is ¥500. From the menu, for less than ¥900 each, you can order a selection of bar dishes, from fish and chips to fried Japanese vermicelli and tuna, fresh basil pizza, and *udon* noodles with homemade meat sauce.

KN Shibuya Building, 7F
13-9 Udagawa-cho
Shibuya District
Tokyo
(03) 3464-1831
http://mm.visia.jp/garageland/

Train: Yamanote Line to Shibuya Station.

Subway: Ginza Line to Yamanote Station.

Directions: To reach the bar, take the Hachiko exit at Shibuya Station, cross the street, and walk to the end of Center Gai shopping street. Turn right, then left. A few blocks past Tokyu Hands department store, the bar is on the right, across from the police box.

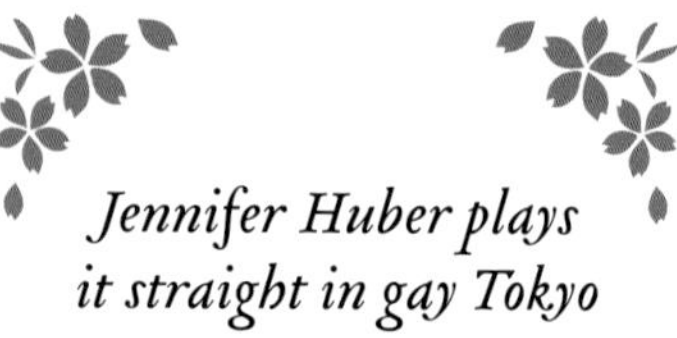

Jennifer Huber plays it straight in gay Tokyo

Using his "gaydar" to guide us through the streets of Tokyo, my traveling companion Matt led us to the center of the city's small, lively gay quarter, Shinjuku Ni-Chome, commonly referred to as Ni-Chome. As if reaching a mountain summit and basking in his achievement, he placed his hands on his hips and confidently declared, "We're here." It might have been his instinct assuring us we were in the right place, or maybe it was all the rainbow flags and stickers in the windows—either way, "here" we were.

With the exception of Ni-Chome, homosexuality seems to be mostly in the closet around Japan, especially in rural Japan where Matt and I had just spent the month. Unsure of the reaction, we hid Matt's homosexuality from our host families. Part of the reason for keeping it a secret was that the families had set him up on several blind dates with young Japanese women. Being a good guest, Matt was always polite and gentlemanly. But since he'd had to unwillingly participate in the Japanese heterosexual dating scene, we spent our last weekend in Tokyo, so that he could experience Japanese gay culture.

We got our first taste of it at Advocates Café, an open-air bar where men and women, both Japanese and foreign, mingle and connect. Here, the men were decidedly gay, and most of the women were straight. Interestingly, the women seemed to feel the need to make their sexual orientation clear when they introduced themselves. Most of the foreigners we met were English teachers living in Japan, and because of that, young Japanese men love Advocates, using it as an opportunity to practice their English with native speakers.

We arrived in time for Happy Hour, and for about ten dollars each, we guzzled bottomless plastic cups of beer. In the hour that we were there, the crowd nearly tripled in size. *Finding Nemo* played on the television screen, but was drowned out by patrons engaged in conversation. We liked the place, but it was time to move on and check out the rest of the neighborhood.

With Matt as our guide once again, we wandered onto a side street, where we passed a pudgy, drag-geisha dressed in a short, red silk dress, hobbling along on wooden sandals. I couldn't resist telling him he was *kawaii*— cute. He giggled shyly, hiding his smile behind his right hand, and continued on his way. We decided to take a chance, and climbed the narrow staircase where we had seen the drag-geisha exit. It led to a tiny, second-floor nightclub. Matt opened the door into a dimly lit pub, and the six Japanese men sitting at the bar turned their heads, cheered, and clapped enthusiastically at his entrance. When I peered around the corner, I was booed!

"Sorry, no girls," the bartender said, as he made an X with his index fingers, signifying that I had made a major faux pas. That evening, as I was to learn first-hand, women are not permitted into many of Tokyo's gay clubs. I'd also been told earlier that very few venues admit Westerners of either gender. According to one of the men I'd chatted with, gay Japanese fear that foreigners are infected with HIV, and exclude them from the clubs.

With my head lowered in embarrassment, I suggested that we head back to Advocates for another hour of drinking and conversation. Most trains stop running at midnight, so at eleven thirty, a mass exodus of Ni-Chome bar hoppers made its way to the station. Matt and I crammed into a train car and headed to our Tokyo hotel. I had heard these crowded cars provide an opportunity for drunk Japanese men to inappropriately fondle women. I didn't have to worry about that. Matt, on the other hand ...

Getting to Shinjuku Ni-Chome (Ni-Chome)

Tokyo's Shinjuku Station is Japan's busiest station and is served by numerous subway and train lines, including the main Yamanote Train Line, which circles the city. At the station, exit out the east doors onto Shinjuku Dori. Advocates Café is about a ten-minute walk.

Advocates Café

This open-air café is open nightly and spills out into the streets during the weekends.

7th Tenka Building, 1F
2-18-1 Shinjuku
Shinjuku District
Tokyo
(03) 3358-3988
http://advocates-cafe.com

Womanly advice

It's estimated there are between two hundred and three hundred gay pubs/bars/clubs within Shinjuku Ni-Chome. Though many don't allow women, I felt comfortable and welcome at Advocates and found everyone there friendly. As for all of the beautiful men you will see, they are gay—trust me.

Getting to know Japan's gay and lesbian scene

The Japan section of *Utopia Asia* is an excellent source, featuring a map of Ni-Chome, accommodations, restaurants, bars, clubs, and shops, as well as local gay and lesbian organizations, help lines, and forums. Related is the *Utopia Guide to Japan*, covering twenty-seven cities, including Tokyo, Kyoto, Nagoya, and Hiroshima.

www.utopia-asia.com/japntoky.htm

Ishikawa Prefecture

Hauquan Chau braves Wajima's "Night of the Mikoshi"

Every August, in the town of Wajima, signs should be put up warning visitors to "Beware of oncoming *mikoshi*!" As day becomes night, the town is transformed from a quiet fishing port into the site of one of the biggest festivals in western Japan. *Mikoshi*, portable replicas of Shinto shrines, are carried through the streets on the shoulders of the townspeople, and the four-day festival culminates in a huge *mikoshi* parade on the final night.

Each shrine in Wajima maintains a portable *mikoshi* with donations from generous businesses. The *mikoshi* parade route includes stops at these businesses to acknowledge their patronage. About an hour before the parade, a pre-festival meeting is held at the restaurant of a patron who offers food and drinks for the participants. Here, the official *mikoshi*-carrying uniforms are distributed: a *happi* coat, *tabi* slippers, and the all-important shoulder pillow to cushion the massive weight of the *mikoshi*.

I had come to Wajima to visit a friend who was teaching there, and when I met up with him downtown that evening, a pre-festival meeting was already in progress. Before I knew what was happening, I was rounded up into the restaurant, where someone handed me a *happi* coat and pillow, and I downed a cup of ceremonial sake. At first, I protested, "No, no, I'm just here to watch." But everything was happening so quickly, and the excitement was so contagious, that I got swept up in the moment. Other foreign teachers from different parts of the world had also been corralled into participating, but by the third round of drinks, it didn't matter who we were or where we were from. We were all united in the goal of carrying the *mikoshi* through the streets of Wajima to the Sea of Japan.

The polished, lacquered *mikoshi*, engraved with gold and set on two girders, gleamed under the street lamps. At the rear, a huge drum was mounted between the girders, where a drummer would stand to strike a marching beat throughout the parade. The task of getting the *mikoshi* onto the shoulders of the team was coordinated by Mr. Fuji, a jovial, sturdy-looking man who used large, sweeping gestures to give orders. "Ready? Up! Up! Slowly!" he commanded in Japanese with a booming voice, as the mammoth structure rose from the ground with the groan of creaking wood.

Crushed under the weight of the *mikoshi*, the cushioned shoulder pillows offered little relief. Being taller than most of my teammates, I felt that I alone was carrying my side. Pain ripped through my muscles, and my tendons stretched to their limits. I felt about to falter, but with the shouts of "*Ganbatte*!" and the cheers of excitement from the crowds, I wasn't going to let my team down. Still, I envisioned the headlines: "Man Crushed by *Mikoshi* at Local Festival" or "Shinto Gods Unfavorable to Festival Participant."

There were twenty of us carrying the *mikoshi*, with ten others available to relieve us along the way. The drummer set our walking tempo as Mr. Fuji waved instructions out front. A wooden-flute player accompanied the drummer, and a pole man marched ahead to lift any electrical lines that crossed our path.

Like the other *mikoshi* teams, which had started at different parts of the city, we had a specific route to follow, with stops along the way at shops or restaurants that had contributed to our shrine's coffers. Far from being a rest, each stop required us to "perform." And how else for a portable shrine to perform than to rock back and forth? One side would quickly bend down, while the other would push up, tilting the shrine to one side. Immediately, the two sides would switch from up to down, repeating the maneuver over and over. From afar, the *mikoshi* looked as if it were bobbing on a sea of people.

At every stop, the kind owners offered huge bottles of sake, and another member of the team carried beer to quench the unending thirst of the carriers. Due to exhaustion, and all this alcohol surging through our veins, control and stability became problematic.

At times, one side would suddenly dip, forcing the other side to compensate with upward pressure. This sudden change would swing the *mikoshi* wildly to one side, toward the crowds, whose grinning expressions would freeze, deer-like, as the lumbering shrine rushed toward them. In response to the frantic gestures of Mr. Fuji, the shrine would veer away from the crowds and equilibrium would again be achieved. The crowds cheered wildly.

Through narrow streets, over curved stone bridges, and under precariously hanging electrical lines, we finally made our way to the park. On the shores of the dark sea, with its waves crashing in rhythm with the now distant drums of the other *mikoshi*, at long last, we set down our burden.

Hundreds of people crowded around the *mikoshi*. Children were lifted onto shoulders to touch the tops of the shrines, karaoke singers bellowed out *enkai* songs, and the smell of grilled *takoyaki* (octopus) floated in the air above the food stalls. We warmed our gullets with more sake, as the lanterns overhead brightened the faces of the high-spirited revelers.

Toward evening's end, the crowds began to diminish, and one by one the *mikoshi* were loaded onto trucks and carried away, back to their shrines for storage until next year. Some members of our team also had to be carried home. The rest got rides back to the restaurant where we had started. Mr. Fuji made his closing speech, followed by a toast with more sake, and a round of applause for a successful night.

Mikoshi festival

The Wajima-*daisai* takes place every summer, from August 23 to August 25. Although the town has dozens of *minshuku* (bed-and-breakfasts) with prices starting at around $55 (¥5,500) per person and usually including two meals, reservations are recommended during festival time. The tourist information office at the Wajima Bus Station can help you find accommodations. You can also contact the Wajima Tourism Association in advance at (0768) 22-6588.

Getting to Wajima

From Tokyo Station, take the Joetsu Shinkansen to Echigo-Yuzawa Station. From here the Hokuetsu Kyuko Line (limited express) will take you to Kanazawa Station. Take the Nanao Line to Wakura Onsen Station, the Noto Railway to Anamizu, and then the Noto-chuo bus to Wajima. If you prefer, you can skip all the transfers to the smaller train lines and catch a Hokuriku Tetsudo express bus directly from Kanazawa Station to Wajima.

While a visit to Wajima is well worth the trip, it's no afternoon jaunt. It's nearly 640 kilometers from Tokyo to Kanazawa, the gateway to the Noto Peninsula where Wajima is located. The bullet train only goes as far as Nagano, and once you get out into central Honshu, the trains run a little more slowly and less frequently than the transit systems in the urban areas. From Kanazawa, it's a hundred-kilometer bus ride to Wajima.

One of the best ways to enjoy an excursion to Wajima would be to take the more leisurely scenic route, as the bullet trains move so rapidly that it's nearly impossible to enjoy the scenery along the way. The plains of central Honshu have a quality all their own, with emerald rice paddies studded with the sapphire-blue roofs of the farmhouse manors. Many of the trains have windows that can be opened to enjoy the fresh air. With Tokyo as a departure point, the castle town of Matsumoto is a good place to stop for the night, and there are places along the perimeter of the fortress to enjoy a view of the city lights coming on at sunset. From Matsumoto, it's a pleasant trip to Kanazawa for an overnight stopover to see the gardens of

Kenrokuen the next morning before continuing on to Wajima.

Chiba Prefecture

Jasmin Young catches a wave in the surf town of Taito

Upon moving to Japan and spending my first three months in Tokyo's concrete jungle, I was pleasantly surprised to learn of the remote town of Taito. My home for eleven years, this little beach community is well known by professional surfers from all over the world. Since there is no reef along the coastline, surfing is safe even for novices, and because of the consistency of the wave conditions along this part of the Pacific coast, Taito is the perfect venue for surfing events.

Here we hold Japan Pro Surfing Association contests, as well as World Qualifying Series and World Championship Tour events. Both are part of the Association of Surfing Professionals World Tour. Many of the world's top surfers compete right here at Taito Beach, so it is not uncommon to bump into legends such as nine-time ASP World champion Kelly Slater or three-time JPSA champion Masakazu Kouno (Zuccho) during competition season.

In Taito you will also find a Japanese surfer named Yama-san. He is the town "organizer," orchestrating just about every event in Taito, from beach cleaning to *matsuri* (festivals). One such classic event that I so look forward to at the beginning of every summer is the Surf Town Fiesta (officially called the Surf Town Festa), an annual, week-long festival that includes many of the major international surfing contests.

What I love about this yearly celebration (besides the delicious food and beer) is that although the surfing competitions are a major highlight, the Surf Town Fiesta also focuses on other important aspects of beach life. Yama-san is a self-proclaimed "*eko*" surfer, which is Japanese English for "environmentally friendly" surfer. He has introduced many important concepts to the local Japanese surf scene, such as recycling, and keeping the ocean clear of the plastics and fishing lines that are the cause of many turtle and dolphin deaths. Yama-san is also passionate about the importance of beach safety, and has introduced lifesaving techniques at the fiesta.

To some, these things may seem like common sense, but because we are in such a remote area of Japan, eco-focused philosophies are new to many of the local surfers and fishermen. I too am an *eko* surfer, and am honored to have a friend like Yama-san, who works tirelessly to promote an appreciation of the environment during the fiesta. It is important that we as surfers not only enjoy the ocean, but also respect it, and the creatures that live in it.

The Surf Town Fiesta is a time for fun in the sun, good food, and friendship. But it is also a time to emphasize the importance of our ocean environment. We welcome pro surfers from all over the world to come and share our paradise, and I hope that our surfing friends will take our message back to their own beaches and help keep our oceans clean.

Getting to Taito

Taito is an easy day trip from Tokyo. From Tokyo Station take the Wakashio Line directly to Kazusa Ichinomiya or the Rapid Line to Soga Station and change to the Sotobo Line to Kazusa Ichinomiya Station. From Ichinomiya, it is a ten-minute taxi ride along the Togane-Kujukuri Toll Road to Taito Beach.

Surf Town Fiesta

One of the first events of the summer, the festival is held yearly around the first week of June. From June until the end of August, beach tents are erected where food, ice cream, and drinks are available for beach goers. The waves are usually small and fun during this time of year, so even novices can enjoy the activities.

Aichi Prefecture

Frank Lev takes you out to the ballgame in Nagoya

After many months in Japan, I finally went to a baseball game. I enjoyed myself, not so much because the players were great, or the game particularly exciting, but because of the differences between the American and Japanese baseball experience.

In my opinion, baseball is a boring sport. It's a mystery to me how some people become infected with a fever that can make them so passionate about the game. Many Japanese have the bug, and I wonder if maybe it's the slowness and dullness that appeals to overworked businessmen. Baseball gives them a chance to relax and do nothing, maybe even snooze a bit in front of the TV.

As for my approach, I take a more spiritual view. To me baseball is the game that most imitates real life. It's generally uninteresting, with a lot of waiting around. However, there are a few intense moments that you have to be ready for. I look upon going to a baseball game as a sort of Zen exercise. You have to maintain your alertness throughout the quiet times in order to be prepared for those magic moments.

When I arrived at the stadium, I bought the cheapest ticket available, partly because I am cheap, and partly because I was told that the bleachers are where the action is. I soon realized that my bleacher seat meant I had become part of a group—or a section and a group, to be exact. Each section of about a hundred fans had a leader with a yellow shirt and a whistle. The section leaders took their cues from the group leader, who stood at the bottom of the bleachers and led the fans in cheers.

There were many different cheers, some of them songs, some chants. The group leader's assistant (a very important job) would hold up cards with the words. The cheers were almost nonstop. As long as the home team Hanshin Tigers were at bat, the fans were cheering. As the opposing pitcher for the Chunichi Dragons wound up for the pitch, they would abruptly stop so that the batter could concentrate. Then they would start right up again. The exuberant energy of the fans more than makes up for whatever deficiencies the players may have. Japanese baseball fans would put any high school football crowd to shame.

The fans are also well armed with cheering paraphernalia. Along with flags, many bring loud noise-making devices, such as hollow plastic bats that can be struck together to make loud bangs. Then there are the trumpets. By the end of the fifth inning, my head had started to pound. I now understood why people would pay up to $80 to sit in the non-bleacher seats. They were quiet.

Among the many idiosyncrasies of Japanese baseball, I found it a little strange to see people eating sushi and noodles. However, I felt right at home with the beer and ice cream vendors. I also noted that at the end of a throw, Japanese players pushed the ball rather than snapped their elbows down. I used to call this throwing "like a girl," but now that I'm more experienced and sensitive, I've changed my view. The girls I knew in my childhood threw like professional Japanese baseball players.

Japanese fans also have a fun twist on the seventh-inning stretch. At the start of the inning, people pull out big balloons with a valve that allows the air to escape slowly. As the third out at the top of the inning approaches, these balloons start appearing like strange flowers in the crowd. Just as the third out occurs, the balloons are released in a frenzy of color and motion. Then, in a matter of seconds, a cadre of young men marches onto the field and snatches them up, and the game goes on.

Best of all, though, is what happens when the home team scores a run. Everyone yells, "*Banzai*!" and then turns around and shakes hands with neighboring fans. I became particularly popular at this time. People seemed especially happy to come over and shake my hand, pat me on the back, or give me a high five. We had many congratulatory opportunities that day, as the Tigers won 8-0.

I stayed until the last pitch, and everyone else remained glued to their seats afterward, because an interview with the winning pitcher was being shown on the big-screen scoreboard. I don't think I'll go to another Japanese baseball game. Once was enough. But I'm glad I got to see this entertaining interpretation of a classic American sport.

Nagoya Dome
1-1 Daiko Minami
Nagoya
(052) 719-2121

More about Japanese baseball
Japan has two baseball leagues with six teams each. The season runs from April through October. To learn more about Japanese baseball, visit the following websites.

www.japanball.com
www.japanesebaseball.com
www.japanbaseballdaily.com

Shizuoka Prefecture

Sugu Althomson spends a golden week in Hamamatsu

While I was living in Hamamatsu, during the nationwide Golden Week celebrations, I heard the Hamamatsu Festival marching tune for three days straight. The city's neighborhood bands filled the streets. First, the whistlers blew their staccato notes, calling the drummers, who beat their drums in reply. Bringing up the rear were the buglers. All the while the crowds chanted along, "*Oisho*! *Oisho*!"

One evening, I was invited to join the festivities. My friend's grandparents wanted their foreign guest to enjoy the full Golden Week experience, so they loaned us their *happi* coats, and we headed off to the main parade with our neighborhood group. Every one of Hamamatsu's neighborhoods has its own group, with a float and band, and as our group encountered another in the street, we began marching around them. Our buglers played louder and our drummers beat faster as we tried to outdo our neighbors.

Hamamatsu has another Golden Week tradition that I love—the kite battle. Locals gather at the beach with their kites, some measuring up to five meters. Each kite is launched by its neighborhood group, which battles the others by using the kites' strings, coated with ground glass. Throughout the day, I observed neighborhoods in different stages of the competition. Some were flying their kites in the air, looking for a fight; some had already lost the fight (and their kites in the process); and some never got off the ground.

The kites are decorated with neighborhood emblems that match the *happi* coats of the launch crew. It takes many members of a group to launch and fly each enormous kite. The kite itself is made of heavy paper lashed to thick bamboo that gives it shape, and then a thick rope attaches the whole rig to a giant spool.

In typical Japanese fashion, the festival also includes tents set up in a park near the beach, selling cotton candy, candied apples, and squid on a stick. Even in this area on our way to watch the kites, we could hear the glorious cacophony of music that we'd been listening to all week. "*Oisho*! *Oisho*!"

Because one of the Golden Week events is Children's Day, families celebrate the births of newborns during this time. One year, I was invited to a private party for such an occasion by the family of the same friend whose grandparents loaned us their *happi* coats. We arrived at their home in the early evening, and were welcomed around a formal table set for a Japanese feast. As I sat there chatting with the family, in the distance, getting gradually louder, came the Golden Week tune—first the call of the whistles and drums, followed by the bugles and chants. It sounded like a gathering war tribe. When the group arrived at the house, it marched in circles in the street, chanting, "*Oisho*! *Oisho*!"

Then the group began calling the family name, until the parents came outside. A barrel of sake was produced, and some of it was poured into a huge, shallow bowl. The husband and wife had to quickly drink the whole bowl of sake. The husband drank with no problem, but the wife balked at the prospect. Next, the grandparents stepped up for the same ritual. After the honorees had their fill, the group replenished the bowl for each of the guests until all the sake was consumed. But the cask was emptied too soon as far as the crowd was concerned, so the bowl was filled and refilled with beer. The group even called up the foreigners a few times to see how much we could handle.

When I first arrived in Japan, my boss told me, "Unless you absolutely have to travel for Golden Week, don't. It's much more fun to stay in Hamamatsu." Good advice. The parades, the kite battles, and of course, the private party, all made Golden Week one of the best festivals of the year. *Oisho*!

Getting to Hamamatsu

Hamamatsu sits between Osaka and Tokyo on the bullet train, about two hours from each. Be careful about which train you take, because not all trains stop in Hamamatsu. Make sure to either take the Kodama Line (the slower train) or the Hikari Line (though it doesn't always stop in Hamamatsu, so double check).

Celebrating Golden Week

During Hamamatsu's Golden Week, from May 3 to 5, there is a booth just outside the north exit of Hamamatsu Station that offers information and the festival schedule in both Japanese and English. To experience the evening parades, just head for central Hamamatsu and follow the sound of the bugles and people yelling, "*Oisho! Oisho! Oisho!*" as loud as they can. You can walk to any nearby street that has been blocked off for the parades.

Kite battles

From the north exit of Hamamatsu Station, walk toward the bus terminal. Take the bus to Nakatajima Sand Dunes: Number 4 from Platform 5. The bus will drop you off at a park. Keep walking through the park and you'll reach the beach entrance. By this point, you'll see many people coming and going and you can follow the crowd. Enter the beach and head to the right for a bit, following the kites in the air.

Family festivities

To join a birth-of-a-child party, start talking to everyone you meet. Fortunately, Hamamatsu receives many foreigners from all over the world, so one does not need much Japanese to speak with locals. With any luck, you'll meet someone who will be happy to invite you. It happens frequently. Most of my friends who tried were welcomed with open arms. From what I understand, the residents and community members are happy to invite as many people as possible to share in their celebration. And of course, many people are also eager to lend their *happi* coats to spread community pride, so at the very least, you can join in the marches. Good luck, and enjoy the party!

Niigata Prefecture

Geoff Reid drums up enthusiasm for Sado Island's Earth Celebration

Navigating through the dusty streets of Ogi Town, we finally found the end of the very long line for the final concert of the Earth Celebration arts and music festival, a performance by Kodo, Japan's premier *taiko* drum ensemble. Without the nervous, pent-up energy I've witnessed in queues of such length, the people in this line were both pleasant and patient, seemingly content just to be in the moment.

When we finally started moving, we gradually left the village behind, entered a forested slope, and started up a path through a weathered Shinto *torii* gate. Our reward for the climb was a view of the Sea of Japan, with the sun just beginning to set. Fortunately, friends had arrived ahead of us and staked out a prime spot in front of the stage using beach towels and blankets. As we shared snacks and sake, dusk came upon us, and the drums began.

The resonance of the great *taiko* drums reverberated through my body and across the hilltop. Feeling an internal echo of such magnitude was a whole new revelation of sound for me. I was transfixed by the primeval beat that drove the complex rhythms, and by the fitness and endurance of the drummers. Their lean muscular bodies soon broke into a sheen of sweat, and their faces contorted in pain from the feverish exertion of the pounding tempo. Though their eyes were fierce, they were also serene, locked into the trance of the music.

After two hours of heart-pounding entertainment, we hiked back to our quiet campsite on the beach, first through a darkly lit forest path, and then on narrow, winding old roads beneath the kind of intense starlight that can only be seen in a place so far from an urban environment. One of the local farmers had left out *suika*—sweet, round Japanese watermelons—for sale in a cart parked alongside the road. We deposited three thousand yen in the tin and selected a few. When we finally arrived back at the beach, a bonfire was already blazing, and an aspiring DJ from New Zealand was setting up a makeshift sound system for an improvised finale to the festival.

Since 1998, the Kodo ensemble has been presenting its "Earth Celebration" arts and music festival on the remote island of Sado. Formerly a place of exile for both artists and aristocrats who displeased the shogunate, and historically the richest source of gold on the Japanese archipelago, the island has vestiges of a rural, but not altogether unsophisticated, traditional Japanese culture that is becoming increasingly difficult to find on the mainland. For a week every August, the island is infused with a bohemian atmosphere, brought on by the convergence of Japanese neo-hippies with musicians and artists from around the world.

I was one of many *gaijin,* foreigners who come from all over the country to escape the confines of teaching English, and to get a taste of the "alternative Japan" that lies mostly hidden outside the metropolitan areas. Sobama Beach was dotted with the camps of resident aliens from all over the globe, many of whom were more than happy to share their inside secrets on Japan, and even offered me tours of their "hometowns" if I ever happened to be passing through.

Perhaps stimulated by the mission statement of the celebration—"to provide a forum for cultural collaboration"—I found both foreigners and Japanese at their friendliest during the festival. It's the kind of event where, if you are as fortunate as I was, you might meet a renowned anthropologist while waiting to embark on the night ferry, and get her insights into the tensions between traditional and modern Japan, or encounter a Japanese jazz musician who reads sagas in their original archaic Icelandic as a hobby.

Memories of my experience at Sado Island later helped sustain me during my year of being the first and only foreigner ever to live in my tiny little backwater town. When culture shock hit hard, it would have been easy to "Japan-bash" whenever I encountered other frustrated foreigners. The temptation to view all Japanese as part of a conformist, rigid, and monolithic culture within the easy enclosures of stereotypes could be very attractive sometimes.

Nevertheless, one of the things that kept me from giving in to the persistent negativity into which many resident *gaijin* seem to fall was having met Japanese people at the festival who lived their lives outside the traditional roles of dutiful salary men or compliant housewives. Visiting Sado Island, reveling in the cross-cultural conviviality and bacchanalian excesses of the Earth Celebration, remains one of the touchstones of my experience living and working in Asia.

Earth Celebration

The festival is usually held the third week of August, and is billed in English as "an international arts festival that seeks an alternative global culture through musical and cultural collaborations from artists around the world." Festival information can be found on the Kodo website.

www.kodo.or.jp/ec/qa_e.html

Getting to Sado Island

Sado Island is located in the Sea of Japan, off the coast of north-central Honshu, approximately forty kilometers from the port city of Niigata. The fastest way to get to Sado, barring an expensive plane ride, is to take the Joetsu Shinkansen from Tokyo to Niigata, and then the jetfoil ferry. Car ferries also leave for Sado from Niigata, as well as Naoetsu in southern Niigata Prefecture and Teradomari in north-central Niigata Prefecture. Extra ferries are added during the festival to accommodate the increased traffic.

Where to stay

There are accommodations available in every price range on Sado, from luxurious *ryokan* and home-style *minshuku* to free camping on the beach. Geoff recommends the Sobama Beach Campground: (0259) 86-2363. It is located across the peninsula, about fifteen minutes by bus from Ogi Town.

An overnight stay costs about $13 (¥1,300) and includes toilets, pay showers, and a sundries shop. Try to book ahead, as the festival is one of the busiest times of year. Also, if you plan on camping, be aware that the winds sweeping down from Siberia over the Sea of Japan can be quite chilly at night, even in August.

Discovering Sado Island

Sado is a sizeable island that offers stunning vistas and landscapes reminiscent of the northern California coast or the Gulf Islands of British Columbia. It offers plenty of venues for marine sports and hiking, as well as lots of unique cultural opportunities, such as touring sake microbreweries or taking a ride in the harbor in a *taraibune,* a giant washtub-shaped boat—a strange vessel that is the symbol of Ogi Town.

Area tourist bureaus

Japanese tourist bureaus offer excellent information for accommodations and other practical information.

Niigata Prefecture Tourism Guide

www.enjoyniigata.com

Sado Tourism Association

www.visitsado.com/en/

Yamanashi Prefecture

Will Raus keeps his feet planted firmly on the ground in Kofu

I was five-foot-nine and 165 pounds the day I became a sumo wrestler.

Dr. and Mrs. Shimizu, my hosts in Japan, own a medical clinic, and every year, Dr. Shimizu holds a sumo training camp for his interns. I have a black belt in taekwondo, and I've always been interested in the martial arts. I was curious about sumo, so Dr. Shimizu invited me to join his students at the Kose Sports Park in Kofu, to embark upon the improbable task of becoming a sumo wrestler.

Each of the five days of training lasted four hours, and began with the setup, in which we got naked and helped each other tie our *mawashi* belts. The *mawashi* is the only piece of equipment that a sumo wrestler uses. There's only one way to tie this thing, and there's no way to do it yourself.

After preparing the surface of the *dohyo* fighting ring with fresh sand, we performed warm-up stretches that ended with *shiko,* the traditional sumo stretch that requires lifting one leg high in the air, then bringing the leg down with force. We worked our way up from twenty *shiko* the first day, to a hundred repetitions on the last day, which was by far the most difficult part of the training.

I didn't really notice the pain caused by the *shiko* until it was too late. At some point in the middle of the second day of training, my thighs started to ache, and when I woke up on the third day, it hurt like hell just to get out of bed. So I reluctantly sat out. I felt bad because I had to weenie out of a whole day of training, but I knew that if I didn't take a day off, I would probably be a wreck by the end of the week. Amazingly, on the fifth day, which was the most demanding, I had no pain whatsoever.

The ninety-minute drills on the basic techniques of sumo were the next and most important part of each training session. We started with how to advance toward an opponent by shuffling forward without lifting our feet, because a sumo wrestler's power depends largely on the stability of his stance. Rounding out a series of different drills, the coach acted as an opponent for each of us to push across the ring and out of bounds.

After the shoving exercises, the coach would comment on my stance and how I could improve it, then he'd get himself into position and we'd do it all over again. By the time the drill was over, I knew how pushing an opponent works, but it's a lot different when a target is actually pushing back. The biggest challenge was learning how to exert force with a flat-footed stance. It was tough to break my taekwondo habit of staying on the balls of my feet for mobility, but by the end of the week, the sumo stance had become second nature to me.

In this phase of the training session, we also learned about the three factors that facilitate a win. The most important is foot placement. If a wrestler's feet aren't planted firmly on the ground, most of his power is lost and he will probably lose. Next is hand placement, which means a firm grip on the opponent's *mawashi* belt, along with a good defense against the opponent's grip. The final aspect is optimal body placement, which should be lower than the opponent's, with the forehead planted firmly on his chest to give a push more power.

After the drills each day, it was finally time for the actual sumo wrestling. There's an old military aphorism that says, "Every battle plan lasts until the battle begins." Sumo is no exception. Even though we'd spent the past ninety minutes going over all the drills, all was forgotten in the throes of battle. Because we'd all been doing the same drills, we were aware of what should happen and what to expect, but once the fight started, it was every man for himself.

Determining the winner is simple—the first person to step out of the ring or touch the ground with anything other than his feet loses. There are also sumo taboos that prohibit punching with closed fists, striking to the groin, pulling hair, and bending back the opponent's fingers.

One of the martial arts principles that I've always embraced is that confidence is the most important element. First, I knew that my opponents weren't out to hurt me. Although the aim of the match was to forcefully remove my opponent from the ring, by the time we started wrestling, we all knew each other, and I felt safe. Secondly, I'd watched sumo on television, so I knew what to expect from that first charge. Finally, I was confident in my abilities as a wrestler, and so I knew that as long as I played it smart, there was nothing to worry about. I guess those three things made it a lot easier to cope with the fact that, at the heart of it, there were a hundred and eighty pounds of sumo waiting to do everything he could to remove me from the ring.

To the casual observer, sumo may look like nothing more than very large men shoving each other around in a ring. This couldn't be further from the truth, as I learned once the matches started. The first of my best-of-five matches was against an opponent who was about my size, so our face-offs turned into grapples as we jockeyed for hand position and tried to get under each other. My opponent had really coarse, bleached hair, and after that match, I had a fierce friction burn across my upper chest. But I ended up winning simply by my ability to hang on at the edge until I found a good grip or a rush of energy to put me back in the game.

Against my larger opponents, I found myself at a big disadvantage, because I was sure that they would barrel into me and knock me flat on my back. Then it dawned on me—they were thinking the exact same thing. In the first charge, my opponent came straight for me ... except I wasn't there. I had slipped to the side, and before he could react, I was behind him, and there was nothing he could do but accept being shoved out of the ring. Of course, that only worked once, but it still made me feel all slick and crafty knowing that my little trick had worked.

The real moment of triumph came on the final day. I had already lost two matches, and I was feeling a little less than confident. In the heat of one battle, my opponent had jammed me up against the straw matting, holding on for dear life. In that moment, only one thing came to mind. I had to push. In one quick movement, I shoved him away, charged under him, set my hands, and pushed. The whole thing happened so quickly that my opponent didn't even have time to react. Within seconds, the match was over, and I had just walked him straight off the edge of the mat.

In the next match, I had the same guy up against the matting, but I felt him regaining his foothold, and I knew that if he managed to get under me, I would have a hell of a time fighting my way back. So in one swift movement, I moved my hands off his belt and under his arms, and lifted him straight off the ground and over the matting. My fellow students all cheered for me, and since I've never had much upper body strength, it was a really cool feeling to pick up a guy my size and hoist him effortlessly over the edge.

When the wrestling was over, each day ended with sweeping and sifting the sand that lined the ring. Once the *dohyo* was cleaned and prepared for the next users, we shed our *mawashi* and happily hit the showers, as sumo is quite the dirty sport. As much fun as the camp was, I always found myself looking forward to the end of a long, tiring, sweaty day, and that final moment when we laid our *mawashi* out in the sun to dry.

Sumo wrestling

For more on professional sumo matches, continue on to the next essay.

Osaka Prefecture

Frank Lev comes face to face with a sumo wrestler in Osaka

When I was living in Kyoto, the nearest sumo tournament was in Osaka and held for just two weeks each year. It would be my only chance to see one before my teaching contract was up. My boss called the arena and was told the tournament was sold out, except for one seat on Tuesday. I would have to travel all the way to Osaka on Saturday to pay for the ticket in person. But I was determined to see a sumo match, so I was willing to do whatever I had to, and pay whatever it cost.

On the day of the tournament, I arrived at the arena in plenty of time to watch some of the lower-ranked sumo wrestlers face off in the large, raised ring. Most of the spectators were seated on cushions on the floor in roped-off areas. These box seats were sold only in sets of four, and most had been snatched up months ago. My ticket entitled me to sit about as far away as it was possible to sit.

I'd been there for a couple of hours when the higher-ranked wrestlers paraded out, dressed in their fighting belts topped with colorful aprons. They formed a circle on the stage to perform their ceremonial dance. Next came the referees, dressed in beautiful *Edo*-style kimono. As the match began, the first pair of wrestlers entered the ring. They had four minutes to perform their salt-throwing rituals for driving out evil spirits, and to psyche out their opponents by delaying as long as possible.

Once this was over, the near-naked giants crouched down into their ready stances. *Bam*! It started. They lunged at each other. *Bam*! It was over. The object of each sumo match is for a wrestler to force his opponent outside the circular boundary that marks the wrestling area, and one of the wrestlers had done just that. Afterward, they retreated to their respective sides and bowed to one another. The loser sulked off, and the winner crouched down to receive his honors from the referee, who bowed and waved his fan. I realized that I would have to pay close attention, or I might miss a match altogether.

The matches were fun to watch, although the action was sporadic. Occasionally, however, one of the wrestlers was thrown completely out of the ring. And sometimes, when the wrestlers couldn't get a hold on each other, they would resort to slapping, which is legal as long as they use an open hand. One wrestler was slapped so hard his nose bled. Instead of stopping the match, the wrestlers fell into a deadlock. All the while, blood was flowing, and the men were turning red from the intense exertion. Finally, the referee stopped the match and the wrestlers returned to their corners. The bleeding was stopped, and the match continued where it left off. In the end the bleeder lost. Both wrestlers got a large round of applause.

Toward the end of the day, as tension mounted and the crowd waited for the final two *Yokozuna* (grand champion) matches, I walked down to the arena for a closer look. I wasn't sure if it was allowed, but I thought, *What the hell, this is my only chance to see* sumo *wrestlers up close*. So I pretended that I was walking to my seat, then I stepped back and stood along the wall. I wanted to get a good picture of the wrestlers lined up for their turns.

I heard a loud thump behind me, and when I wheeled around, standing in the corner was the largest man I have ever seen. I felt only one thing: terror. The wrestler was like a bull, and I was intruding on his space. One of the managers hurried over and let me know in no uncertain terms that I should return to my seat at once. I didn't argue. I got back just in time to see that same man pick up his three-hundred-pound opponent and throw him out of the ring.

Finally, it was time for one of the *Yokozuna* to fight a lower-ranked opponent. The excitement in the hall was at a crescendo. All eyes were on the two men. They squared off, performed their rituals a few times, and then lunged at each other. The champion was much larger than the other, and they came together with a thud. They tugged and grunted. The bigger wrestler had legs like a rhino, and he leaned his weight into his opponent, bearing down on him, but the smaller man held his own.

Suddenly, the smaller man swung around quickly and twisted the *Yokozuna* until he lost his balance and fell to the ground. It's rare for a *Yokozuna* to lose. The crowd went wild, shouting, cheering, and even throwing seat cushions into the ring. But, of course, this is Japan, so it was orchestrated pandemonium—cushion throwing is the accepted way for spectators to show excitement.

After a few minutes, the arena settled down and the second *Yokozuna* came out. Amazingly, he also lost to a lower-ranked wrestler. Again, amid shouting and cheering, the cushions flew. Afterward, people were talking animatedly about what an amazing day this had been, because they couldn't remember the last time both champions had lost in the same day.

Turns out I was lucky to see such an exciting and rare day of sumo. Also turns out I was hooked. I watched the rest of the two-week tournament on television, checking in each night for the highlights.

Attending a sumo match

There are six tournaments a year in Japan: three in Tokyo, one in Osaka, one in Nagoya, and one in Fukuoa. Each tournament lasts two weeks. For general information on sumo and obtaining tickets, visit the following website.

www.sumo.or.jp/eng/

Nihon Sumo Kyokai Ticket Sales Office

1-3-28 Yokoami
Sumida District
Tokyo
(03) 3622-1100 (Japanese)

Train: Sobu Line to Ryogoku Station.

Subway: Toei Oedo Line to Ryogoku Station.

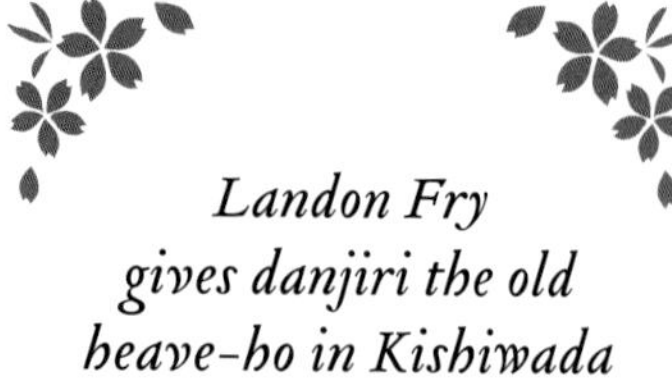

Landon Fry gives danjiri the old heave-ho in Kishiwada

Japanese spectators lined the streets, staring eagerly down the side of an old *ramen* shop, which was closed for the festival weekend. I fixed my eyes in the same direction, and was stunned as four metric tons of meticulously crafted wood on enormous wheels moved sluggishly into view. Sweat poured from the people pulling at the thick rope. Rhythmic cheers echoed down the streets, while *taiko* drums thundered from inside the massive vehicle. Flutes added melody, and atop the golden roof, a man hopped back and forth jubilantly. Kishiwada's Danjiri Festival was in full swing.

I made my way to the next street corner, where the *danjiri* approached a sharp right turn. It stopped for a moment as the team pulling it moved into position, and then a great drum crescendo accompanied orchestrated screams, as the *danjiri* continued on its journey. As the *danjiri* rounded the corner, men spilled out of their seats on the side, grasping at anything they could to avoid smashing against the asphalt. It tilted slightly, rolling along on just two wheels. The spectators gasped and held their breath as the *danjiri* finished its turn, and crashed back down on all four wheels.

Sadly, such success is not always the case. Nearly every year, someone at the festival is killed or seriously injured. While no one wishes for such a tragedy, people flock to the city and gather in droves at the street corners to watch the impending doom of the *danjiri* riders. With thirty-three teams pulling *danjiri* all over the city from six in the morning until dark for two days straight, the chance of an accident is high.

By nightfall, I was lucky enough to get in on the action. All the *danjiri* were making their final rounds of the city, and were now lit up and rolling along the streets like giant fireballs. The group of Americans I was with managed to make its way into a spot with the Naka-Machi team. An older man, worn from a day of *danjiri* pulling, showed us how to pull the thick rope and avoid letting it touch the ground, and how to scream properly. Not any scream will do. In addition to pitch volume, the proper word—"*Soorya*!"—must be called out. As best I could tell, the word doesn't have any particular meaning, but is used as a chant during labor to coordinate work. Two groups traded screams back and forth, compelling our feet to move in unison.

Spectators lined the city streets with cases full of *chu-hai*, a strong Japanese spirit, handing out drinks to anyone who is working to pull a *danjiri*. The *chu-hai* is offered more as a command than a suggestion, so it is important to drink slowly, unless complete inebriation is your goal.

I saw the *danjiri* through to the end of the line, which, fortunately, was the train station. Along the way, I learned that, as a foreigner, the most important factor is not being too shy to ask permission to join in. The only thing Japanese spectators seem to enjoy more than watching the *danjiri* go by is watching silly tourists pulling them.

Danjiri festivals

A *danjiri* is basically a large cart shaped like a shrine or temple. Danjiri festivals began in the early 1700s as a way to pray for a plentiful harvest. They are held around the country in mid-September. Kishiwada's is considered the most famous.

www.city.kishiwada.osaka.jp/danjiri/english/

Getting to Kishiwada

Kishiwada is an easy day trip from Osaka. Take the Nankai Main Line from Osaka to Kishiwada Station. The Danjiri Information Center is to the left of the station entrance. Here you will find English language information about the festival and free headbands.

Nara Prefecture

Alan Wiren gets into Muro's dragon spirit

A great, serpentine cave winds through volcanic rock toward the heart of Muro Mountain. Peering into the long, narrow mouth, it is easy to understand how this place inspired legends of an awesome dragon spirit. The cave opens just above a stream that splashes down the mountain in a series of waterfalls to the tiny village of Muro. The village is set beside the ancient Muro-ji, a temple which, along with the cave, is rededicated to the dragon spirit every year.

When I first came along the strip of tarmac that runs beside the river gorge into Muro, I was greeted by a village elder. Gripping a can of beer in one hand, he said, "We're having a festival today!"

Nearby, others were pounding rice into fist-sized *mochi* balls, and piercing harvest vegetables with bamboo skewers for decorations.

"Everyone will gather at the bridge around noontime," the man told me.

Spanning the river that separates the temple from the village, the bridge is a crimson arch. True to the elder's word, at midday various villagers began to arrive. Some wore business suits, others kimono. One had on a blue robe and a tall, four-cornered hat. He held two freshly cut lengths of bamboo: a thick one with a stoppered hole at one end, and another smaller, open-ended one that formed a cup. He grinned as he dispensed sake from the vessels.

On the other side of the bridge, just beside the temple gate, a golden filigreed and betasseled *mikoshi* shrine, designed to be carried though the streets, was surrounded by excited children in bright blue *happi* coats. The crowd on the bridge was joined by four young men in black pants and T-shirts, who carried two heavy, wooden masks with long hair, fearsome eyes, and menacing teeth. They also held two broad blue banners spangled with white moons and stars. Some older men arrived in more somber attire, and soon, they all formed a knot at the temple side of the bridge, waiting for permission to enter.

In accordance with tradition, Muro-ji's head priest must be asked seven and a half times before allowing anyone to pass. The sun was strong and the men with the masks had begun to sweat by the time consent was finally given. They donned the masks and banners, each set covering two men and turning them into a single beast, and they led the throng through the Muro-ji gate.

Inside the temple complex, the wooded mountainside rose steeply, and the festival party climbed broad stone steps to a clearing where a pair of centuries-old wooden buildings with shingled roofs stood. There are stairways beyond that wind up the mountain, passing by more historic buildings, including the smallest outdoor pagoda in Japan, but our procession went no farther.

Instead, we turned to a tiny shrine set off among the trees where the dragon's dedication ceremony is performed. Then the chimeras stepped forward to perform a Chinese lion dance that has been passed down and preserved through the generations.

When the dance was done, our entourage retraced its steps, hoisted the *mikoshi* onto the shoulders of a group of men, and paraded through the village to the Shinto shrine called Ryuketsu, the Dragon's Cave. Here the lions really came to life. Their dance lasted nearly an hour, as the articulated jaws of their masks clacked open and shut. At times, they appeared to be wounded by a long Japanese sword, suffering shuddering death blows, and then, after a miraculous recovery, they brandished the sword as if vanquishing all enemies.

When the dance ended, the lions nipped at the heads of the children to bring them good fortune. Then, at last, along with all the others, I ran to catch the balls of *mochi* that the elders threw into the crowd.

More about Muro

Muro is an attractive destination at any time of year. The village is home to an art park where abstract stone sculptures have been placed in a whimsical arrangement by Israeli artist Dani Karavan. It makes an ideal spot for a picnic. Muro Temple is known for its plum, cherry, rhododendron, and hydrangea blossoms in the warmer months, when the mountain air provides relief from heat and humidity. In autumn the flame of the maples on the temple grounds is soon followed by winter snowscapes, and Muro's traditional inns make cozy hideaways.

Getting to Muro

An easy day trip from Osaka, Muro is part of Uda in northeastern Nara Prefecture. From Osaka, take the Kintetsu Train Line to Muro-guchi Ono Station. Take the bus to the Muro-ji-mae stop. From there it's a five-minute walk to Muro-ji.

Festivals in Muro

The Dragon Festival is held in mid-October. Muro also celebrates many other festivals. A tea ceremony in mid-November is an ideal time to visit, with the maples at the height of their autumn colors. A flower festival from April 20 to May 10 showcases rhododendrons, and on April 21, a Memorial Ceremony is held for Kukai, the Buddhist monk who is attributed with founding the Muro-ji.

Aomori Prefecture

Paul Sharp floats through Aomori's Nebuta Festival

I came to the beautiful coastal city of Aomori just to see the Nebuta

Festival, where giant papier-mâché characters from Japanese history and folklore are brought to life every year. The festivities hadn't even begun, yet somehow I was already late. Even though the sun was still bright and the parade still hours away, spectators were already gathering.

Under the covered arcade, families had staked out the best viewing spots, and early arrivals spread picnic blankets while waiting for their friends. I noticed that the stadium seating provided the finest vantage point, but an usher used charades to explain that I couldn't enter. Then, when he realized that I speak Japanese, he clarified that the seats cost thousands of yen and were already sold out.

When the floats finally appeared, they crept in from side streets, and I had to squeeze between a mailbox and a telephone pole to watch their arrival. As each took its place in the middle of the street, I waited with the crowds for some kind of signal. All of a sudden, the floats lit up, their colors amplified against a dark cityscape. Beginning to move, seemingly by their own volition, they became luminous, animated sculptures.

The first float depicted a warrior battling a dragon, with the scene intensified by drumming, chanting, and gongs. I had to capture the lifelike beauty with my camera. It was difficult to avoid obstructing other spectators when trying to snap a shot from just the right angle, but as long as I kept moving, nobody seemed to mind.

Next, I chased a demon, then turned to find a tiger, and a *Kabuki* character as big as a whale. Thinking back to the stadium seats, I wondered why anyone would want to sit still in the midst of all this excitement. I was soon invited to dance by a group of kids, while the grown-ups banged on portable gongs, yelling encouragement. They were all neighbors who had created a float featuring a big, fierce Buddha. Dancing in the summer heat soaked my shirt with sweat, so someone offered me a cold drink. Finally, the kids let me sit down, and they slowly danced away.

Despite the action still going on around me, I couldn't resist the aroma of the food stalls any longer. I filled my bag with beers from a convenience store, and weaved along through the crowded sidewalk, trying nearly everything. Bypassing the octopus balls for the time being, and promising myself a chocolate banana later, if I still had room, I satisfied my cravings with fried chicken on a stick, cabbage pancakes, and fish-shaped cakes filled with chocolate.

By now the parade must have circled past me three times, and the forty-plus floats all started to look alike. Every few minutes, a massive figure fighting a dragon or a samurai threatening the sky with his spear, glided past. Everything was still just as beautiful, but as the festival began to wind down, I no longer felt the need to watch so intently, and I was able to relax. I chatted with a group of Japanese tourists who were picnicking beside me. They offered me a drink and some dried squid. Later, I passed around some beer from my bag.

When the parade finally ended, I felt drained. The crowds dispersed, and eventually the floats and their retinues left the main road. I trailed behind one group, and then another, as they pushed their floats home. Massive garage doors were closed on the floats, and the groups continued with their own festivities right in the middle of the streets.

A local party broke out when the people in the group I was following reached their neighborhood. They invited me to join them for a beer outside a little corner shrine, where fifty or so people were laughing and chanting festival songs. Everyone was so excited from the night's events that I couldn't follow what was being said. Cheerfully, an old man asked me how I liked Nebuta, but I didn't know quite enough Japanese to explain with much clarity. In the end, with one thumb up, he asked me in English, "Nebuta good?"

I answered with both thumbs up. "Very good."

Aomori Nebuta Festival

The festival is held in Aomori during the first week of August. For more information, contact the Aomori Tourism and Convention Association and visit the festival website.

Aomoriken-Shoko-Kaikan, 4F
2-2-17 Hashimoto
Aomori
(017) 723-7211
www.nebuta.or.jp/english/index_e.htm

http://apti.net.pref.aomori.jp/index-en.html

Getting to Aomori

Aomori is on the north end of Honshu and is best done from Tokyo as a trip of a few days or longer. Take the Tohoku Shinkansen from Tokyo Station to Hachinohe Station. Transfer to the Tohoku Main Line to Aomori Station.

Hokkaido Prefecture

Tim Patterson celebrates the sea urchins of Teuri Island

With blue sky overhead I walked along the harbor to the northern tip of Teuri, a small island off the northwest coast of Hokkaido. Cats prowled the dusty street, slipping in and out of ramshackle wooden sheds and squabbling with seagulls over fish scraps. Gulls are called "seacats" in Japanese, a fitting description given the noise they make, which sounds just like a cat begging to be fed.

At the end of the street, where the road dead-ended into a sea wall, an old woman sat in the shade of her doorway, shucking sea urchins. She smiled and fired off a few questions in the local dialect, accepting my stumbling replies without batting an eyelash.

Older people in the countryside often simply assume that I speak Japanese, while younger, more cosmopolitan people who have encountered Westerners before are shocked when I manage to say hello. It occurred to me that to this woman, I was probably only slightly more foreign than the Japanese college students from Tokyo that I had met on the morning ferry to the island.

"Here for the sea urchin festival, are you then?" the old woman asked. "There'll be an *enka* singer performing tonight. She came all the way from Iwate, if you can believe that. And fireworks afterward of course. Where are you staying? Camping? Ha! Well, the inns are full anyway and it won't rain for another day or so. Good weather this year, isn't it, and plenty of urchin too. Don't take too long walking or we'll eat it all!"

As we talked, the woman kept right on shucking urchins, splitting them with a knife, scooping out the edible yellow gonads and dropping them into a pan of fresh water. The shells, each about the size of a baseball, went into a large bucket, where their spines scratched helplessly against the plastic.

Leaving the old woman to her work, I rounded the cape and started off down the wild western shore. Bits of Russian, Korean, and Japanese garbage had washed up amidst the boulders on the beach, and big driftwood logs lay piled in the shadows at the base of the cliffs. Sea roses and orange lilies clung to grassy hollows amidst the tens of thousands of nesting birds, which were too absorbed with their own family squabbles to pay me any mind. Fishing boats motored about offshore, outlined white against the dark blue of the northern sea, and far off on the horizon a small puff of clouds marked the peak of Rishiri Island, an extinct volcano rising more than seventeen hundred meters above the ocean.

After downing a Sapporo beer and taking a quick swim in the cold salt water, I boulder-hopped my way back to the village, where the annual sea urchin festival was now in full swing. The festival marks the beginning of the short summer season in northern Hokkaido, and is the biggest party of the year for the island's hardy year-round residents.

A young fisherman with a shaved head and big hoop earrings called me over to his stand, where I bought a plate overflowing with wedges of fish, scallops, hunks of octopus, and thinly sliced squid for a little less than four dollars. "Take these too," he said, handing me three sea urchins, which he pulled out of a tank and sliced open just as the old woman had done. "Try it raw," he said, and gave me a little wooden ice-cream spoon. "But just eat the yellow stuff."

While the rest of my seafood cooked on the grill, I struggled to scoop out the slimy yellow globes of sea urchin and then let them dissolve on the back of my tongue. In most sushi restaurants raw sea urchin is expensive and elaborately prepared, served on little mounds of rice wrapped in seaweed, but the taste was better this way, stronger, a pure distillation of the northern sea.

Getting to Teuri Island

Highway 233 up western Hokkaido Island is Japan's answer to California's Highway 1. The ribbon of blacktop hugs the coast, winding beneath windswept bluffs and through fishing villages clustered by gravel riverbanks. This is a windows-down, music-rolling, road-trip highway, and if you don't have a car, just stick out your thumb. I've never had a bad experience hitching in Japan.

Teuri is about two-thirds of the way up the coast, accessible by ferry from the town of Haboro. In the summertime the ferry runs twice a day. I like to camp on Haboro Beach the night before and catch the morning boat. There's no train service to Haboro, but a bus provides direct service to the ferry port from Sapporo. The bus takes about three and a half hours. For a timetable, as well as information on island bird watching, visit the following website.

www.teuri.jp

Sea urchin festival

The festival is held in early August. For accommodations, there are several family inns in Teuri village, a youth hostel, and a free public campground. For more on tourism in the surrounding area, visit the following website.

www.asahikawa-tourism.com

General Japan

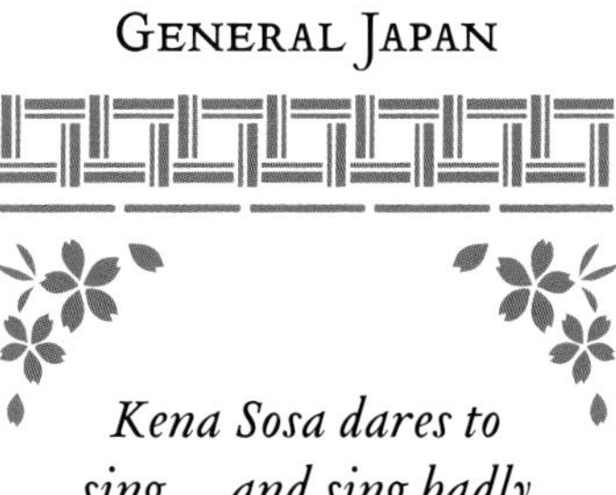

Kena Sosa dares to sing ... and sing badly

I had heard about karaoke in the United States, and though I was curious, I didn't have the courage to go alone, and I could never gather the troops to come with me to be my cheering section. So, my first karaoke experience was with friends in Japan.

I expected what I had seen in movies and on television: standing alone in front of a group of bar hounds, humiliating myself. Being *hazukashii* (shy), I was terrified of singing in front of a crowd of strangers. However, in Japanese karaoke bars you are not wailing for people you don't know. Instead, my friends led me into a booth, where I discovered that karaoke in Japan is quite different from its mutant American counterpart. In Japan, you rent a private booth with those you choose to share it with—friends, co-workers, teachers, neighbors. Whoever they are, chances are they all love karaoke.

Karaoke is like a national sport: loved by nearly everyone in the country. Whether your stay is long or short, if you don't go to a karaoke bar, you can't really say that you've been to Japan. In the language of its birthplace, *kara* means "empty" and *oke* is the English-turned-Japanese abbreviation of "orchestra" (*okesotura*). The concept of karaoke is that you have no back-up band to cover up your superstar voice ... or complete lack of singing skills. People in Japan do not really care if you sing well or not. They go to karaoke because it is fun.

I eventually discovered that the only things Japanese karaoke booths have in common with each other are the basics: a music menu, a sizeable couch, a monitor, and the karaoke machine. Other than that, the sky's the limit. Some karaoke places have nice, comfortable rooms, most of which are themed. Since I was introduced to karaoke, I've been in Elvis-themed booths, graffiti-adorned booths, and my favorite, a booth with Styrofoam walls painted to look just like a cave, cool and refreshing.

Another motivating factor for those who are shy like me is that karaoke bars are just that—bars. From your wacky karaoke keypad, you can order all kinds of drinks, and if you're lucky, you'll find a place that is *nomihodai*, all you can drink. If not, I recommend a Japanese drink called *chu-hai*, which is a mixture of spirits and juice or soda. Having a *chu-hai* close at hand will give you the courage to pull off a bad rendition of your favorite tune.

But back to the dreaded singing part. The songs appear on the monitor in both Japanese and English, so there are no worries about language barriers. You can pick whatever you like. And in Japan, among friends, the reassuring thing is that you don't have to go it alone.

For my karaoke debut, I was joined by a friend. The song we chose was "Stop in the Name of Love" by The Supremes, which was silly, because we soon realized that we only knew the chorus. Nonetheless, it broke the ice, and once I got used to the idea that no one was judging me, I could ham it up and get into the karaoke spirit: Dare to sing, and badly! Sing your heart out. And rest assured that no one back home will ever find out.

Karaoke etiquette and advice

- Queue up for only one song at a time.
- Join in for duets if invited.
- Don't be afraid to ham it up and get silly.
- Never boo or heckle other singers.
- Applaud after every song.

Finding a karaoke club

Many of the smaller karaoke bars are tucked away on neighborhood streets. However, Japan has several karaoke chains, such as Karaoke-Kan, Karaoke 747, and Big Echo with outlets in many cities, all of which have private booths and a selection of international songs. Rates are usually posted on the exterior of the building; expect around

$5 (¥500) per hour per person at peak times during the evening and on weekends. Many karaoke clubs offer discounted rates during off-peak hours.

Karaoke-Kan

Featured in the movie *Lost in Translation*, this popular karaoke club is about a five-minute walk from Shibuya Station.

K&F Building
30-8 Udagawacho
Shibuya District
Tokyo
(03) 3462-0785

Train: Yamanote Line to Shibuya Station.

Karaoke 747

Grand Tokyo Kaikan, 6F
33-1 Udagawacho
Shibuya District
Tokyo
(03) 3463-7478

Train: Yamanote Line to Shibuya Station.

Big Echo

7-4-12 Roppongi
Roppongi District
Tokyo
(03) 5770-7700

Subway: Hibiya Line to Roppongi Station.

Geisha in Tokyo's Sanja Matsuri parade

Retail Therapy

An insiders' primer to boutiques and markets

During my time teaching English in Tokyo, I worked at a conversation salon, where students of similar fluency were assigned to tables of three or four, to practice casual conversation with a native speaker. One of the most common icebreakers, especially with beginners, was, "What is your hobby?" Almost to a one among young Japanese women, the answer would be, "Shopping." No matter how many times I heard that reply, I was always amused.

I hardly considered shopping a hobby, and I'd never had much patience for endless hours of browsing in search of nothing in particular. However, after a few months in Tokyo, I found that I gradually abandoned my real hobbies (cooking, sewing, gardening, playing guitar, reading, studying *kanji*) and spent most of my free time shopping instead.

Over the next two years, I wandered the covered shopping streets of the Ikebukuro District. I joined the slow parade of youthful consumers down Takeshita Dori in the Harajuku District. I squandered entire afternoons at Tokyu Hands, and I spent many a lunch hour exploring the fourth floor of Kinokuniya Bookstore. Over time, I noticed a subtle shift. I was enjoying shopping for fabric more than I enjoyed making my own clothes with it. Eventually, I stopped sewing altogether, and began buying clothes in all the bargain outlets I'd discovered. It was time to face it. Shopping had become my hobby too.

For travelers in Japan, shopping is so obvious that it needs no explanation. You can't walk a block without discovering yet another irresistible item to part you from your yen. But because nearly everything in the country is notoriously expensive, a little guidance is helpful to keep you from breaking the bank. Fortunately, our contributors are full of savvy insights.

Sara Francis-Fujimura knows of a countrywide shopping opportunity so budget friendly that she can turn her kids loose

Shoppers at the Ueno fish market in Tokyo

to buy anything they want while she stocks up on chopsticks, fireworks, and squid snacks. And Jennifer O'Bryan frequents a boulevard lined with reasonably priced culinary supplies, purchasing items typically used in restaurants for unique gifts for friends back home. In his exploration of Japan's little-known secondhand shops, Stefan Chiarantano forages for intriguing collectibles with a heartbreaking history, while Mark Schilling picks up pop culture knickknacks, both new and used, at Tokyo's *manga* mecca, Mandarake.

As in many Asian countries, shopping in Japan is as much about the experience as it is about the purchase. Alice Jackson can't imagine a visit to Tokyo without stopping at the Oriental Bazaar, where she has been hunting for treasures since 1957. Sara Francis-Fujimura feels that her shopping trip to Hirata every summer is as much about understanding Japanese culture as it is acquiring a few new items. In a twist on the classic purchasing experience, Jasmin Young spins her souvenirs, a set of teacups, with a pottery maker in the beach town of Awa Kamogawa. I also often find that shopping is a way of getting to know a place, such as the town of Wajima, where the age-old industry of hand-crafted lacquerware unites shopping opportunities with a unique look into an ancient cultural tradition.

If you're traveling in Japan, there's no getting around it, you're going to shop, and you're likely to discover some pretty wonderful venues all on your own. Until then, our contributors offer a few excellent places to start.

Tokyo Prefecture

Alice Jackson is a regular at Tokyo's Oriental Bazaar

Each time I visit Tokyo, I love to shop at the Oriental Bazaar. Over the decades, I've purchased wood-block prints, *obi* sashes, silk fans, cloisonné jewelry, a pharmacy sign, a cast-iron teapot with a bamboo hanger to suspend it from the ceiling ... You could even say that my home has been designed and decorated by Oriental Bazaar.

My first shopping trip to the bazaar was in 1957, while I was living and working in Tokyo. Because it is located on one side of Meiji Shrine, and our housing area was on the other side, on the weekends we would walk through the shrine and gardens taking pictures, and then go shopping. That always made for a nice Saturday or Sunday afternoon.

During that first school year, 1957-1958, I bought the decorative screen that now hangs in my dining room. Amazingly, I still remember exactly how much I paid for it. (Would you believe, just fifteen dollars!) In those days, even though our salary was just a few thousand dollars a year, we lived in the Washington Heights military housing complex, and our rooms cost us only five dollars a month. Add to this an exchange rate of 360 yen to the dollar, and we could buy anything we wanted.

On a trip to Japan in 1974, I purchased the teapot with its bamboo pole, and the drugstore sign that hangs above my fireplace. We had the sign translated, and it says something to the effect that ginseng should be taken for the common cold. Of all my purchases from the Oriental Bazaar, the folding screen, the teapot, and the drugstore sign are the three that I treasure most.

As I continue to return, I've noticed that the Oriental Bazaar now attracts more foreign shoppers. It was never so crowded in the 1950s. It is also larger in size; I don't remember a third floor. There are now fewer hand-crafted Japanese goods, and more mass-produced items made especially for tourists. But Japanese department stores can be very pricey, and although they may have better quality, for me the Oriental Bazaar is still the perfect place to shop, especially for young people on a budget.

At my age, I am just about done with shopping. Perhaps my tastes are changing, or maybe I am trying to be more selective. I now look for good buys on *obi* sashes, which I use in my home as table runners. Nevertheless, I still like to visit the Oriental Bazaar to explore everything on display. It's always fun to look. Even after all these years, it beckons me with its enormous red *torii* gate, and I always look forward to browsing whenever I visit Japan.

The Oriental Bazaar

The Oriental Bazaar is located in the Harajuku shopping area on Omotesando Boulevard, about halfway between Harajuku and Omotesando Stations. This four-story emporium caters mainly to foreigners, and is usually crowded with people speaking many languages. It carries nearly every type of souvenir or gift that a traveler might want to buy, including new and vintage kimono, cotton *yukata*, woodblock prints, fans, chopsticks, porcelain, dolls, jewelry, lamps, and antique furniture. The merchandise is arranged according to price, with the inexpensive souvenirs in the basement, the mid-range items on the middle floors, and the more expensive merchandise, such as furniture and antiques, on the top floor. Although I doubt that all of the antiques are genuine, they look authentic, and the prices are reasonable. The Oriental Bazaar also offers shipping.

5-9-13 Jingumae
Shibuya District
Tokyo
(03) 3400-3933

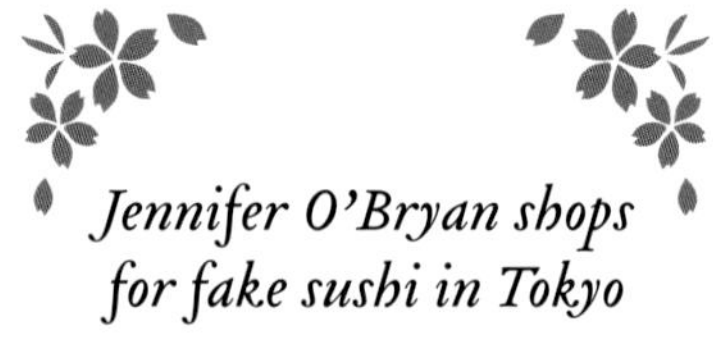

Jennifer O'Bryan shops for fake sushi in Tokyo

During my stay in Tokyo, I observed that plastic food displays are ubiquitous in the windows of Japanese restaurants, and I wondered where the proprietors bought the glasses of fake Asahi beer, faux *bento* boxes, and mock curry beef bowls they put on display to tempt customers in from the sidewalks. The Kappabashi restaurant supply neighborhood in Tokyo's Asakusa District, that's where.

On my first venture into this area, I knew I was in the right place when I gazed toward the sky and saw a giant, mustached, white-toqued chef's head atop the Niimi Building. Exit 3 at Tawaramachi Station had landed me at Asakusa-dori, a boulevard that runs right through the heart of Kappabashi.

Anything a restaurant owner could possibly want can be found here, and some of the approximately one hundred and fifty shops are so small that they specialize in only one type of supply. During my visit that day, I found a shop that offers only chefs' uniforms, another that sells only bakery supplies, and one so specialized that food strainers are the only merchandise it carries. If I wanted to open a 1950s-themed diner, there is another store that sells an impressive array of Americana, from vintage posters and neon wall clocks to those glittery, red vinyl stools, a classic trademark of the American luncheonette.

Along the way, I browsed in a shop called Nishimura, which just sells *noren,* those curtains that hang in restaurant doorways to advertise the type of food offered inside. I found another shop called Kondo Shoten that specializes in bamboo wares, and one called Kappabashi Soshoku, which offers a variety of red paper *chochin* lanterns. In the pottery stores, I marveled at the abundance of porcelain piled high on shelves in narrow aisles, making for some dicey moments as I sucked in my stomach and held my breath, hoping nothing broke as I squeezed by.

After several fascinating hours spent idling in Kappabashi's many shops, I finally found the one I'd come for: Maizuru, one of Tokyo's largest and oldest purveyors of faux food. This plastic food emporium features replicas of every dish imaginable, from spaghetti with meat sauce and crisp garden salads to exotic sushi delicacies. And although it offers custom-made items, I was happy to make my selection from their regular inventory.

Predictably, I was powerless to resist Kappabashi's temptations. At the end of the day, I headed home with eight teacups, two iron teapots, five pairs of chopsticks, four chopstick rests, a dispenser that keeps water warm for tea and soups, and, naturally, a delightful assortment of plastic sushi that looks as tasty as the real thing.

Getting to Kappabashi

Take the Ginza Subway Line to Tawaramachi Station, which is about a five-minute walk from the heart of Kappabashi. Once you arrive at street level through Exit 3, look for the sign that reads: "Kappabashi-dogu-gai," and for the giant chef's head atop the Niimi Building. The following website offers shop descriptions, detailed directions, and a small map of the district.

www.bento.com/phgal-kappabashi.html

Shopping tip

While plastic food is a big draw for tourists, Kappabashi is also a great place to pick up Japanese-style kitchen wares, such as lacquer *bento* boxes and chopstick rests. Irregular factory-produced pottery items are inexpensive and are often displayed in bins outside of shops, with beautiful teacups selling for as little as ¥200 apiece.

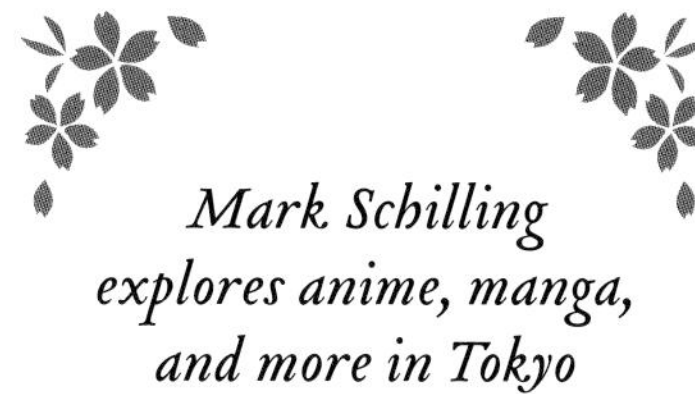

Mark Schilling explores anime, manga, and more in Tokyo

Are you into the *anime* and *manga* side of Japanese culture—a casual fan, or maybe even one of those committed *otaku* who collect memorabilia, dress in *manga* costumes, and go to the conventions? Or do you just want a weird Japanese *tchotchke* or two to take to the folks back home? If the answer to any of these questions is yes, and you happen to be in Tokyo, check out Nakano Broadway.

Located in Nakano, a sub-center just west of downtown Tokyo's Shinjuku District, Nakano Broadway is in the Sun Road Street Mall, housing a warren of shops catering to every imaginable *otaku* obsession. Though it totals five floors, including the basement, the real action is on the second, third, and fourth floors.

Here is where you'll find the nerve center, Mandarake. It began as a used-comic store in 1987, but has since expanded to more than a dozen shops in the building and ten other stores around the country.

Mandarake's main business is still buying and selling *manga*, and nearly all of its stock is for the Japanese-literate reader. But it also has other shops that sell everything from the tiny figures of *anime* characters that children buy from vending machines, to robots and other toys from the early postwar period, which are priced into the stratosphere. In other words, there are Japanese pop culture products of every description, for every budget.

Mandarake is now well known abroad—partly because it is good at publicizing itself. I've twice interviewed the chain's affable founder and president, Masuzo Furukawa, who both times was dressed down in a stocking cap and jeans, like one of his part-time employees. But my reasons for liking Nakano Broadway are somewhat different from the typical Mandarake devotee. I don't need it for *manga*, since most of the titles I buy are available in any large bookshop. I also don't need it for pop culture knickknacks, since most of the ones I have are *omake* (freebies) from the local convenience store. I am the opposite of the max-out-the-credit-card *otaku* that Mandarake mainly caters to.

I like Nakano Broadway because there is so much more to it than just the well-publicized Mandarake. It also has shops selling all types of subcultural stuff, from old movie posters and cinematic memorabilia to warriors, castles, and other gear used in role-playing games. I stock up on the former, and am content to admire the obsessive detail of the latter.

There are also restaurants and coffee shops, including the noteworthy "maid shop" on the third floor, which not only serves dozens of flavors of good ice cream, but in the evening allows customers to play games and sing karaoke with the shop's "maids," who are waitresses dressed in maid costumes. Though intriguing, this is one service of which I have yet to partake.

Some of the shops are fairly new, while others have been in business for decades—and look it. Most, however, are offbeat or outright odd. Browsing them is like taking a stroll through the strange and wonderful side of the Japanese creative mind. Think of it as a free museum of Japanese popular culture. Free, that is, until you spot that must-have movie poster or classic *anime* figure that you just can't live without.

Mandarake

Nakano Broadway, 3F
5-52-15 Nakano
Nakano District
Tokyo
www.mandarake.co.jp/en/shop/
http://bwy.jp/ (Nakano Broadway)

Train: Chuo, Sobu, or Tozai Lines to Nakano Station.

Directions: When choosing a train, be careful. The Chuo/Ome Special Rapid starting from Shinjuku and the Chuo Commuter Special trains do not stop at Nakano. Once at the station, go out the north exit and cross the roundabout to the Sun Road Street Mall. Walk down Sun Road about five minutes until you come to Nakano Broadway. Head for the second floor to begin your explorations.

Ishikawa Prefecture

Celeste Heiter pictures herself trading places in Wajima

On Honshu's west-central shore, on Noto Peninsula on the Sea of Japan, is the lovely hamlet of Wajima. It's a quiet little town overlooking a fisherman's wharf, and on any given day, to the casual observer, not much appears to be happening there.

Our first day in Wajima dawned brightly, and we were up in time for Asaichi, the morning market, where locals sell fresh produce, homemade pickles, local handicrafts, paper fans, and folkwear. By noon, we had wended our way downtown, where shop after shop after shop was piled to the rafters with every kind of lacquer item imaginable, from chopsticks to whole suites of exquisite furniture. However, with all that merchandise to tempt me, I think I showed remarkable restraint. At the end of the shopping day, I returned to our *ryokan* with only a pair of wooden *geta* sandals with padded silk thongs that I still have in my closet to this day, and a pair of deep green-and-gold lacquer chopsticks that are among my favorite souvenirs of Japan.

Our two-day visit to Wajima was all too brief, but we had the good fortune to find the best lodgings of any place we stayed in all of Japan. The inn was an old wooden building, and from the street, it appeared quite unremarkable. But once inside, the *genkan* (where guests remove their shoes) revealed a quadrangle of traditional rooms overlooking a small garden in the center. Our room on the upper story was especially large, with expansive *tatami* floors, lots of extra futons and pillows, and large window screens that could be propped open with a stick for a view of the garden below.

The proprietor was a quietly gracious young woman named Yuko who spoke good English for someone so far out in the provinces. Yet her demeanor betrayed a hint of sardonic wistfulness—something unfulfilled or unrequited. In little snippets of conversation with Yuko over the next couple of days, I learned that at nearly thirty, she was still unmarried, and had resigned herself to spending the rest of her days running the family business with her aging mother. To her, it seemed as if she would be stuck in that little town forever ... a tender trap indeed.

On the last evening in Wajima, we donned our *yukata* (cotton kimono) and walked down to the beach to witness a *taiko* drumming performance that had originally been a means of frightening away invading enemies. As we sat there in the firelight on the dark beach, the drummer in his gruesome mask and wild headdress, and the *toom-toom-tum* of the great *taiko* drum, were quite intimidating. Afterward, the spectators, most dressed in *yukata* with wooden *geta* on their feet, made a mass exit toward home. The rattle of hundreds of *geta*, clicking along the streets of Wajima, still echoes in my memory.

The following morning, we enjoyed a traditional breakfast of miso soup, pickled salad, dried fish, and white rice. Afterward, as we bade a reluctant farewell to Yuko, the fleeting thought crossed my mind that I could be quite happy living her life there in Wajima. In that same moment, something in her eyes told me that she would gladly have traded places.

Getting to Wajima

For information on traveling to Wajima, go to page 122.

Shopping in Wajima

Asaichi and Yuichi

These lively morning and afternoon markets take place on a few blocks of Asaichi-dori, surrounding the riverbank and the seashore. The markets are lined with more than two hundred vendors selling local crafts, fresh produce, seafood, pickles, and dried foods.

Lacquerware

With around eight hundred lacquerware workshops, the town of Wajima, where lacquer trees once grew in abundance, is known for its elegant lacquerware. The city streets are lined with one shop after another, featuring an endless array, from economical bowls and chopsticks, to opulent *bento* boxes and tea sets, folding screens, and fine furniture. One of the many establishments that offer tours in English is Omukai. Call (0768) 2-1313 for an appointment. Wajimaya, which is open Monday through Saturday, serves a modestly priced lunch, and reopens at seven for a *taiko* drum performance. More on Wajima lacquerware and the town's lacquerware museum can be found at the following websites.

http://shofu.pref.ishikawa.jp/shofu/wajima_e/index2.html

www.jnto.go.jp/eng/location/sit/ishikawa/1703.html

Where to stay

Yuko's *ryokan* is called Heguro. Ask for it and other *ryokan* suggestions at the Wajima Tourism Association. The tourist information office at Wajima Station can also help you find other accommodations.

Wajima Tourism Association

20-1-131 Kawai-machi
Wajima
(0768) 22-6588 (Japanese)

Wajima Station Tourist Center

The tourist center is in the bus station, which was formerly the train station.

(0768) 22-1503/4277

Drumming in Wajima

Gojinjo-daiko, a *taiko* drum ritual, is performed at the Nafune Festival, held at the end of July and beginning of August. Nafune is about a twenty-minute bus ride from Wajima Station. Performances are also held at Wajima Bunka Kaikan and the Kasuga Shrine on Sosogi Beach from late April to late November.

Fukushima Prefecture

Sara Francis-Fujimura gets to the heart of Japan in Hirata

I believe that the heart of Japan isn't in the big cities and tourist centers, but in the small hubs of daily life. That's why I head to Monzen-machi in Hirata each summer to do my shopping. Sure, I can buy fruit and vegetables at the local grocery store, but going to Monzen-machi is always a cultural adventure.

A small, agricultural town twenty kilometers west of Nagoya, Hirata doesn't get a lot of *gaijin*. This is immediately apparent when I walk down the crowded Monzen-machi marketplace, toward Gifu Prefecture's most famous business shrine, Ochobo Inari Jinja. Being five-foot-eight, blindingly white, and traveling with two grade-schoolers chattering loudly in English, I couldn't blend in with the locals if I tried.

I'd love to be just like any other wife out buying *kabocha* (pumpkin) and *nasu* (eggplant) for the evening's dinner, and I conduct my business in as much Japanese as I can, but I still can't disappear into the crowd. Elderly men chat me up in English in the middle of the street. Mothers scold their preschoolers for staring at us. But I realized just how much of an oddity I was the day the locals stopped staring at a trio of junior sumo wrestlers buying veggies to look at the *gaijin* trio instead. Though the added attention can sometimes be uncomfortable, the cultural experience at Monzen-machi far outweighs any inconvenience.

A bright, orange-red *torii* marks the opening to Monzen-machi. Inside awaits a rainbow assortment of locally grown fresh fruits and vegetables at economical prices, at least by Japanese standards. Most stores offer free samples of their wares, and my kids and I nibble until our bellies are nearly full on rice crackers, pickled vegetables, and tiny shrimp. Not one of us is brave enough to try the seasoned crickets.

We usually make a day of it, stopping in at one of a dozen restaurants and cafés for local favorites such as *unagi* (eel) and *tonkatsu* (fried pork cutlet). You definitely won't find any California rolls here. For the more gastronomically adventurous, Monzen-machi has other unique foods beyond the crickets. My father-in-law once convinced me to try deep-fried chicken cartilage from a street stall, but even he couldn't talk us into deep-fried pig intestines. There is also a traditional teahouse beside the Ochobo Inari Jinja Shrine. And on certain days, chanting men rhythmically pound *mochi* at the sweet shop next door. It's the only place I've ever seen purple *mochi*.

Several stores offer the usual touristy clutter, and impulse buys directed at children, but there are also a few stores owned by skilled craftspeople working in wood, paper, fabric, and ceramics. Though I've been to Monzen-machi a dozen times now, I never fail to leave with at least one more handmade Japanese keepsake that I couldn't pass up.

My refrigerator back home in Arizona looks like an aviary, thanks to the bird store near the entrance. Every year my children return with a new handcrafted, feathered, papier-mâché bird magnet. Some of the birds have a sensor chip, and my kids love tripping them all until the cheeping can be heard halfway down the street. With each bird at an affordable one hundred yen, they happily spend their small allowance on this unique souvenir. Now that the owners have added faux beetles to their collection, my bug-loving son Andy agonizes over his choice.

Though I'm not a superstitious person, I always stop at Ochobo Inari Jinja, which roughly translates as "thousand-generation protection." This Shinto shrine is said to bring good fortune. According to my mother-in-law, business owners from all over the region, even prostitutes from Nagoya, come to make offerings and pray for good business. Here, an *oba-san* sells *abura-age* (special fried tofu) to throw as an offering—a fitting gift considering the patron spirit of this Shinto shrine is the *kitsune* (fox), and foxes are fond of *abura-age*. I usually make a small offering and leave my *meishi* (business card) in hopes that my business will continue to grow and prosper. As a freelancer, I can always use a bit of extra luck.

Traveling to Hirata is always worth the trip. Whether I manage to blend in or not, I get to load up on fresh vegetables, fill up on tasty snacks, treat my kids to a special souvenir, and pray for the prosperity of my business. And the best part is that I get to do it all in the heart of Japan.

Getting to Hirata

With fewer than ten thousand people, Hirata (which has been incorporated into the city of Kaizu) does not have a public transportation system. It is an easy day trip from Nagoya. To reach Ochobo Inari Jinja/Monzen-machi from Nagoya, take the Higashi-Meihan Expressway to Kuwana, then take Route 258 North. At Nanno-Cho turn east toward downtown Hirata-Cho. The shrine and shopping area are three kilometers past downtown.

www.city.kaizu.lg.jp/english/english_top.jsp

Lost and found

Tucked near the back of Ochobo Inari Jinja is a large, red, corrugated steel box. Despite the piles of shoes, clothes, and other clutter inside, don't confuse it for a trash can like I did the first time I saw it. Whether you have lost your wallet, or your husband, the mystical box will make the missing object or person return to you. For example, if you lose your wallet, place a new wallet in the box. If your husband has strayed, place a pair of his shoes inside. The box is rumored to have a dark side too. Once, there was a straw doll, a few *meishi*, and a photo inside—all used to curse the people they represented. As a result, a sign appeared on the door warning visitors that cursing people at this shrine is strictly prohibited.

Chiba Prefecture

Jasmin Young spins a tale of making pottery in Awa Kamogawa

For the past eleven years, I have been working as a designer and teacher in the quiet little beach town of Misaki. What many travelers don't know is that there are a lot of opportunities for fun along Japan's Pacific coastline that don't require getting into the water.

In Awa Kamogawa, there lives a Japanese *sensei* named Mr. Hasegawa. Among many things, he is a master of making pottery and blowing glass. His home and pottery shop, which he built by hand, sits on a mountaintop, just minutes from the Awa Kamogawa Train Station.

Two and a half hours southeast of Tokyo, Awa Kamogawa is a vibrant town, with magnificent views of the Pacific Ocean. With the beautiful coastline, and arguably the most consistent surf on the East Coast, it is frequented by surfers and fishermen. But spinning pottery is a little-known pastime in this area, and offers a nice break from the humid lowland summers.

My Japanese husband introduced me to this little slice of heaven last year. Mr. Hasegawa gave us a private one-hour lesson, and a big lump of clay that he happily helped me to mold into as many pots and cups as my heart desired. I was even allowed to choose the color of the glaze for my creations. After careful consideration, I decided on a subtle aqua with a hint of blue that matches my kitchen tiles perfectly. Mr. Hasegawa doesn't speak much English, but he managed to communicate that I was the pickiest student he'd ever had!

After a thrilling hour of spinning, Mr. Hasegawa invites his students to his Japanese-style coffee room overlooking the ocean. The room is filled with homemade wooden furniture (another one of Mr. Hasegawa's talents), and he offers complimentary *ocha* (green tea), and delicious fruit and Japanese cakes that he prepares daily.

A visit to Mr. Hasegawa's little pottery paradise is a wonderful experience, and one I highly recommend. I cannot wait to go back next year, as I have already prepared a list of things I want to make. Until then, I hold fond memories of spinning pottery with Mr. Hasegawa, and my husband and I drink lots of delicious teas from the beautiful cups we made.

Spinning pottery

A one-hour lesson (including clay) is ¥3,000 per person (about $30). Mr. Hasegawa burns and glazes your pots for you, and ships them COD anywhere in the world within a couple of weeks. You will need a Japanese speaker when calling to book your lesson. Feel free to contact me at Jasmin Designs (website below) for help with this, since Mr. Hasegawa is now a friend of mine.

(080) 1170-7243 (Mr. Hasegawa)
www.jasmindesigns.com

Getting to Awa Kamogawa

Awa Kamogawa is an easy day trip from Tokyo. From Tokyo Station take the Wakashio Line directly to Kazusa Ichinomiya Station or the Rapid Line to Soga Station and change to the Sotobo Line. Awa Kamogawa is the last stop on the Sotobo Line.

Mie Prefecture

Frank Lev commits petty larceny on Mikimoto Island

I have a small confession to make. Sometimes I steal things.

While my stealing is petty and doesn't hurt anyone, I know that it is wrong. But sometimes I still do it. I think it happens when I feel lonely, angry, or bored, as a way of escaping these feelings. And it works.

There is a certain excitement I feel when I steal something. Will I get caught? What will I say if I get caught? And there's a certain thrill in having put one over. Plus I get to keep what I steal, and so sometimes have a very unusual souvenir, like the one I took from Mikimoto Island.

After three months in Kyoto, walking the straight and narrow to my job, shops, and safe nightlife hangouts, avoiding encounters in which I would have to speak to Japanese people, I suddenly realized that I'd better start traveling, or I would never really see Japan. After much deliberation, I decided to visit Mikimoto Pearl Island on the Ise Peninsula. Located just twenty meters offshore, the island is named for the man who developed the process for making cultured pearls.

At fifteen dollars, the admission price onto the island seemed steep, but in retrospect, it was worth every penny. Mikimoto is a perfect example of a Japanese tourist attraction. It is completely manufactured, and great pains are taken to see that you have a good time.

The tour begins with the pearl museum, which features the history of oysters and pearls, an explanation of the culturing process, and even a demonstration of the delicate culturing operation every ten minutes. In another part of the museum the focus is on the finished pearls, displaying a staff of women who sift through thousands of pearls to find matches for a perfect strand. Of course, there is a store that sells pearls. And I bought a strand. That's not what I stole.

The *ama* divers—women who dive down into the bay for the oysters, dressed in white cotton suits that cover their entire bodies, including little bonnets for their heads—are the best part of the tour. Every half hour a boat comes out with two or three divers. They perform for rows of cheering tourists, who go wild when they come up with an oyster. The young women wave good-naturedly from the water, while another diver is available for photo opportunities.

On my visit, I got so involved in the museum that I lost all track of time. At four fifteen, when I looked out the window, the sky was ugly. By four thirty it had started to rain. The attendants began putting out umbrellas for people who wanted to continue watching the divers. I hadn't brought one with me because I had wanted to travel light. I picked up an umbrella and opened it. It was nice. The metal halter slid smoothly on its track like a well-oiled gun. The fabric was a distinctive pink and black, with "Mikimoto Pearl Island" written in large fancy English script on one side. Although I wasn't feeling particularly lonely, angry, or bored this day, as soon as I saw the umbrellas, my first thought was that maybe I could steal one.

I walked beneath the stands used for viewing the divers and waited until the women emerged and everyone was watching them. Seizing the moment, I furtively slid the umbrella into my right coat sleeve, tucking the tip into my pocket. It was a bit uncomfortable, but it worked.

The show ended a few minutes later, and I made my exit with the rest of the crowd. No one stopped me or seemed to notice anything unusual. The attendant at the door bowed low and thanked me. Maybe she thought it rude that I didn't bow back, but really, I couldn't. She probably just thought that I was a foreigner who didn't know any better.

Once outside it had really started to rain, so at a safe distance from the museum, I took out the umbrella. Then it struck me. Everyone in this town either worked at Mikimoto Island or was involved with it in some way. Everyone knew what the umbrellas look like and would recognize the logo. It occurred to me that, since every door has an umbrella rack out front, I could swap the stolen umbrella for a less conspicuous one at the next umbrella stand I passed and let someone else worry about the wrath of Mikimoto. But I suddenly felt sad about losing it. I had worked hard to get it. It was a great souvenir and I didn't want to part with it.

I decided that if anyone stopped me and asked me about the umbrella, I would just say that I found it. So I opened it, with its fluorescent colors screaming "Mikimoto Pearl Island," but no one came running after me to demand it back. The people I passed on the street just glanced at it and walked past. I passed a policeman. He looked up, but didn't do anything.

Then it occurred to me what was probably going on. The Japanese were too polite to say anything. Even though it was obvious that I was walking around with an umbrella that I had lifted from the museum, they were more concerned with avoiding conflict than getting that stupid umbrella back. It would be rude to cause another person to lose face by catching him in a lie or an act of thievery.

I tested out my theory that night at the youth hostel. The clerk asked me if I was a member. I lied, saying that I was, but that I had lost my card. He gave me the members' rate. Then I stole his pen with him looking right at me. He didn't say anything. I tried the same kind of thing in other places, always with the same result. Now I don't feel like stealing things anymore. What's the point? It's too easy here. No one will even try to catch me. I guess I'll have to find a new way to get my thrills in Japan.

Getting to Mikimoto Pearl Island

From Tokyo Station (about four hours), take the Tokaido Shinkansen to Toba Station. From Osaka Station or Kyoto Station (about two hours from either starting point), take the Kintetsu Line to Toba Station. Mikimoto Island is a five-minute walk from Toba Station.

Shopping for pearls

Although we don't condone Frank's actions, we do recommend visiting Mikimoto Pearl Island and purchasing one of its many treasures. Pearl Plaza is located on the first floor of the main building, and features an abundant array of pearl jewelry and other pearl-related gifts and souvenirs.

1-7-1 Toba
(0599) 25-2028
www.mikimoto-pearl-museum.co.jp

General Japan

Stefan Chiarantano forages for traditional kokeshi dolls

My love affair with secondhand shops began in my early twenties, when I started to add to my wardrobe with finds from Goodwill. I'd pick up a tie, a shirt, or a blazer to complement the clothes that were already in my closet. Then my shopping habits blossomed into buying books from used-book stores, and pieces of furniture from secondhand stores. So, you can imagine my joy when I found I could indulge my passion for hand-me-down shopping in Japan.

Purchasing used goods is not common among Japanese shoppers, who prefer to buy the best and latest merchandise available. Nevertheless, I discovered that secondhand shops were springing up all over the country, and that there were already several in the little town of Komagane where I was living. It was while rummaging the shelves of one of these thrift shops that I first discovered *kokeshi* dolls. Hidden behind other assorted objects, their vibrant colors caught my eye. I picked one up and was reminded of the Ukrainian wooden dolls I'd seen back home.

Japan today is awash with so much Western culture and influence, I thought that perhaps this doll was the Japanese version of a traditional Occidental figurine. It was made of wood and had a cylindrical head and body, hand painted in bright hues. But unlike the Ukrainian versions, it had no hands or feet. I found this difference peculiar. In my limited Japanese, I asked the shopkeeper what it was. A *kokeshi*, she told me, is sold mainly as a souvenir to commemorate a visit to a tourist attraction. When I mentioned the Ukrainian dolls, she said there is no connection. *Kokeshi* dolls are distinctly Japanese.

My gut feeling told me that there was more to *kokeshi* dolls than being simple mementos, so I asked some of my Japanese acquaintances about them. I was shocked by the answer. In feudal times, food was often scarce, and natural disasters such as typhoons, earthquakes, and tsunamis caused dire circumstances. Many families farmed in inhospitable areas, and lived in constant fear of famine and pestilence. With many mouths to feed, and no other means to ease the burden of an unwanted pregnancy, the Japanese sometimes resorted to infanticide.

But the pre-Meiji Japanese weren't without feeling, my acquaintances assured me. They very much regretted their actions, and the tradition of *kokeshi* dolls grew from their sorrow. The *kokeshi* served as reminders of their lost children, for whom the parents offered prayers, and asked forgiveness for terminating their brief lives.

Infanticide was outlawed during the Meiji period (1868-1912), and as Japan prospered, the practice faded altogether. But history lives on in the *kokeshi* dolls, although the earlier versions were cruder, fashioned by hand, and not nearly as fancy or colorful as those manufactured today as souvenirs.

I have bought many of the *kokeshi* dolls that I found while foraging through secondhand stores. Some I've given as gifts to friends, and the ones I've kept are grouped together on my bookshelf. I cherish them because they remind me of Japan's tragic history, and the way the Japanese dealt with a painful and complicated issue. *Kokeshi* also symbolize for me that through hardship and struggle, a nation and its people can transform from a primitive feudal society into an economic superpower. They are icons that evoke an era before Westernization and industrialization swept the country. They also remind me of my love for secondhand objects, and the joy that comes from giving them a new home.

Shopping for kokeshi dolls

Kokeshi dolls may be purchased in department stores, museums, gift shops, and certain tourist sites, as well as at market fairs (secondhand dolls). You should also keep an eye out at the Oriental Bazaar (see page 149) and hundred-yen stores (see page 163). Outside Japan, the dolls may be found on eBay.

Miyagi Zao Kokeshi Museum

The Miyagi Zao Kokeshi Museum features a display of five thousand traditional *kokeshi* dolls. Visitors can also watch the process of manufacturing *kokeshi* dolls, paint their own, or purchase them from the gift shop. Not on the beaten path, the museum is located in the Tohoku region of northeast Honshu and is worth visiting if you are touring in that area.

36-135 Aza-Shinchi
West Urayama Mountain
Togatta-Onsen
Zao Town
(0224) 34-2385

http://travel.japan-tohoku.com/enarea.htm

Reading up

To learn more about *kokeshi* dolls, purchase a copy of *Kokeshi: Wooden Treasures of Japan, a Visual Exploration*, by Michael Evans and Robert Wolf, published by Vermillion Press.

Thrift shops

Thrift shops are called "recycle shops," and they are growing in popularity. So much so that there are now chains of recycle shops in cities throughout Japan. However, up until recently, thrift shopping has not been common because it carries a certain stigma. Most Japanese people disdain purchasing used items, and often throw away perfectly good merchandise simply because they want something newer and better. Once a month, each neighborhood has *sodai gomi* day, in which residents place their cast-off household goods at the curb for pick-up by garbage collectors. They will even snip the cords off electric appliances to deter scavengers. Nonetheless, budget-conscious people, especially foreign residents, go out for a walk on the evenings before *sodai gomi* day and help themselves to the items left on the streets. Many *gaijin* completely furnish their apartments by going curb shopping late at night. To locate some of the recycle shops around Japan, check out the following website.

www.frugaljapan.com/Main/Ency008

Sara Francis-Fujimura revels in Japan's hundred-yen shops

Undoubtedly the best-kept shopping secret in Japan is its hundred-yen (*hyaku-en*) shops. They are *nothing* like our dollar stores back home. Everything is priced at one hundred yen, and at an exchange rate of about one hundred yen per dollar, I can stock up on everything from toothpaste to fireworks to squid snacks, all at a fraction of the usual retail price.

Being a budget-conscious parent, I love to watch my kids' faces light up when I tell them they can buy anything they want at one of these stores. I purchase all of my sushi-making tools and *bento*-making equipment there. I also routinely stock up on expensive-looking stationery, ornate chopsticks, and last season's Hello Kitty doo-dahs, to bring back as small presents that won't break the bank, and also won't take up a lot of room in my suitcase.

Scrapbookers and paper crafters will love the decorative *washi* paper, stickers, and other inexpensive art supplies available at most of the stores. They are also great places to try out new foods, particularly snacks. Wonder what dried cuttlefish tastes like? Buy a bag, and if it's not your taste, pitch it.

Much to my husband's chagrin, I've never found a hundred-yen shop that I didn't like, and I've certainly never come home without a few "I-just-couldn't-pass-it-up!" buys. Of all the shops I've discovered, my favorite is Apio at Ogaki Station in Gifu Prefecture. I've been known to spend hours treasure hunting there.

My Japanese friends laugh at my confessions of spending more than ten thousand yen (one hundred dollars) at a hundred-yen shop, but the bargains are just too great. And ... shhh! Don't tell my American friends, but most of their souvenir gifts came from one of these shops as well.

Hundred-yen shops

Hundred-yen stores can be found all over Japan. The best places to find hundred-yen stores are in the larger train stations. There are also plenty of mom-and-pop versions, and department stores often have a section (and sometimes a whole floor!) of hundred-yen buys. Daiso is the biggest hundred-yen chain—their website below contains a full listing of stores, including many in Tokyo.

www.daiso-sangyo.co.jp/english/

Apio

If you happen to be in the Nagoya area in Gifu Prefecture and feel like some bargain shopping, make a detour to Apio, which is in the Ogaki Station in the city of Ogaki. The train station is served by the Tokaido, Kintetsu Yoro, and Tarumi Lines.

Into the Wild

Outdoor experiences for adventurous travelers

I've never been much of a rugged gal, but while I lived in Japan, I couldn't get enough of the outdoors: long walks in Tokyo's parks and gardens, train rides into the fertile farmlands, and intrepid treks into untamed nature preserves. I was fortunate to visit Japan's wine country in the Fuji foothills, Lake Chuzenji in Nikko National Park, the secluded Kamikochi wilderness area in the Japanese Alps, the vast Kansai Plain from Matsumoto to Kanazawa, and the remote Noto Peninsula.

Beyond the cities lies the Japan of coffee table books: mystic mountains, deep forests, emerald rice paddies, and the legendary seascapes of the famous "floating world" artists Hiroshige and Hokusai. I saw as much of this as I could, but through their adventures, the contributors to this chapter made me realize how much more there is still to explore.

I was so busy appreciating Japan's marvelous transit system that I didn't think to rent a car and take to the open road like Nolan Webb, who drove the back roads of Kyushu. Although I rode my bicycle around the streets of Tokyo, it didn't occur to me to venture farther afield like Michael John Grist, in his quest to find the mountainous source of the Tama River. And since Japan was still enjoying its economic heyday when I lived there, the eerie, abandoned Sports World that Michael also discovered hadn't yet fallen into ruin. While I did enjoy Sunday fishing on a small river near the city of Kofu, and visited several pleasant *onsen* during my travels, Diana Lee's *ayu* fishing trip to Kitani-kyo, and Elizabeth Sharpe's soak beneath the watchful eye of a water sprite at the Yagen Valley hot springs, are reminders of how rich and varied these experiences can be.

Some of the contributors to this chapter write about places I still dream of visiting someday, although I hope I don't confront a typhoon on Mt. Fuji, as Sugu Althomsons did. But I would like to see the Japanese macaques that Jennifer Huber encountered at the Jigokudani Wild Monkey Park, and

Japanese maple tree in autumn

I long to pay homage as Quintin Winks did when he cycled the Pilgrimage of the Eighty-Eight Temples on Shikoku Island. As for Arin Greenwood's travels by snowshoe through the wintry landscape of Hokkaido, I doubt I'll make it that far, so I am grateful for the chance to experience it through her eyes.

In this chapter, each contributor inspires me to go back to Japan for my own further exploration of its geography and geology. At times, I will follow in their footsteps, but I also look forward to charting my own new map into the wild.

Yamanashi Prefecture

Michael John Grist seeks the source of Tokyo's Tama River

Tokyo's Tama River has been a steady part of my life for as long as I've been in Japan. I've been playing Ultimate Frisbee on its banks in the suburb of Futako Tamagawa for more than five years. I once walked alongside it from my old apartment in the Minami Osawa neighborhood all the way to the Shibuya District. I barbecued by the riverside with all my old GEOS Language School students in the town of Fuchu for my farewell party. I nearly got swept away while crossing through its rapids on the way to Canadian Mike's birthday party, and I first flew my power kite on the wide floodplain at Keio Tamagawa.

I've walked alongside this river on dates with girls. I've partied, camped, and watched movies on generator-powered movie projectors beside its banks. The Tama River has always been there for me like a steadfast and loyal friend, and from the moment I bought a bicycle, riding to its source in the foothills of Mt. Fuji seemed like a grand idea.

The Tama River begins as a mountain stream from Mt. Kasadori in Yamanashi Prefecture—just one of the mountains in the Mt. Fuji foothills. It flows down the slopes into Lake Okutama, over the highlands of western Tokyo, through the city itself, and out into Tokyo Bay near Haneda Airport. Throughout its long history, the Tama River has been devastatingly destructive to surrounding landscapes and property, which are prone to flooding in the summer rainy season. Even Japan's modern flood defenses cannot fully control the Tama. Last year my Frisbee field on the floodplain was rendered unplayable during a typhoon.

On my quest to reach the source of the Tama River, I set off from my apartment in the Ikebukuro District on a Saturday morning in May with my friend Jason. We slogged along congested roads under the Shuto Expressway as we blitzkrieged our way through Shibuya, down to Futako Tamagawa, and onward to the river. It was a beautiful sunny day, and the riverbanks were lined with groups of young people barbecuing, picnicking, and paddling in the shallows. Here, I took off my shirt, and set to the work of grinding out the route that lay ahead.

Forty kilometers later, we'd passed through all the zones that were familiar to me. The river was still wide, and although the cityscape that lines its banks began to give way to more greenery, it was still present, as there's nowhere in Tokyo Prefecture where you're really away from the urban sprawl.

As we began our ascent into the mountains, the bike path dwindled away, and there were posted signs with maps showing that it was possible to take a nature trail up through a forest to a road on the other side. But that road led away from the river, so we were loath to detour too far. Instead, we scoured the area for more signs, and found one that directed us to another road that looped in a ten-kilometer route, bringing us to an old cross-hatched metal bridge across the river.

Although our goal was finding the source of the river, Jason got it into his head that we were close to Mt. Mitake, and since that place had special meaning for him (something about a girl), he wanted to camp up there. Near the bridge, an old man confirmed that the mountain was less than ten kilometers away. I was none too keen on the idea of a pedaling up the mountain, since we had originally intended to camp by the river. Jason's plan to carry the bikes was madness to me. But there seemed to be no place to camp near the river's banks, so off we went.

This stretch proved the hardest of the day: ten kilometers of gradual snaking uphill against a fierce headwind, bikes laden with our gear, and us already tired. Little did I know that this was only the beginning of our suffering.

At the base of Mt. Mitake, we decided to board the cable car in Chichibu Tama Kai National Park and ride it to the top. It was insane, but at this point, insanity seemed the only way to go. A few hundred meters up the road toward the cable car, the incline grew very steep, and it was no longer possible to ride, so we had to get off and push our bikes. I emptied out my water supply to lighten my load.

After thirty minutes of upward struggle, we reached the cable car just in time to take one of its last runs up the mountain. The station attendant eyed us as if we were crazy, but allowed us—and our bikes—onboard the empty carriage. Kilometers of beautiful dense forest rolled past the windows as we ascended, this time happily not by our own steam.

To reach a place to camp, it appeared we would have to port the bikes from the top of Mt. Mitake along a narrow ridge to the top of Mt. Hinode. Carrying our unwieldy bikes every step of the way, we navigated treacherous mountain paths: an obstacle course of tree branches and jutting stones. The ground was wet and muddy, the inclines were seemingly endless, the light was fading, and we were exhausted. But at this point, going back would have taken much longer than going forward, so we pressed on.

We reached the peak of Mt. Hinode in a slow drizzle, but were rewarded with a glorious night view over the blackness of the sloping forest, all the way down to the distant lights of Ome Town. There we laid down our bikes and collapsed in the shelter of a pagoda-like wooden building. We pitched our tent and ate the sandwiches and trail food we had brought, carefully rationing Jason's remaining water.

We had the mountaintop to ourselves, and as the night closed in, we were cocooned in an ethereal mist, a fuzzy-white shell of fog and moonlight that narrowed our field of vision to a few hundred meters, blocking out the town lights and isolating us completely. It was immensely gratifying, if a little daunting, as we sat there in the mist, chatting quietly for a few hours before retiring to the tent to sleep.

The next day we were awakened by the dawn, and the arrival of early morning hikers, mostly old folks and a gaggle of kids on a school trip. They were startled at our presence on the mountaintop with bikes, and in the cold light of day, I too thought that it had been utter madness to have brought them up there.

By now, we were out of food and water. We decided to skip the cable car this time, and the haul across the ridge and down Mt. Mitake took over an hour. The hikers we passed expressed surprise when they saw us carrying our bikes down the mountain, and when we finally reached the road that led back to the Tama River, we greeted it like conquering heroes returning home.

Despite our thwarted attempt to reach its headwaters, now when I think of the Tama River, along with the memories of barbecues, rapids, movies, parties, and romantic walks, I'll also remember the long, beautiful ride along its wide banks, the struggle up Mt. Mitake to the cable car, the absurdity of shouldering my bike from one mountaintop to another, and finally the unreality of camping in total isolation in a cocoon of silver fog. Sure, we didn't reach the source of the river, but that's okay. It just leaves a new adventure, and more great memories, for another day.

Bicycling the Tama River

Our trip from Ikebukuro to the top of Mt. Hinode and back took nine hours and totaled 158 kilometers on our bikes. When riding on city streets and rural roads, wear bright clothing, make sure your bicycle has reflectors and working lights, and ride against oncoming traffic. Motorists will probably not yield to you, so you have to swing out and around them well in advance to avoid collision. For general information on bicycling around Japan, visit the following website.

www.japancycling.org/v2/

Train travel to the Mt. Mitake cable car

If you're not up for a big bike ride, take Tokyo's Chuo Line west from Shinjuku Station to Tachikawa Station. Transfer to the Ome Line and get off at Mitake Station. Located at the base of Mt. Mitake in Chichibu Tama Kai National Park, the cable car can be reached by a shuttle bus from the station.

Camping

We camped in an undesignated area at the top of Mt. Hinode, but there are campgrounds in the vicinity, which are clearly marked on a map at Mitake Station.

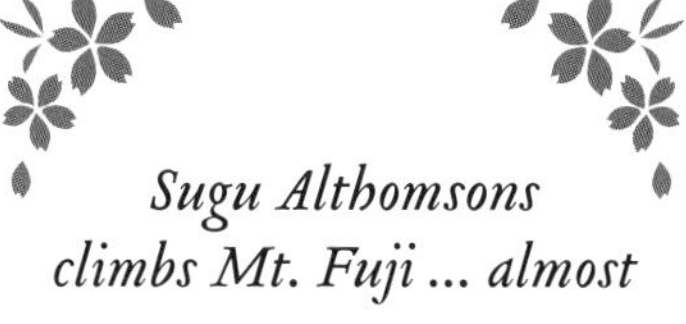

Sugu Althomsons climbs Mt. Fuji ... almost

Every time I read about Mt. Fuji, I found inspiring stories detailing pilgrimages up its slopes, and the beauty and tranquility of the summit at sunrise. People of all ages, from all walks of life, make the trek to witness that singular view, so why not me? I'm young and healthy. Climbing Fuji-san should have been easy.

I had been in Japan for less than a month when I planned my hike up the mountain, just in time for the tail end of the hiking season. My friends arranged everything, including a car, and as we drove, we talked about how we could trim the hike from the average six hours to five. We would be hiking all night, and wanted to reach the summit before the sun rose.

From the town of Shin Fuji, the road to Mt. Fuji ends about halfway up its lower slopes at Station 5, one of ten rest stops, some with overnight lodging huts, along the path to the summit. We parked, and I got out of the car and tried to take a picture of the city lights below. But they were blurry, and I saw that the lens was wet. My clothes were damp too. The rain was falling so gently that I hadn't felt it.

When we arrived at the foot of the trail, we heard rumors of a typhoon, but our group's masculine pride wouldn't allow us to chicken out. We could handle a little rain. Then I saw the other hikers preparing to challenge the summit, all wearing rain gear. That's when I started to panic.

My shipment of winter clothes from home hadn't arrived yet, so I'd brought the warmest clothes I had, a pair of baggy jeans and a long-sleeved, button-down shirt, which I had planned to save for the chill that waited higher up. I now realized that my T-shirt was already inadequate, so I put on my "warm" shirt.

With foolish bravado, we started up the trail, but no sooner had we set foot on the barren lava, the typhoon started for real. With the wind howling and the rain pouring, I could only see the ground a meter or so before me. I lost track of time as we hiked for what seemed an eternity, grimly facing the twenty-sixth typhoon of the season, determined to reach the summit.

Trying to make the best of the situation, we laughed and joked. But when we caught our first glimpse of Station 6, we made a run for it. All we could think about was getting inside and having something warm to drink. The exorbitant prices of beverages and snacks would be worth it, if it meant we could enjoy the shelter. But it was already crowded to capacity when we reached it, so we decided to forge ahead, confident that we were continuing where others had not.

The first steps away from Station 6 seemed immensely steeper, and my soaked jeans made it unbearable to lift my mud-crusted feet, but we still trudged onward, growing quieter and humbler with each step. Farther up the trail, even more hikers had beaten us to Station 7, and when we asked to enter, the station attendant locked the door with us on the outside. He obviously felt no pity for anyone foolish enough to climb Mt. Fuji under these conditions.

We had no choice but to continue. Another eternity of holding onto a flimsy rope guide, praying that the wind wouldn't uproot the stakes from the ground. Another eternity of my shoes filling with gritty lava. Each station was more crowded than the last, with yet another impassive station master, and a steeper climb beyond it.

By the time we reached Station 7.9, we desperately began calculating. We had only been climbing for about three hours, and I had been shivering for two hours and fifty-seven minutes. It would take us three hours to get back to the warmth of the heater in the car. The farther up we climbed, the longer we would be soaked in the rain, the longer the trek back down. We all looked at each other, none of us wanting to say it.

Finally, someone spoke. "You know, we wouldn't actually *see* the sunrise. The clouds would just get a little brighter."

That's all it took. We quietly nodded in reluctant agreement, and turned back.

Even though we didn't make it all the way to the summit, climbing Mt. Fuji was an experience I will never forget. And next time, I'm going to do it right. I won't be so arrogant. I will pack warm clothes. I will take the whole weekend, so I can stop at every rest station. And I'm *never* going in a typhoon!

Getting to Mt. Fuji by bus

There are six trails to the summit of Mt. Fuji. I took the most popular and easily accessible, the Kawaguchiko Trail, which can be reached by bus from Tokyo's Shinjuku Station. During the peak climbing season, buses depart frequently throughout the day from the west side of the station, in front of the Yasuda Life Insurance Building, Number 2 Building, bus platform 50. The trip takes about two hours. Reservations are necessary and can be made through the Keio Kosoku Bus Yoyaku Center (03-5376-2222).

Once you reach Kawaguchiko Station, another bus (forty-five minutes) will take you to the Kawaguchiko Fifth Station, about halfway up the mountain. During the official climbing season, buses travel directly from Shinjuku Station to Kawaguchiko Fifth Station.

Getting to Mt. Fuji by train

To reach the Kawaguchiko Trail by the local (slower) train, you can take the Chuo Line from Tokyo's Shinjuku Station to Otsuki Station, and then transfer to the Fuji Kyuko Line to Kawaguchiko Station. From Kawaguchiko Station, take the bus to Kawaguchiko Fifth Station, as described above. An alternative, which I took, is the more expensive bullet train from Tokyo bound for Nagoya to Mishima or Shin Fuji. From there, change trains to get to Kawaguchiko Station, where you can proceed by bus up to Station 5.

Clothes and gear

For the climb up Mt. Fuji, you will need a pair of sturdy, comfortable, well-broken-in walking shoes, since the paths are steep and rocky in places, not to mention slippery in wet weather. The weather is variable at the summit, so a waterproof raincoat or poncho is recommended, as well as a warm jacket and gloves for cooler overnight temperatures. You should also wear sunscreen and a wide-brimmed hat. Bring plenty of water, and a supply of nutritious snacks. A flashlight is helpful if you plan to do any hiking after dark. A small oxygen bottle, which may be purchased at the Kawaguchiko Fifth Station, will help with altitude sickness.

Timing your ascent

From Kawaguchiko Fifth Station, the ascent to the summit takes five to seven hours, and the descent takes three to five hours. Mt. Fuji is a popular destination, especially on weekends and holidays during the climbing season (July and August), so expect large crowds and slow going. The most practical and common timetable for the ascent is a morning bus ride from Tokyo, followed by a light lunch at Kawaguchiko Fifth Station, and a climb up to one of the mountain huts. Stop for dinner and an overnight rest, and wake several hours before sunrise for the hike to the top to watch the sun come up at the summit. Finally, descend back down to reach Kawaguchiko Fifth Station in the afternoon. A slower climb not only makes your hike more enjoyable, but helps prevent altitude sickness.

Staying in a mountain hut

Located at the rest stations, huts are only open in July and August, and cost from $50 to $70, depending on the inclusion of meals. Reservations are highly recommended. For assistance, contact the Fujiyoshida City Hall International Affairs Desk at (0555) 24-1236 from 9:30 a.m. to 5:30 p.m. on weekdays.

Organizing your trip

For current bus times, detailed access maps, climbing guides, phone numbers for individual huts, and more, check out the following websites.

www.city.fujiyoshida.yamanashi.jp
www.yamanashi-kankou.jp/english/

Nagano Prefecture

Jennifer Huber gets mugged by a monkey in Jigokudani

On our trip to Japan, my traveling companion Matt and I were on a mission. We did not come for majestic Mt. Fuji or sacred Buddhist temples. We had seen the famous *National Geographic* photos showing Japanese macaques, also known as Snow Monkeys, soaking in steamy hot springs, and we were on a quest to find them.

Every week we stayed with a different family in Shizuoka and Yamanashi Prefectures, and each family asked, "What would you like to do?"

Our first response was always the same: "See the monkeys."

The host families couldn't understand our fascination. They would laugh and ask, "Why would you want to see the monkeys? They are like the raccoons in your country. And ... they're mean!"

It was hard to believe such a thing about the fuzzy, pink-faced monkeys, and we worried that we would never get to see the elusive creatures. After all, it was common during the trip to be told about an incredible activity or tourist sight, followed by, "But we don't have time to visit."

Each day that we were denied seeing the monkeys, our sense of purpose grew stronger. The Japanese macaques had become our forbidden fruit. After a month in Japan, our exchange program ended and we still hadn't seen them. So Matt and I extended our stay to make a trip to Jigokudani Wild Monkey Park on our own.

After three hours on a train from Tokyo, we finally reached the base of the mountain and began our ascent, through the woods, along a muddy, cliffside trail, toward wild monkey territory. At the entrance to the park, we stopped at the gift shop for some rice cakes. The store clerk handed them to Matt in a crisp, white paper bag, and we headed into the park. My eyes were scanning the hillside for monkeys when a screech pierced the quiet mountain air. There was a rustle in the bushes, and from them a fuzzy, tan monkey bolted toward Matt. Screaming, it lunged for the bag.

Matt jumped back, squealed, and held the bag above his head. With outstretched arms, the monkey leapt toward the bag, grabbing at the air in hopes of snatching the rice cakes. With each leap, it shrieked and flashed its fangs.

As I stood watching, I couldn't help thinking that if not for the sharp teeth the scene would have been comical. Jumping from side to side, holding the bag atop his head, Matt looked as if he were playing a game of keep away with a small child. But this was serious. Our Japanese host families were right. The monkeys *are* mean!

Help soon arrived, when a man ran up yelling something in Japanese. He motioned his arms, and the meaning of his instructions quickly became clear. Matt followed his mime and hid the bag in his jacket. It was that simple. Once the monkey could no longer see the bag, it scampered back into the bushes to await its next victim.

Unnerved, but undeterred from our mission, we hiked onward to the summit, where we saw hundreds of tan, furry lumps that we soon realized were monkeys. At long last, we'd found our macaques!

As we sat on the rocks, trying to blend into the scenery, we observed the monkeys enjoying life in their natural habitat. Some sat on the mountainside, picking nits from each other's fur. Others played tag, screeching at times, perhaps indicating that someone had cheated at the game. The females walked cautiously by us, with their babies clinging tightly with tiny fingers. And as we'd hoped, a few macaques soaked in the steamy hot springs, just like the photos we'd seen in *National Geographic*.

Our visit was much too short, but we were satisfied at having seen our elusive monkeys. It was now time for our journey back to Tokyo to catch our flight home to the States the next morning. Hiking down the mountainside, we passed a Japanese family of four heading toward the park entrance. Their two small children were eating pretzels, and I tried to warn them about the ambushing monkey. But all I knew was the Japanese word for monkey.

"*Saru*! *Saru*!" I shouted.

The family must have mistaken my words of caution for excitement at seeing the monkeys. With smiles and nods they replied, "*Hai, saru, hai.*" I gave up. They would just have to fend for themselves.

Jigokudani Wild Monkey Park (Jigokudani Yaen Koen)

The park is open year-round with limited hours in the winter. It is an easy day trip from Nagano, but should be done as an overnight trip or longer from Tokyo.

6845 Yamanouchi-machi
Shimotakai-gun
(0269) 33-4379
www.jigokudani-yaenkoen.co.jp

Directions: From Tokyo Station, take the Joetsu Shinkansen to Nagano. The Nagano Dentetsu train will take you to Yudanaka, where you will take a bus or taxi to Kanbayashi Onsen. From the *onsen*, it's about a thirty-minute walk to the park entrance.

Shizuoka Prefecture

Michael John Grist trespasses in Izu-Nagaoka

Abandoned in the 1990s, Sports World occupies an idyllic position at the crown of the Izu Peninsula, overlooking a wide swath of richly forested mountains and valleys. In its heyday it was a sport and relaxation haven, featuring tennis courts, miniature golf, a dive pool, restaurants, a hotel, a huge wave pool, a spa, and a gym. Now it's the haunt of the occasional skateboarder and graffiti artist, or curious tourist like me.

At around ten at night, I arrived at nearby Izu-Nagaoka Station, and spent over an hour walking to Sports World, where I planned to set up camp and explore the following morning. I had decided not to use taxis, on the off chance the driver realized I was intending to trespass and notified the police. Also, the long walk served to better sever me from everyday reality, readying me for my solitary plunge into the depths of the ruins.

It was very dark when I arrived. I made my way through the first barricade and walked along the moon-swept, empty car park. At the ticket gates there were barbed wires, but I easily slipped underneath them. The entrance to the Games Center was veiled in darkness. Stars were visible in the sky, which almost never happens in Tokyo. I wanted to head for the mini-golf course, thinking it would be a good open place to camp. I walked by graffiti-covered walls and ruined cars, including one flipped on its roof, and down a long open road covered over with grass and weeds. To my left was the golf course, completely overgrown.

I experimented with my flashlight. I wore it on my head, but this too severely limited my vision to only the direction I faced. I also worried that it would draw attention to me. I was never concerned about ghosts or monsters when in a *haikyo* (ruin)—only about meeting crazy people. Who else—besides me—would be in a place like that at an hour like that?

Fortunately, there was light enough from the moon to get by. I was able to reach the bottom of the park and the big wave pools, and decided that rather than set up camp right away, I would head up to check out the hotel. The path was completely overgrown, so I had to push my way through the greenery. At times I thought I heard voices, and froze. At other times a strange pig-like grunting sound came from the end of the biggest wave pool. I hurried on.

At the hotel, I entered the first room I saw. Its door had a chain bolt, and I put it on immediately, then walked through the room. I checked the sliding door. It had been smashed at the lock, but the lock still seemed to work.

I was amazed at how well preserved the room was, about thirty square meters, immaculate and clean. Apart from some shards of glass by the screen door and a few dead cockroaches, it looked exactly as it must have fifteen years earlier, when it was abandoned. The bathroom was sparkling, the toilet paper in a neat triangle, the toilet with a paper welcome sign on it, and the complimentary toothbrushes and shampoos all in place. In the main room, the TV sat with its remote controls neatly aligned beside it.

For a while, I enjoyed the wonderful moon-lit view of distant mountains, the complex's central lake, and the ghostly silhouettes of the other hotel blocks around me. Slowly, though, as I spent more time silent, unmoving, and alone, the stillness of the place crept over me.

I felt a sense of fear, prompting me to lock the screen door, draw the curtains, and drag chairs and tables in front of the entrances. But there was also a sadness, that the place was empty, and that I was there by myself, as if Sports World wanted more people, more life, more color. I went to sleep, and dreamed of my room being broken into by people I knew, and our adventures among the ruins.

The next day dawned glorious. I opened my curtains wide to a spectacular mountain view, the lake and overgrown jungle of palm trees on the golf course all bathed in bright hot sunlight. I stepped out onto the balcony with my tripod to take photos and videos of the place.

As I panned across the vista, I spotted a man in a blue uniform and cap striding along on the far side. I immediately thought, *He's a security guard and he'll kick me out.* I stared at him for a moment, unsure of what to do and not wishing to draw attention to myself by retreating back into my room. Eventually I ducked, and watched him walk away through a gap in the rail.

I didn't see him again, but I laid low for a while. I ate my breakfast, then left the room. I fought my way back down the tangled paths. At the wave pools, which were coated with red rust and algae, I dallied and looked around the creeper-covered restaurants. At one, in a corner of the complex where the outer fence met a small road, a girl appeared at a hole cut in the fence.

I had my tripod set up to take a photo of a solitary cash register. She crept through the hole with a camera in her hand.

I smiled and said hello in Japanese. She said hello back, then asked me if it was okay to come in and take some photos. I said, "Sure." She went on past me.

I walked up the main thoroughfare, stopping to look into the dive pool. Back at the Games Center back lot, I saw the girl again, on some kind of modeling photo shoot with three friends. We didn't say anything, just regarded each other with curiosity and then moved on.

Getting to Sports World

Sports World is an easy day trip from Tokyo. Take the Kodama Express Train from Tokyo to Mishima. Transfer to the Izu-hakone Tetsudo-Sunzu Line to Izu-Nagaoka Station. From the station you will have to walk, as Michael did, or hire a car. Ask the staff at the car rental office for directions. (Editor's note: Since we don't officially condone trespassing, once you get to Sports World, we'll leave the breaking in part up to you.)

Japanese ruins

Japan's many *haikyo* are quickly becoming famous—both within the country and around the world. It's no surprise as there are just so darn many of them, often at ridiculous scales, with ridiculous design motifs, all left exactly as they were when abandoned. In other countries, these giant theme parks and gorgeous old museums would probably have been torn down or preserved for the sake of history, but not in Japan. Here they molder, rot, and sink into the past as the world moves on around them. Exploring these places, especially in a country with such an opaquely difficult language, can require a fair bit of resourcefulness, but tracking them down is well worth the effort. To get started, check out Michael's website. Good luck!

www.michaeljohngrist.com

Nippon no Haikyo

This is one of the guidebooks I use to find *haikyo* all over Japan. It has maps, photos, and some history for almost all of the included *haikyo*. The drawback is that it is only in Japanese. However, with basic *hiragana* writing system and map-reading skills, you should be able to put it to use. The book is published by Indivision (ISBN: 978-4-9903712-0-3).

www.indivision.cc/ (Japanese)

Yamaguchi Prefecture

Diana Lee is hooked on ayu fishing in Kitani-kyo

When the Japanese summer gets too sultry and unbearable, all I can think about is something cool. I want to eat something cool, or drink something cool, or jump into something cool ...

I remember one such summer. While most Japanese swarmed crowded beaches and water slides, my friends took me on a short drive away from Tokuyama, a coastal town at the southwestern tip of Honshu, Japan's largest island. We climbed up a winding road and arrived at the remote Kitani-kyo watershed region, where campers pitched their tents upstream along a tributary, and sportsmen fished downstream along the Nishiki River.

Located in Yamaguchi Prefecture, Kitani-kyo is one heavenly escape, blessed with water, rocks, and trees. Once the snow starts to melt in April, the Nishiki River carries volumes of cold, clean water down the mountains. This massive river draws anglers to fish for one of Japan's favorite catches: *ayu* (sweetfish). As a popular Japanese dish, it is eaten three ways: fried, broiled with salt, or as sushi.

With sharp teeth and a sleek bodies like river trout, *ayu* feed near riverbeds, are fiercely territorial, and will attack any other fish entering their habitats. Decoy fishing is the secret to catching the aggressive *ayu*. Interestingly, a live *ayu* is attached as bait to snare other *ayu*. With four hooks dangling from its belly, and a fishing line running through its gills, the weakened bait is still lively in the water.

On my first attempt at *ayu* fishing, surrounded by the beauty of nature, I watched anglers skillfully and patiently snaring *ayu* before gently pulling them out of the water with their nets. Every fisherman flashed a broad grin as he lifted the prize catch dangling at the end of his line.

After a series of wild overhead throws, flinging the line into treetops, or bashing the poor live bait against the boulders, I was lucky enough to master the casting rhythm and plop the bait into the water. I was luckier still to ensnare a few *ayu*, and I also smiled broadly at my first catch of the day.

Kitani-kyo is an ideal place to escape mental stress, sweltering heat, and daily monotony. In the early mornings, instead of waking to alarm clocks and roaring traffic, we awoke to the sounds of gurgling water and chirping birds. In the hot afternoons, instead of hanging out by the water cooler, we took a dip in the deep refreshing pool. And in the evenings, instead of falling asleep in front of the TV, we enjoyed grilled *ayu* as we counted the stars that lit up the night.

Getting to Kitani-kyo

For details about traveling to Kitani-kyo, we recommend contacting the Yamaguchi Tourism Office.

2-1 Kameyama-cho
Yamaguchi
(083) 934-2810
www.city.yamaguchi.lg.jp/kanko/org/eng/
kanko@city.yamaguchi.lg.jp

Staying at Kitani-kyo

The best times to visit are summer and autumn, although Diana suggests avoiding July, which can be rainy. There is camping with car parking, but no toilet facilities. You will need to bring your own camping and fishing gear with you.

Cormorant fishing

From June through August, you can witness the ancient tradition of cormorant fishing at the Kintaikyo Bridge in Iwakuni. This unique practice entails the skillful use of birds on leashes to catch *ayu. Ayu* dishes are often served during the performances, which feature fishermen in classic costumes. For more on standard *ayu* fishing techniques, check out the following website.

www.biwa.ne.jp/~y-ogura/hyper/hyper.html

Aomori Prefecture

Elizabeth Sharpe soaks in the Yagen Valley hot springs

Winters on the Shimokita Peninsula in Aomori Prefecture are glacier cold, and this day was proof. Snow blanketed the low boulder wall that enclosed the hot spring, and strands of my wet hair had frozen into icicles. But I was toasty warm. My cheeks were rosy, not from the frigid air, but from the heat of the mineral-rich water of Yagen Valley's Kappa No Yu, where I crouched low, so far down that my shoulders were submerged, the water lapping around them like a soft massage.

As I soaked, my eyes rested on a small statue sitting at the pool's edge. It represented the hot spring's namesake, a *kappa,* a water sprite that is said to have saved a monk who was lost and injured. After the *kappa* immersed the monk in the hot spring, the monk was soon healed. How much of the tale was true, I didn't know, but I didn't doubt the water's restoring virtues.

In tales, *kappa* live in rivers, ponds, lakes, and hot springs like the one in which I was relaxing. They are a Japanese version of bogeymen, only more complicated, for they can be both good and evil. The evil part was puzzling, since the odd creature that seemed to be looking at me was rather cute. It was about the size of a small boy, with a face like a frog. Its mouth jutted out slightly, almost like a beak. On its back, it bore a shell, like a tortoise, and its hands and feet were webbed, perhaps for swimming in the waters it called home. Even more curious was the small, round indentation in the crown of its head, with tufts of hair growing around the rim. I'd been told that the water it contained gave each *kappa* its energy and power.

While I'd heard that *kappa* could leave a bather rich in good fortune, they are also mischievous and dangerous. According to one legend, they pull victims into the water to weaken and drown them, and then reach into the alimentary tract to pull out the liver, their favorite delicacy. That was gruesome, I thought, looking warily at this *kappa's* deceptively comical features.

But a Japanese friend told me if I ever saw a *kappa*, I could trick him and stay safe. "Bow to him," my friend said, "as any respectful Japanese person would. Because the *kappa* is terribly polite, it will bow back. When it bows, the water on its head will tip and pour out. Once the water is gone, the *kappa* is powerless and can't hurt you."

I loved the idea of this mythical half-man, half-beast living in one of the most beautiful hot springs in Japan. He'd chosen his home well. Kappa No Yu lies within a virgin forest, along a tributary of the Ohata River. I could hear the gurgling of the stream as I lay back against the smooth rocks that lined the pool. They were cool against my neck and scalp. Above me, I could see the tops of the Hiba Cypress, and the bared trunks of the leafless trees that grew along the river's bank, their branches cloaked thick with snow. As more snow fell, the soft flakes tickled my face and stuck briefly to my eyelashes before melting away. I breathed out slowly, watching the mist form around my breath, swirling up with the steam that rose from the spring.

I suppose that *kappa* tales are told to children to keep them from misbehaving, to warn them away from hot water, and to remind them to be polite. But I did not fear the *kappa.* Instead, I felt blessed with the good fortune of skin softened, wrinkles smoothed, muscles relaxed, and my mind rejuvenated with every visit.

Yagen Valley hot springs

Kappa No Yu is the largest and best known of three *rotenburo*, or outdoor hot springs, in the Yagen Valley. Two of the three—the original Kappa No Yu and another smaller bath merely called Yu—are mixed, which means that both men and women bathe together. A third bath, Meoto Kappa No Yu, has large segregated pools separated by a tall wall. Meoto means "couple," which explains the male and female *kappa* sitting side by side atop the wall.

All three baths have relatively rustic dressing rooms that sit alongside the *rotenburo.* In the mixed baths, there are two dressing rooms, with one side for women and the other side for men. Only Meoto Kappa No Yu has a bathroom, as well as a small restaurant that sells noodles. It's also the only one with limited (and varying) daytime hours. The other two baths are open twenty-four hours and are free.

Getting to the hot springs

Aomori Prefecture is considered *inaka*, or in the boondocks. Even more *inaka* is the Shimokita Peninsula, making Yagen Valley an off-the-beaten-path gem. To reach the valley's hot springs, begin at Mutsu up on the ax handle of the peninsula. You can take a bus to the hot spring's general area, but unfortunately, they are infrequent in this part of the country. Traveling by car is convenient, and you'll get to see more of what Aomori has to offer.

From Mutsu, take Route 279 to Ohata Village (fifteen to twenty minutes). Once you reach Ohata, turn onto a smaller road and follow signs for Yagen Spa (another fifteen to twenty minutes). You'll come to a bridge with a small tributary of the Ohata River running beneath it. Turn off toward Kappa No Yu into a parking lot, which is shared with the Kokusetsu Yagen Yaeijo campground.

To get to Meoto Kappa No Yu, continue past the bridge from where the Kappa No Yu turnoff is located. On the right, you'll see the shop with a parking lot in front. The baths are behind the shop. Yu, the smallest hot spring, is just before Meoto Kappa No Yu, on the right side of the road. It's easy to miss, so drive slowly.

Where to stay

Hotel New Yagen is the largest and most popular traditional-style Japanese hotel in Yagen Valley, and is only a few kilometers from the baths.

6-1 Ohatamachi Yagen
Mutsu
(0175) 34-3311
www.newyagen.com (Japanese)

When to go

While warm summer weather and brilliant autumn leaves make the Yagen Valley popular during these times of year, Elizabeth believes going to a *rotenburo* in the winter is by far the best experience. Consider a trip to Kappa No Yu after a full day of skiing or snowshoeing on Kamafuse Mountain near Mutsu. The hot mineral waters are bliss for tired, aching limbs. Plus, you might catch a glimpse of the Japanese macaques (Snow Monkeys) that live in the local forests. They enjoy the hot springs when humans aren't around. For information about sightseeing, culture, hot springs, and more in the area, check out the following website.

http://apti.net.pref.aomori.jp/index-en.html

Hot springs by night

Kappa No Yu is a treat at night. A long, wooden staircase leads down to the bath close to the river's edge. After dark the staircase is lit by lanterns, adding a romantic ambience to the steam rising up from the hot water. Still, the lighting is dim and the dressing rooms are dark, which makes visiting during a full moon advisable. Nothing quite beats a soak in an outdoor bath under a starry sky.

Hot spring etiquette
To read about hot spring etiquette, go to page 215.

Shikoku Island

Quintin Winks cycles Shikoku's eighty-eight temples

There are no atheists in a Japanese tunnel. This thought springs to mind as I pedal in. Trucks dominate every centimeter of road. I'm forced onto a lumpy sidewalk barely wide enough for a single pedestrian. There's no barrier between the traffic and me.

Terrified, I pedal through darkness as the roar of a truck becomes deafening. The light at the end is still six hundred meters away, and I marvel at the irony of dying violently in a polluted tunnel while on an ancient Buddhist pilgrimage.

Yet moments later I'm spat back into the serenity of the Pilgrimage of the Eighty-Eight Temples. It's a journey that leads visitors into a forgotten Japan, along a twelve-hundred-kilometer route through an ancient landscape on Shikoku, the southeastern-most island of Japan's big four.

The traditional way to complete the pilgrimage is on foot, which takes between fifty and sixty days. Unable to spare that much time, my two friends and I choose touring bicycles and tents. Cycling and camping give us the most freedom, while submerging us in the country and culture.

In the three weeks it will take to complete the pilgrimage, we will ride into a dozen more tunnels, each time scared witless. But they're a requisite for our journey through this part of Japan that has slipped from the consciousness of much of the Western world. As we follow the ancient route, the complexity of this nation's cities, the crush of people, seething industrial machines, and outlandish fashions will be replaced by humble farmers and peaceful villages.

Just hours into the pilgrimage, the rush of Tokushima has faded as much in my mind as it has from view. By evening we've seen a half dozen more Shingon temples. In the cities we're able to visit this many in a single day, but between them the temples spread out. Sometimes it's as much as sixty kilometers from one temple to the next.

The landscape unfolds quickly on a bike, and I'm often surprised that we're in the mountains, then on the coast, then back in a city. At the same time, riding is slow enough that I can enjoy the Japanese spring: clacking bamboo forests, saffron sunrises, shadowy gorges, and seas of deliciously perfumed cherry blossoms.

We pedal on, headed for the humid coast. The hills give way to coastline and sub-tropical jungle as the last few drops of rain splash on shiny pavement. Ahead, a monkey cockily crosses the highway before disappearing into the dripping forest.

Onwards down the coast, I watch local surfers glide along walls of liquid glass rolling in from the North Pacific. Remote villages shelter behind imposing tsunami barriers, and rare is the temple that's located within sight of the water. Those that are offer sweeping views of the ocean, but most are nestled high in the nearby mountains.

The hills, of which there are many along the pilgrimage, are sometimes more remarkable than the temples they lead to. At times we pedal up monstrous inclines, devoid of switchbacks or relief. Temple Sixty-Six is the highest, some 911 meters above sea level. But the gradual climb past mountain views to this hilltop retreat makes this stretch the most memorable.

Much of the road winds through forest and alongside precipitous cliffs, eventually reaching a grassy plateau. A little farther on, having snaked through a weathered cedar forest, the road arrives at two enormous old-growth trees marking the temple entrance. Of the temple itself, there's little to deserve a recollection, except for the moody statues all over the grounds.

Intricately carved from stone, they're eerily lifelike. Some are laughing, others frowning, and still others smile cheekily. They represent a spectrum of human emotions and characters, and it's said that among the hundreds on the property, there is at least one in which you'll recognize your own true face. Walking among these strange stone people leaves me with a disconcerting feeling that as I pass by, they're moving, pointing, and perhaps even laughing at me.

Over the course of three weeks, the temples pass as in a dream. By the end of each day I can't even remember which one is which, though many have unique features that etch themselves in my memory: a pilgrim on his fifty-third circuit, a thousand-year-old tree, the Buddha's giant, knotted sandals, and a rainbow of koi swimming in a pitch-black pond. And I realize as I reach the end that this pilgrimage is not about the individual temples. It is the cumulative experience that I will carry with me when my journey is over.

Following the pilgrimage

For the Pilgrimage of the Eighty-Eight Temples, also known as the Shikoku Pilgrimage, on Shikoku Island, most pilgrims begin at temple number one near Tokushima and head south along the east coast in a clockwise direction. There are temple signs, stone markers, and small wooden signs all along the route.

Quintin recommends the Deca route map, published by Giga, which can be found at any bookstore on Shikoku, and probably any good bookstore in Osaka or Tokyo. It is a map book of Shikoku, with all the temples listed. The International Centers in the island's four prefectures also have good English maps for their areas. For walkers, there are numerous, thorough maps for sale at the big temples and at pilgrims' outfitters in the big four cities—Tokushima, Kochi, Matsuyama, and Takamatsu. The maps are in Japanese, but you will be able to read the road, kilometer, and temple numbers. A popular title is *Shosai Chizu Cho*. Good websites include *The Temple* Guy and *Shikoku Henro Trail*.

http://thetempleguy.com/akimeguri/shikoku/
www.shikokuhenrotrail.com

Getting to Shikoku

Osaka's Kansai International Airport is the nearest international hub to Tokushima. From here, a train will connect you with the ferry to Tokushima. The inexpensive train leaves Kansai regularly and stops at the ferry terminal a half hour later. From there, it's a two-hour ferry ride.

Where to stay

Each of Shikoku's four main cities has a wide array of options, from exclusive hotels to budget hostels. Most towns in between will also have some places to stay, as do about a third of the temples on the pilgrimage. Temple accommodation is typically priced mid-range (from $100 to $200 a night) and includes a vegetarian breakfast. There are also lots of free, basic shelters for pilgrims along the way. Some just have a roof over a wooden floor; others a hearth, *tatami* mats, and even places to cook.

For those in search of an inexpensive alternative that offers the most freedom, there is camping. Japan's camping laws are extremely relaxed and permits are not required to pitch a tent anywhere on public property. But camping in town requires some ingenuity, especially for those looking to sleep until a reasonable hour; of course, you should avoid bedding down on the steps of a town hall or a school field. If you do choose camping, it can be done quite comfortably. The famous Japanese *onsen* (hot spring spas) are located all along the pilgrimage, and are a wonderful place to get clean and soak away any aches and pains. Along with restaurants, corner stores are plentiful, and the food is very good.

When to go

March and early April are the best times to go, for a number of reasons. First, the cherry blossoms are sweeping across the landscape, perfuming the air. The temperature this early in the spring is also perfect for riding. Snow may occasionally still fall at higher elevations, but those embarking on the pilgrimage any later run the risk of oppressive heat and humidity.

A Henro Pilgrimage Guide to the 88 Temples of Shikoku Island, Japan

Written by Taisen Miyata, this book is not always in stock Amazon.com. It can also be ordered from Bishop Taisen Miyata.

Koyasan Buddhist Temple
342 First St.
Los Angeles, California
90012 USA
(213) 624-1267
www.koyasanbetsuin.org

Kumamoto Prefecture

Arin Greenwood hits the trail at a Takamori dude ranch

Dinner is surreal, as we might have expected—we are, after all, at a dude ranch in southwestern Japan. The dining room at Blue Grass looks like an Old West log cabin ... west of the Mississippi by way of Tokyo, that is. On the walls are photos of rodeos; on the floor are low, Japanese-style tables. The shop next to the dining room sells cowboy boots, but you have to take off your own shoes before entering to look at them. I am reading horse magazines while eating *udon*, tempura, and pickles. My boyfriend Brian eats his steak with chopsticks.

Yuki, the woman who is serving our food, tells us that in 1991 her father started Blue Grass as a cowboy-western ranch because he likes America and horses. Although he has never been to America, he calls himself Bear. In fact, except for Yuki, the staff all have Western names. She doesn't even like horses, and would have moved to the city, but couldn't because her sister married an American and left home to live in Wisconsin. Someone had to stay and help Bear with the family business. Yuki seems surprisingly sanguine, considering.

After dinner, Brian and I head outside to play with Budd, the ranch sheepdog. Then we go to bed on a futon mattress that rests atop an elevated bed frame. While I'm falling asleep with my head on a buckwheat pillow, I wonder about Blue Grass—is it cowboy western as in lifestyle, or even western, as in regional America? Perhaps Bear should brush up on his geography.

The next morning, Brian and I drink coffee, eat eggs, and wear slovenly clothes. We are definitely Westerners, but not at all cowboy western. We're about halfway through our breakfast when into the dining room walk eight or so Japanese who are spectacularly "Wild West western." They wear fringed suede vests, neat denim shirts, and leather belts with buckles the size of Texas. Yet they eat miso soup and fermented fish and drink green tea. "You can dress them up like cowboys," I giggle, "but they're still Japanese at heart."

"They're guests from Tokyo," Yuki explains. "We're taking them riding in the mountains." And their clothes? "They bought some from our shop. The rest they got in America."

After breakfast, it's time for me to ride. I meet Cassie, my guide, an easy-going woman in jeans and well-worn boots. Cassie introduces our horses. Hers, Peter Pan, is ironically twenty years old and getting crabby. Montana, my horse, is enormous, just like the state.

"Can we run?" Cassie asks.

"*Hai*," I say. Yes.

Surrounded by volcanic mountains, brilliant green rice paddies, and rustic farms, we ride away from Blue Grass at a clip. It's exhilarating and fun, though Montana seems bouncier than I remember horses being back home. When I ask Cassie, who used to be called Toshie, where she learned to ride, she tells me that she spent a year in Australia, where she developed a love of horses. When she came home to Japan, she got a job at Blue Grass.

"Is cowboy-style riding big in Japan?" I ask, and learn from Cassie that there are numerous ranches throughout the country. I look around at the endless mountains, acres of rice paddies, row upon row of green tea fields, and cow pastures aplenty, and it's no wonder to me that Japan has adopted this Western tradition.

Back at Blue Grass I walk—painfully—past the riding ring where an American flag flies next to a Wisconsin flag, and a Japanese cowboy wrangles a stallion. While I realize that Blue Grass may not be truly cowboy western, in its own way it is authentic and sweet. Bear took the three things he loves best—horses, his vision of America, and his daughters—and brought them all together to create this strange and wonderful place.

Blue Grass

Blue Grass is open year-round, but you should try to go in the fall during the Country Gold International Music Festival, a big weekend event staged by Japanese country-and-western singer Charlie Nagatani.

2814 Takamori
Takamori-cho
Aso-gun
(0967) 62-3366
www.aso-bluegrass.com (Japanese only)
www.countrygold.net/us/ (Music festival)
www.realwestern.com (Western activities in Japan)

Miyazaki Prefecture

Nolan Webb follows the road less traveled in the Kyushu Highlands

My map showed hardly a town along the road between Miyakonojo, about an hour from the Pacific, and our target, the Takachiho Gorge, deep in the mountains up north. As fields and paddocks petered out, the paved way narrowed to a single lane of traffic in either direction. Autumn hues painted a colorful backdrop as my Japanese partner and I drove past blurs of flaming red *momiji* (maples), and the fluorescent yellows of ginkgo trees, so bright and abundant in this southern region.

At a fork in the road, the map indicated that our narrow route joined with Highway 265, which cuts right through the heart of the Kyushu Highlands. Yet here we found no major thoroughfare to take us the last two hundred kilometers. At first we wondered if we hadn't made some mistake, or that perhaps this small, unremarkable road would eventually widen, but our hopes were to be proven wrong. From that point onward, Highway 265 became a single-lane, unkempt, and nearly abandoned road.

We thought we had given ourselves enough time to reach the gorge by late afternoon, but after a half hour of plodding and winding, we faced a decision: turn back now and start again the next day, or inch forward in hope of reaching our destination before sundown. In the midst of a long weekend, with time to spare and a tank of gas at our disposal, we decided to push on.

At thirty kilometers per hour, swaying as we banked each curve, we continued along until the road straightened and climbed to a steep mountain pass. From this vantage point, I expected to see towns and crisscrossing roads in the valley below. Instead, an unpopulated punchbowl of evergreen forest, glazed over with a thin layer of incandescent fog, lay before us.

On this stretch there was no evidence of human life, not so much as a discarded wrapper or old bottle. Finally, we glimpsed what appeared to be an inn, blackened with decay. Around the next bend we saw a few smaller buildings along the grassy banks of a shallow river, the first signs of habitation in two hours of steady driving. A rusted sign marked the name of the town in archaic brushstrokes, cryptic even for a Japanese native.

We stopped and got out to explore, and while wading through the overgrown pathway toward the complex, we came upon a pair of primitive, humanoid figures that were better fit for Easter Island than a roadside in rural Japan. The mossy, mysterious eyes of these waist-high statues seemed to follow us as we slowly made our way toward tiny classrooms, each barely large enough for ten students.

Windows with shark-toothed panes of broken glass lined one wall. On another hung a paper fish, a faded crimson and buttercup-yellow carp. A dismantled television sat in the corner, next to a dusty arithmetic book. Cobwebs fluttered from the water-stained ceiling into the shadows of the rotting hallway. The air was as musty and thick as in a cellar. A small barren field spread out from an open doorway, and we could picture the long-departed schoolchildren, their heads bobbing above the tall grass along the river.

Farther down the road were more abandoned buildings, shack-like abodes that formed a little village. Here and there we found remnants of a simple working life: old bicycles with granny baskets, a rusted motor, a stack of lumber, a pile of cracked pipe fittings. The town looked as if it had been abandoned overnight, as if the residents had awakened in the shadow of an erupting volcano, or a bursting dam, and would be back before long to reclaim their land.

Intrigued, but with no one to answer our questions, we pressed onward. After navigating two more mountain passes, we encountered an old woman.

"How far to Takachiho?" we asked.

She squatted next to our car window. "Half a day if the weather holds, but you'll never get there tonight." Under a wide-brimmed straw hat, she was sullen, stony-faced, and unsurprised to see us, as if foreigners came down from the hills just any old day of the week.

Another half hour put us at Shiiba, a town which was small but at least had living residents, not to mention three or four provincial roads leading out in all directions from the center of town. We had reached civilization. At a small inn, we were greeted by a middle-aged innkeeper with a scarlet headband and the smile of an old friend. "Lost, are you?" he asked, peering at us over a newspaper, through reading glasses perched at the end of his nose.

"Not exactly ... but kind of ... I mean, we know where we're going, but we were just a little surprised that ..."

"Surprised that it would take so long, I bet," he interrupted. "I imagine you probably got a little distracted, what with that ghost town and that old road. City people usually do."

"That's right. Exactly right, in fact."

"Happens from time to time. This route was pretty important back in the day. Traders used it to travel between the castles, until Meiji times." But when we asked what happened to the old town in the hills, he was vague. "The decline must have started back when they ran out of trees to cut down, but nobody seems to remember much about it anymore. People say the town was like a mountain stream that just dried up one summer." He paused for a moment to tighten his headband. "That's not the only town, either. Dozens just like it in these valleys. Vanished. Forgotten."

The man agreed to take us in, but not before gently ribbing us for our lack of a reservation, as he said he would have prepared a feast for us had he known. The next day brought with it gentle mountain rain and a pleasant morning's drive to Takachiho Gorge. The bright turquoise waters and fiery autumn hues enveloped us as we let our rented paddleboat drift along the river. It was a spectacular scene, to be fair, but as we started our drive back south along the coastal freeway, what we found most unforgettable was that road through the mountains and our glimpse of its lost mysteries.

Exploring Kyushu Island

Miyakonojo, the starting point for this trip, is approximately midway between the regional capitals of Kagoshima and Miyazaki. Head north toward Aya town, known for its vineyards and wine tours. From here Highway 265 should be easy to find. Either ask locals or check a MapArt bilingual mapbook, which shows the major roads through Kyushu and is available at most major convenience stores.

Traveling by car

Most of southern Kyushu is crisscrossed with hundreds of old roads, many dating back to samurai times. In this part of the country, a car is absolutely indispensable. It is strongly recommended that you begin with a full tank of gas, since twenty-four hour gas stations are rare in Japan, even in many urban centers. Also, let a few friends know where you're going. Even travelers equipped with mobile phones may find themselves without an adequate signal and thus cut off from the outside world. For more information on car rental, plus plenty of great travel tips, visit the Japan National Tourist Information website.

www.japantravelinfo.com

Hokkaido Prefecture

Tim Patterson treks Hokkaido's Playground of the Gods

My first view of Daisetsuzan, or the "Great Snowy Mountains," happened on the way to Asahidake Onsen Village, a cluster of hot spring hotels. The road climbed east from Asahikawa through stands of white birch and bamboo grass. It was a misty morning, and the high peaks were veiled by clouds, but for a moment, the shroud parted to reveal the rust-colored face of Asahidake.

At 2,290 meters, Asahidake is the highest mountain on Hokkaido, and its summit—my destination—was crowned in crystal ice. White plumes of steam rose from vents beneath the peak, making it seem as if the mountain itself were giving birth to clouds. The indigenous people of Hokkaido, the Ainu, call this volcanic mountain range Kamui Mintara, meaning "Playground of the Gods." Much of it has been designated a national park, the biggest and wildest in all of Japan.

The road ended at Asahidake Onsen Village. Even here, well below tree line, the air carried a chill, and I put on my wool hat for the ropeway ride. As the cable car swung high over a sea of vivid autumn foliage, I noticed my fellow passengers affixing small brass bells to their daypacks. The sound is said to scare away brown bears, but I couldn't help but wonder if a hungry bear might not regard it as a dinner bell.

Hikers stepped off the tram, tinkling like Santa's reindeer. A network of trails looped through wind-beaten scrub pines and around dark alpine ponds. Above, the vegetation gave way to bare rock. Cinching my pack tight, I set off along the trail that led past the steam vents and along a ridgeline.

The morning clouds lifted, revealing green hills that tumbled down to Asahikawa, and the bucolic villages of Biei and Kamifurano, the latter known for its lavender fields. As I stopped to drink some water and admire the view, a tiny girl with a determined look in her eyes pulled herself over a rock and scampered past, followed a minute later by her mother and father. Feeling sheepish, I set off again, passing the girl just beneath the peak as she waited impatiently for her huffing parents.

After a two-hour climb, a line of peaks ran to the south, and all of Hokkaido lay spread out below—wild forest to the east, a patchwork of farmland to the west. I felt exalted and privileged to be standing at the topmost point in the Playground of the Gods. Wind whipped over the summit as I took a celebratory shot of whiskey.

Following my lunch of rice-balls and pickled plums, I continued down the far side of the mountain, traversing a Martian landscape of windswept yellow rock, until I reached the turn-off for Nakadake Onsen. I soaked for a blissful hour, feeling each muscle loosen and relax. Then, reluctantly, I pulled on my clothes and hurried three kilometers down the trail, back to the ropeway, just in time to catch the last tram down the mountain.

Getting to the summit

This excursion could be done as a day trip from Sapporo, but you would be rushed. To enjoy the experience, give yourself a full day for the mountain, at least. Take the Hakodate Train Line from Sapporo Station to Asahikawa Station. From there, take the Chuo bus to Minamikawa and transfer to the coach bus that goes to Daisetsuzan National Park. A ropeway will take you partially up the mountain. From the point where the ropeway drops you off, it is approximately a two-hour hike to the summit. For more information, visit the following website.

www.outdoorjapan.com

Lodge Nutapukaushipe

Located within Daisetsuzan National Park, this lodge is unpretentious on the outside, ramshackle and rough-hewn, but inside you'll find the casual elegance that exemplifies the best sort of country Japanese hospitality. Slurp down a steaming bowl of miso *ramen*, relax with a stack of *National Geographic* magazines in the homey lounge, and soak in a delightfully old-fashioned wooden bathhouse. The service is far from formal. With its laid-back vibe, this is a comfortable place to rest after a long day in the mountains—highly recommended!

Higashikawa District
Asahidake Onsen Village
(0166) 94-97-2150

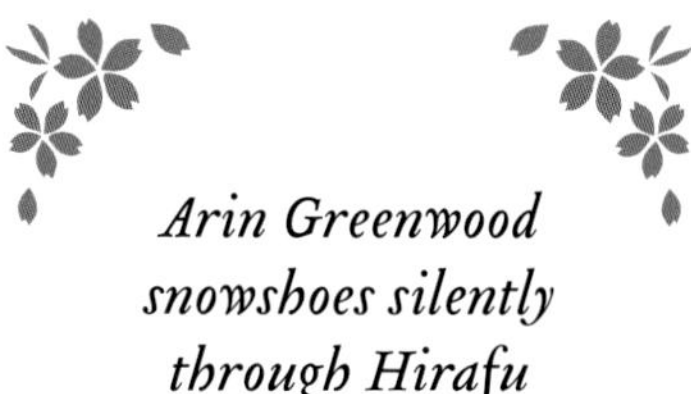

Arin Greenwood snowshoes silently through Hirafu

Levi is a patient snowboard instructor with the misfortune of being *my* instructor here in Hirafu, in the Niseko mountains of Hokkaido. He straps me to my board and gently launches me down a tiny incline, but having both legs attached to a single piece of fiberglass is disconcerting, so I fall again ... and again. Levi compliments me on my ability to get back up.

Phaael is my instructor on day two. He wants to take the chairlift up a smallish hill to "see my stuff." When it is our turn to get on the lift, the chair whacks me from behind, and I fall face first into the soft, powdery snow. My stuff is mortifying. Finally, I make it on, and from the chairlift I watch the snowboarders. They are funky; they look awesome. One, in a super-cool hat adorned with rabbit ears, does a miraculous somersault over a large jump. I am wearing unflattering snow pants that I bought on eBay and an unstylish hat, and I fall off the chairlift at the top of the hill.

On day three, suffering with a tremendous pain in my legs, I hobble through town with my boyfriend Brian to get to the slopes. The snow is ideal. We are surrounded by pretty mountains and pretty trees, and the streets are lined with cafés that serve great local cheese and wine, and colorful inns with names like Potatochips, Tomato, and If. A whimsical sign shows a potato skiing—even potatoes love Hirafu's snow! I could love Hirafu too, if it weren't for the infernal snowboarding.

On the slopes, I fall off the lift again. Brian glides down the hill, schussing and swirling, making himself—an excellent snowboarder—hateful. I inch down the hill on legs that I wish could be amputated. I make myself fall so I can sit and rest. At the bottom I say tartly, "I'd like to practice alone."

On our last day in Hirafu, my legs are almost okay again. Brian wants me to give snowboarding one more shot. But in town I'd seen a flyer that read: "Snowshoe. Enjoy Nature!" So I reply to Brian, "I'd like to. Really, I would. But I've signed up for snowshoeing."

Mieko Shiraki, my snowshoe guide, picks me up in her gray station wagon. On the drive to Mt. Yotei, she tells me she's climbed Mt. Kilimanjaro, hiked to base camp on Mt. Everest, and is a professional tree-climbing instructor. Her snow clothes are not trendy.

When we arrive at the snow-covered slopes of the volcano, Mieko laces me into a pair of lightweight snowshoes made from two pieces of bent cedar. She says they were made by an eighty-year-old man here on Hokkaido. "He's one of the last few who know how to make these. Fifty years ago, there were no cars here. This is how people got around in the winter."

"Not anymore," I snarl. "Now they get around on snowboards."

Mieko and I begin our outing on a meadow of virgin snow, lightly supported on its powdery surface. Walking in snowshoes is slow and quiet and peaceful. And it doesn't confine my legs!

Mieko and I climb a tree-covered hill, looking for fox trails, listening to a woodpecker tapping holes in a tree, and admiring patches of blue sky and snow-frosted birch. We snowshoe down the other side to sit by the frozen waters of Half Moon Lake. As Mieko pours steaming tea and serves cookies, she reminisces about her outdoor adventures, and wonders why more people don't snowshoe anymore. Not enough excitement, she thinks, not enough of a thrill.

At twilight, the trip to the car takes us back over the hill and across the meadow. Snow is falling lightly and my legs no longer hurt. That evening in Hirafu, I rejoin Brian for cheese fondue and hot spiced wine, delighting in the perfection of the day ... and the use of both legs.

Getting to Hirafu

Express buses travel from Sapporo's New Chitose Airport and from Sapporo Station. The ride takes around three hours and passes through some wonderful scenery. You can also take the train from the airport to Kutchan, a town near Hirafu, and catch a bus or taxi at the Kutchan Station.

Snowshoe treks

For more information on snowshoeing with Mieko Shiraki, go to *Discovery U.* Click "English" and then "Winter."

www.discoveryu.join-us.jp

Where to stay

There are numerous small guesthouses in Hirafu. We stayed at Niseko Grandpapa, a Bavarian-style inn that is close to the ski slopes. Some of the rooms have private baths, while others have shared baths. Amenities include a breakfast buffet, a restaurant serving fondue (perfect for après-ski), and a fireplace in the common room. The proprietor is a chef and an artist whose woodblock prints are part of the décor.

http://niseko-grandpapa.com/

Young at Heart

Experiences for all in the family

The people of Japan treat their children like gold. Throughout the year, festivals are held to celebrate sons and daughters, from newborns to young adults. In mid-January, Seijin Shiki marks the passage of Japanese children into adulthood. Springtime brings Children's Day, with separate customs for boys and girls, and during the summer season, miniature *mikoshi* shrines, crewed by little ones, are paraded through the city streets. As the year winds to a close, on the fifteenth of November, Shichi-Go-San honors children ages seven, five, and three.

From Hello Kitty to Tokyo Disneyland, there is no end to the adorable and whimsical products and places designed to entertain and delight children. In some neighborhoods, residential streets are blocked off from traffic so that kids can play on sculpted animals, jungle gyms, and seesaws embedded in the pavement. Department stores devote entire floors to children's toys and clothing. Nearly every park, large or small, has a playground.

When it comes to sightseeing, what is endlessly fascinating to adults is often mind-numbingly boring to a child. And if you're really just a big kid masquerading as a grown-up, you're eventually going to crave a little fun yourself. With this in mind, the contributors to this chapter offer suggestions sure to keep all ages entertained.

In an interesting twist on a hands-on activity, Jennifer O'Bryan goes solo at a Tokyo cathouse—literally—where felines lounge around soaking up attention from visiting cat lovers. Both Kate Glynn and I rediscover the forgotten pleasures of theme parks, Kate on the oldest roller coaster in Japan, and me on the refreshing water slides of Hydropolis.

For suggestions on family bonding with your spouse and kids, you can count on Sara Francis-Fujimura, who spends quality time riding historic streetcars and a steam locomotive. Annie Donwerth Chikamatsu also finds a way to get closer to her loved ones, as they picnic and play at Tokyo's Showa Kinen Park.

Boys carrying a shrine at an Omikoshi Matsuri festival

From chilling out at Ice Cream World to exploring the famous Ghibli Museum, the activities here will entertain both young and old. As for the bravest activity of all—traveling abroad with your children ... and living to tell—take your cues from Heather Poppink, whose advice on taming the savage beast once known as her precious toddler is sure to be appreciated.

Tokyo Prefecture

Jennifer O'Bryan says "hello kitty" in Tokyo

On the eighth floor of the Tokyu Hands department store in the Tokyo suburb of Ikebukuro, the employees lounge in beds, play with toys, and clean themselves obsessively ... and customers pay a small fee to watch them!

While cute animals, both live and animated, are wildly popular in Japan, many landlords don't allow pets, and even if they did, long hours at the office make it difficult to care for an animal. To tap into the market of wannabe cat owners craving furry companionship, Nekobukuro was born. The name is a play on words, with *neko*, which means "cat," combined with *bukuro,* the last two syllables of the suburb in which the store is located.

As someone who is embarrassingly obsessed with my feline friends, and who missed their aloof affection while I was working in Japan, I excitedly made my way to the department store's pet supply floor. As the automatic doors slid open, a pre-recorded "meow" welcomed me to the "cathouse." I had expected to see the bank of cages common in most pet stores. Instead, I found the cats on display in a long enclosure designed to look like a subway car, with a cat conductor at the helm.

From hairless Sphinx to Silver Tabby American Shorthair, the cats were rotated from their subway cubicles, so only a handful roamed freely in the interactive playroom at any given time. A television shaped like Hello Kitty showed videos of the cats, and toys were laid out to entice them to play. An overhead catwalk for hasty escapes from prying hands connected the main room to a second room, where the kitties could perch atop three-meter-tall scratching posts for catnapping and keeping a wary eye on grabby visitors.

Most of the cats demonstrated the typical indifference of their species, sprawling across the furniture, and lounging in the cubbyholes. When I dangled a feather in front of one, he briefly lifted his head, looked at me, and went back to sleep. However, a couple of them did compete for my affection, rubbing against my legs and meowing loudly. In the hallway leading to a second room, a bulletin board displayed photos of and information about each cat, but it was in Japanese, so I never learned the name of the adorable Scottish Fold that took a shine to me.

On my visit I was fortunate enough to be there for the four thirty snack hour. Nekobukuro attendants passed out tasty morsels among the visitors, which we used to lure the less sociable cats from their hiding spots. The treats grabbed their attention for a few fleeting seconds, until they devoured the food and moved on to the next person. No doubt, it's a familiar routine for these felines.

While playing "cat lady" in Nekobukuro, I also discovered that it's quite the romantic spot for couples out on dates. All around me, as I watched young lovers flirting with the cats and with each other, I suddenly realized that I was the only single person there. But that was okay. Even though I had no date of my own to canoodle, my hour with the kitties gave me a chance to witness a clever response to the difficulties of owning a pet in a crowded city, and more importantly, provided a much-needed fix for my feline fetish.

Tokyu Hands Ikebukuro

If you come with kids, take note that the department store also has one of the biggest toy departments in Tokyo.

1-28-10 Higashi-Ikebukuro
Toshima District
Tokyo

Train: Yamanote Line to Ikebukuro Station (Seibu exit to East Ikebukuro).

Subway: Yurakucho or Marunouchi Line to Ikebukuro Station (Seibu exit to East Ikebukuro).

Directions: Follow the signs for Sunshine City, which is a huge shopping complex next to Tokyu Hands. Nekobukuro is located on the eighth floor.

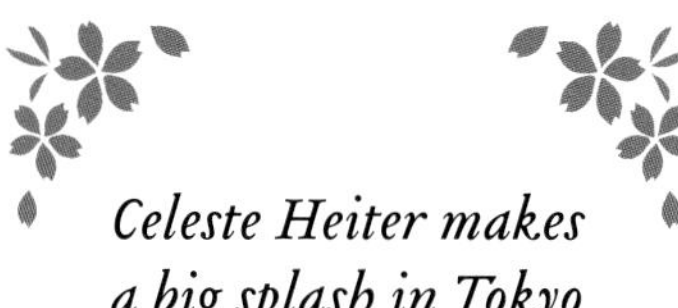

Celeste Heiter makes a big splash in Tokyo

As part of my apartment rental agreement, I taught English every Friday afternoon at the landlady's after-school *juku,* a private classroom where several groups of Japanese students came once a week to improve their conversational English. Admittedly, there were countless other ways in which I'd rather have spent my Fridays off, but I was fond of the children, and Toshimaen, a homey little neighborhood centered around a quaint amusement park, was a perfectly fine place to spend a couple of hours at the end of each week.

In the summer months, my classes finished just at dusk, and I would wander into the admissions area of the park to spend a little quiet time before catching the train back home to the suburb of Ikebukuro. Through the front entrance, I could see games of chance and vendors selling corn dogs and cotton candy. The centerpiece of the park was an elaborately gilded, old-fashioned carousel with carved horses and velvet-lined chariots.

Since it was always so late when I finished the classes, I didn't have enough time to go in. Until a group of my students invited me to spend a Saturday afternoon with them, I had no idea that this beguiling little amusement park was the gateway to a huge aquatic fun land called Hydropolis.

Hydropolis features seven swimming pools, a surfing pool, a network of slippery waterslides, and a suite of classic amusement park rides with names like Flying Pirates, Top Spin, and Corkscrew. Unfortunately, no one had told me to wear a swimsuit. Instead of slipping and sliding down the chutes and tubes, I wandered around the grounds, chatting with my students and nibbling on carnival food.

A couple of months later, in the relentless heat and unbearable humidity of summer, I heard the siren call of Hydropolis. So one sweltering Sunday afternoon, I rounded up about a half dozen of my fellow teachers, not one of whom was under thirty, to join me in acting like a kid for a day.

Toshimaen's many amusements, although enticing, offered no temptation from our single-minded purpose: to spend every possible minute in the cooling waters of Hydropolis. Up, up, up we climbed the narrow wooden stairs, to wait our turn for the swirling, schussing Mr. Toad's Wild Ride through the slippery chutes to the splash pools that awaited at the bottom.

Soaked to the skin, with our fingertips shriveled up like raisins, and our legs aching, again and again we made the vertical climb to the top of each slide for another trip down the chutes to the cool waters below. Like obsessed skiers, trying to make one last run before dark, we didn't leave until we'd squeezed every drop of fun from our day at Hydropolis.

Toshimaen

3-25-1 Koyama
Nerima District
Tokyo
(03) 3990-8800
www.toshimaen.co.jp (Japanese)

Train: Seibu-Ikebukuro Line from Ikebukuro Station to Toshimaen Station at the very end of the line.

Directions: The entrance to the park is right in front of the station exit.

Kate Glynn takes a wild ride near a Tokyo temple

Centered around Sensoji, also known as Asakusa Kannon Temple, the Asakusa District is one of those neighborhoods where the feel of old Tokyo—in the days when it was called Edo—still lingers. Shops filled with traditional wares line both sides of the Nakamise shopping street that leads to Sensoji's inner gate. Each time I visit, I still marvel at the compound's five-storied pagoda and the temple's seventh-century-style architecture. If I didn't know already, I would never guess that it's a 1950's reproduction. The original was destroyed in the firebombing of Tokyo during World War II.

Once I've explored all that, I head for Hanayashiki, a tiny, kitschy amusement park that reminds me more of Coney Island than Disneyland. Set on a plot of land no bigger than a parking lot, with buildings towering around it on every side, Hanayashiki dates back to 1853 and has no high-speed, special-effects-flashing, upside-down-spiraling, hair-on-fire rides. The biggest thrill here is the Space Shot, where visitors politely take off their shoes and arrange them on the pavement before they're rocketed up a sixty-meter rail, and down again, with a split-second view of Asakusa rooftops at the top.

Back on the ground, I walk through the *obakeyashiki* (haunted house). The ghosts and ghouls are papier-mâché, but I think of it as a cultural experience, since the Japanese believe that a spine-chilling, goose-bump-inducing scare is supposed to cool you off on a sticky summer day. Next, I like to indulge in a wonderfully greasy plate of *yakisoba* noodles before I hop on my favorite attraction—the roller coaster. Yes, you read that right, a greasy snack followed by a roller coaster ride.

Not to worry. It's the oldest roller coaster in Japan and goes about forty kilometers per hour. There are no loops, flips, or spirals to make you lose your lunch. The fun, or rather, the terror, on this ride, comes not from speed, but from the proximity of the surrounding buildings. Hanayashiki is so small, and the roller coaster so close to the perimeter, that I always feel as if I'm about to slam into the side of a building or the chimney of a public bathhouse.

The metropolis of Tokyo abounds with sights, from the temples and shrines that are the windows into its ancient past, to the sleek boutiques, where fashionistas sashay like harbingers of a freakish, uber-modern future. But here in Asakusa, Hanayashiki offers a uniquely nostalgic peek into Tokyo's forgotten childhood.

Hanayashiki

2-28-1 Asakusa
Taito District
Tokyo
(03) 3842-8780 (English spoken)
www.hanayashiki.net/e/index.html

Train: Yamanote Line to Ueno Station. Transfer to the Ginza Subway Line to Asakusa Station.

Subway: Ginza Line to Asakusa Station.

Heather Poppink tames a little lion in Tokyo

Hunched over my son's stroller in the middle of a quiet corner store, I was straining to read the *kanji* characters below each selection of thinly sliced meat when my darling two-year-old began to bellow like the King of the Jungle. Try as I might, as he squirmed in his stroller I was unable to appease his growing frustration with the snacks and toys I'd brought along for incidents such as this. Mortified by the disapproving stares of the other shoppers, I quickly threw my food items back onto the shelves and pushed his stroller out into the street.

Going home wasn't an option. After that outburst, I knew I didn't have the patience to cope with him in the confines of our apartment, and he was clearly going to be a restless companion for the long list of errands I had planned for the remainder of the day. It was time for the secret weapon I'd heard other expat mothers whisper about: Tokyo Dome City.

My little lion was still fussing and fretting in his stroller when we boarded the Marunouchi Subway Line to Korakuen Station. The train was filled to capacity with crowds of locals and tourists. When it finally stopped at Korakuen, a large group veered toward the sports arena for a baseball game, while the rest of us headed down a freshly paved sidewalk toward the outdoor amusement attractions that surround the complex.

The path ended at a large open area of shops, restaurants, and amusements. A roller coaster clattered along its track, while a Ferris wheel spun in fits and starts. There were arcade games, and dancers dressed as puppets performed on a stage. When we came to a merry-go-round, I finally set my son free from his stroller, and he charged toward it with shrieks of delight.

The hours passed quickly as we made the rounds from one activity to another, and what had begun as the seething rage of a caged animal was now a dynamo unleashed in the body of a giddy two-year-old. But with my own energy beginning to wane, I realized that I faced the challenge of wearing him out, lest he pitch another tantrum when it came time to leave.

I had one more ace up my sleeve: Toys' Kingdom, a huge interactive play space. If Toys' Kingdom couldn't tame him, I figured nothing would. When we peeked into the first room, wide-eyed and grinning, we saw the treasures laid out before us: kiddy rides, cars, trains, huge building blocks, and an indoor playground. My son wriggled out of my grasp and dove right into the train section, while I planted myself on a comfortable bench.

About an hour later, I announced that it was time to see the rest of Toys' Kingdom. I might as well have told him I was canceling Christmas. Tears poured from my toddler's eyes. He roared like a wild animal and ran in the opposite direction, clinging to a piece of train track. I felt like tearing my hair out, vowing that I would never take him on another outing.

I carried him kicking and screaming down a hall to the next playroom. His protests rang through the building. My cheeks flushed with embarrassment. But his agonized cry soon became a squeal of ecstasy at yet another brightly colored array of toys. I supervised him from a distance, although I no longer dared to hope that Toys' Kingdom would reward me with a docile child.

Two hours later, though, the tide finally turned. Bleary-eyed, I barely recognized what was happening. His running had slowed to a walk. His eyelids drooped. He came to my side willingly, resting his head against my arm while I helped him with his shoes. We waved goodbye to the toys, his lips parted in a yawn, and he was soon asleep in his stroller, purring like a kitten, with a blissful calm gracing his angelic face.

Tokyo Dome and Toys' Kingdom

Both venues are located in Tokyo Dome City, adjacent to Suidobashi Station.

www.tokyo-dome.co.jp/e/e/
www.tokyo-dome.co.jp/omocha/ (Japanese)

Train: Chuo Line to Suidobashi Station.

Subway: Mita Line to Suidobashi Station or Namboku or Marunouchi Line to Korakuen Station.

Jennifer O'Bryan chills out at a Tokyo ice cream emporium

My only real food weakness is ice cream, and whenever I visit a new country, seeking out local chilled desserts is always at the top of my list. In Italy, I reveled in rich, custard-like gelato. In Singapore, I cooled down on sweltering afternoons with fruity shaved ice. And when I lived in Japan, I was a regular at Ice Cream City.

This nirvana for sweet treat lovers can be found in the Namja Town entertainment center in the Sunshine 60 Building, one of Tokyo's tallest skyscrapers. Created by Namco, a major Japanese video game company, Namja Town has devoted its entire third floor to all things ice cream.

Here I learned all about the history of Japanese ice cream, and discovered frozen desserts from a variety of other countries, with the thick, gooey Turkish ice cream being among my favorites. When time came to order, I gave it my best effort to sample as many flavors as I could from among the more than three hundred traditional, exotic, and seasonal varieties. Of course vanilla, chocolate, and strawberry are offered for the less adventurous, but I was drawn to the more intriguing flavors, like cucumber, red bean, or purple sweet potato.

If you want bragging rights, you can line up to try soy sauce, Indian curry, chicken, horse flesh, ox tongue, oyster, octopus, eel, or sea urchin flavors. Or perhaps you'd like a small cup of Dracula garlic ice cream to cleanse the palate after a scoop of crab ice cream on a waffle cone. You can also enjoy the art of ice cream at Ice Cream City, with trompe l'oeil versions made to resemble savory foods like sushi or curry rice. For a real treat, order a dish of pearl ice cream, which comes with the chance of finding a real pearl!

Ice Cream City

Namja Town
Sunshine City
Building 2, 3F
3-1-3 Higashi-Ikebukuro
Toshima District
Tokyo
(03) 5950 0765
www.namja.jp/ (main website, in Japanese)
www.namja.jp/img/pdf/guidemap.pdf (online brochure in English)

Train: Yamanote Line to Ikebukuro Station (Seibu exit to East Ikebukuro).

Subway: Yurakucho or Marunouchi Line to Ikebukuro Station (Seibu exit to East Ikebukuro).

Directions: Follow the signs to Sunshine City. You can't miss it. The Sunshine 60 Building is sixty stories tall.

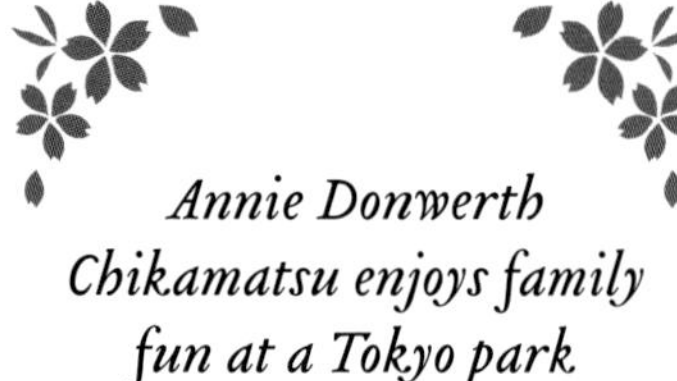

Annie Donwerth Chikamatsu enjoys family fun at a Tokyo park

I heard of Showa Kinen Park years ago, when my two children were toddlers. There were tales of wide open spaces for running and playing, pools and man-made streams for wading, dragons and a Mayan temple for climbing, not to mention the Bounce Dome for, well, bouncing. It sounded like a wondrous place for us to escape from our one-room living situation.

Heading out with small children in tow is not easy in Tokyo though. The train system reaches far and wide, but out where we live, many places were filed on my list entitled "You can't get there from here," because of the number of train changes involved. Back then, carrying strollers and heavy children up flights of stairs was a major deterrent. So Showa Kinen Park was designated a Papa Trip, one that would require the car. But like most Japanese papas, ours was overworked and preferred to catch up on sleep on his days off. Necessity and easier options took us other places. It was years before we headed out to the park.

By then the kids were older, but they still found much to appreciate. They were too big (read: old) to ride the park's train and roll around on the rainbow hammocks, but they giggled through the fog-swathed Foggy Woods, admired the walkway of kid-made tiles, and climbed the chiseled Mayan temple and "jewel"-encrusted dragons. They played a round of miniature golf, and cooled off in the wading streams. They strolled through the poppy fields, and even bounced in the Bounce Dome. I don't think you can ever be too old to bounce. By that time, though, Papa was taking a nap under a nearby tree. Actually, there were quite a few papas napping.

There was too much for us to do and see, especially when we had to figure in time to keep everyone watered and fed. We should have printed a map of the park from the website. We missed the dragonfly marsh and bird sanctuary, the traditional Japanese garden and buildings, and the replica of a farm village from the 1950s and '60s—all interesting attractions I would have liked to photograph.

Little Brother wanted to rent bicycles and cruise around the scenic cycling course, but by the time we came across it, there was just no time. We all came away feeling that Showa Kinen Park is a place well worth more than one trip. It was also noted that it may well be worth the time to make lunch boxes beforehand to cut down on standing in line. The park is huge, so it never felt crowded except when we were in line to enter, eat, and exit.

On our way out of the park, there was a steady stream of people moving toward the station to go home. As we sat in the car in one of several lines to exit the parking lot, I looked over at the other cars to see kids and moms settling in for a cozy nap. Our kids were already nodding off in the back seat. Papa was drinking a second can of black coffee that he bought at the park's exit, and I readied my camera to shoot fields and cityscapes in the sunset. Unfortunately, I fell asleep and missed that too. Papa made it home wide awake.

Showa Kinen Park

The park is an easy day trip from downtown Tokyo. Take the Chuo Line from Tokyo's Shinjuku Station to Tachikawa Station. Change to the Ome Line, get off at Nishi (West) Tachikawa Station, and follow the walkway that leads to the Showa Kinen Park entrance. Maps of the park are available and are recommended.

3173 Midori-cho
Tachikawa
(042) 528-1751
www.showakinenpark.go.jp/english/

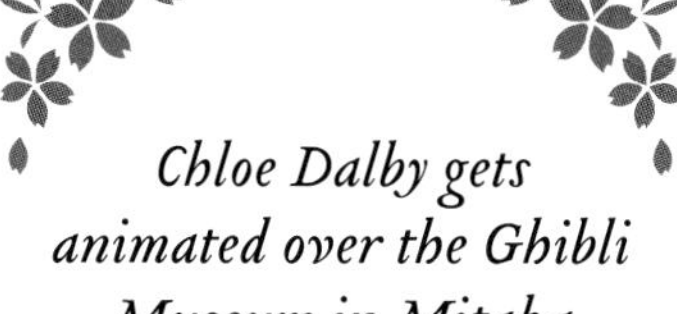

Chloe Dalby gets animated over the Ghibli Museum in Mitaka

Japanese animation inspires fierce reactions. People adore it or they loathe it. I understand. But while I dislike the cloyingly cute cartoons, I appreciate this Japanese art form in independent films, and especially in the work of Hayao Miyazaki.

Miyazaki and his staff at Studio Ghibli are some of the most sophisticated animators of our time. Studio Ghibli films flirt with magic realism that never entirely reveals itself. Even as a child, watching Miyazaki's 1988 film *My Neighbor Totoro* changed the way I experienced cinema.

I learned to pick up on the subtleties of environment—in Miyazaki's worlds, the ordinary transforms into the extraordinary, and alternate realities creep beneath stones and behind branches. Thus I was not surprised when I arrived at the red pine grove at Mitaka's Inokashira Park to find a utopia of the imagination. Within the first five minutes at the Ghibli Museum, I felt spirited into one of Miyazaki's animated fantasies.

The first hints of the Studio Ghibli sensibility are the illustrated buses that ferry visitors from the Mitaka Train Station to the museum. They are decorated as the famous Cat Bus from *My Neighbor Totoro.* At the museum itself, you will find an actual Cat Bus, a furry tour de force that, I learned mid-clamber, is only open to children ages twelve and under.

Slightly deflated but undaunted, I found many other diversions for all ages, starting with the first floor's exhibit on the history of animation. Among the optical illusions and flickering old-time animations (all featuring Ghibli characters), the stroboscope was drawing the biggest crowd, and for good reason. Crowded with figurines in various poses, a circular table spun, and the figures appeared to come to life in the flashing strobe light. Campy animation at its three-dimensional finest.

The exhibit "Where a Film is Born" is by far my favorite. Visitors have the opportunity to peek into a romanticized working studio of a fictional animator, a tableau frozen in time as if the artist had just left the room to take a short walk or make a cup of tea. The walls are lined with illustrations and sketches, the bookshelves are overflowing with embellished tomes and curios, and desks are laden with open sketchbooks and watercolor paints glistening in the warm lamplight.

The five rooms in "Where a Film is Born" give insight into the process of traditional animation, while never losing the magical spirit characteristic of Studio Ghibli. This atmosphere runs through each exhibit and is woven into the fabric of the museum. Wherever I wandered there was something that drew me onward. Even the washrooms are worth a visit.

The interior of the Ghibli Museum has an unusual configuration. The interconnecting displays have been likened to a maze, but I think that the rooms follow a creative train of thought, guiding you through bridged passageways and up spiral staircases, from one curiosity to another. Certainly they reflect Miyazaki's intention: "*Maigo ni narou yo, issho ni*" ("Let's get lost together").

Don't forget to duck into the Saturn Theater in the basement to watch a Studio Ghibli original animated short. And in case you don't find a special souvenir at the museum's Mamma Aiuto! gift shop, you can exchange your reservation ticket for a special keepsake ticket, made from a strip of real 35mm film once used in a theater. Take it to the Straw Hat Café and enjoy a cup of tea while you try to figure out what film your ticket is from.

Visiting the Ghibli Museum

The museum is located within Mitaka Inokashira Park on the edge of Tokyo. Entrance requires advance purchase. Tickets are available in Japan at any Lawson convenience store. To buy tickets outside of Japan, refer to the Ghibli Museum official website.

1-1-83 Simorenjaku
Mitaka City
www.ghibli-museum.jp/en

Train: From Shinjuku Station take the Chuo Train Line to Mitaka Station

Directions: The museum is a fifteen-minute walk from the south exit of the Mitaka Station. You can also take the Cat Bus from the station to the museum.

My Neighbor Totoro

To read a review of this film, go to page 243.

Aichi Prefecture

Sara Francis-Fujimura travels back in time in Inuyama

Like many Japanophiles, I have spent a lot of time in Tokyo and Kyoto learning about feudal Japan, that famous era of shogun and samurai. But the most entertainingly educational museum I have ever been to in the country is Museum Meiji-Mura in Inuyama.

A visit to this museum is like a trip back to daily life in Japan after Commodore Perry and his black ships sailed into Edo (Tokyo) Bay in 1853, throwing open Japan's gates and ending the country's more than two-hundred-year self-imposed isolation from the rest of the world. It's a fascinating time period, when traditional culture collided with modern Western innovations.

At Museum Meiji-Mura, over sixty Meiji-era (1868-1912) buildings have been relocated or replicated on the museum's expansive grounds. Though the history lesson went straight over my children's heads, Meiji-Mura is family friendly. To my kids, aged five and seven at the time, it was a fun place to ride on trains and streetcars, chat with each other on one of the

NTT-sponsored videophones, and chase dragonflies through fragrant flower gardens. The highlight for our family was visiting the Shichijo Police Box. The friendly *omawari-san* outfitted our children with old-timey police hats and posed with them for the perfect Kodak moment.

We contemplated a romantic horse-drawn carriage ride around the grounds, but passed. And we weren't brave enough to attempt the penny-farthing bicycle with the giant front wheel and tiny back one. Instead, when our feet got tired from walking around the nearly hundred-hectare site, we jumped onto one of the streetcars, which were still in service in Kyoto up through the 1970s. My train-loving husband Toshi also relished riding on the velvet-covered hardwood seats of the museum's working steam locomotive, restored to its original Meiji-period condition.

If you are looking for an activity off the normal tourist path that is fun as well as educational, a trip to Museum Meiji-Mura is an excellent choice. I didn't see another foreigner the whole day, which made me wonder if the museum isn't one of the best-kept cultural and historical secrets in Japan.

Museum Meiji-Mura

The museum is an easy day trip from Nagoya.

1 Uchiyama
Inuyama
(0568) 67-0314
www.meijimura.com/english/index.html

Train: Meitetsu Inuyama Line from Nagoya Station to Inuyama Station. From here, take one of the Meitetsu buses that run several times per hour.

Where to eat

After working up an appetite with all the walking, instead of lunching at one of the high-priced restaurants nearby, Sara and her family enjoyed a picnic lunch of croquettes on the lush lawn between the Imperial Hotel and picturesque Lake Iruka.

Savvy souvenirs

Many sites in Japan have free, fist-sized rubber stamps of their attractions available for stamping. Be sure to outfit your kids with a small notebook so they can collect rubber-stamped images of the Meiji-Mura sites during your visit.

Toy vendor's cart in Tokyo's Shitamachi neighborhood

Boys dressed in blue, girls dressed in red

When in Rome

Lessons on living local and making yourself at home

In his book *Be Here Now*, Ram Dass writes, "To him that has had the experience, no explanation is necessary; to him that has not, none is possible." Although he was not referring to Japan, no truer words can be spoken about Japanese culture. The only way to truly understand it is to fully immerse yourself in it.

It's not uncommon to feel like an outsider when you first arrive, but given the chance, the Japanese people are more than willing to invite you into their world. And what a world it is! Whenever I try to describe or explain it, the word *paradox* always springs to mind. It seems that no matter what statement I make, my next thought seems to contradict it.

If I say that Japan is the most beautiful land on earth, I need only remind myself of the bleak February landscape between Narita Airport and Tokyo Station that was my first impression of this "most beautiful" country. If I say that Japan has some of the world's most impressive ancient architecture, I remember my disappointment when I learned that many of its landmarks had been burned to the ground, and what I was looking at were nearly new replicas. If I say that the Japanese are the friendliest people I've ever met, I think back to the time when a cantankerous old woman refused to take money from my *gaijin* hand.

Regardless of these contradictions, my Japan experience was the happiest and most cherished of my life. I made irrevocable friendships and indelible memories, I saw as much of the country as my time and budget allowed, and I experienced every tradition and celebration that I possibly could. While I'm sure that your time in Japan will be as enjoyable as mine, it's almost certain that you too will have at least one "paradox moment" during your travels. In this, you will not be alone, as the contributors to this chapter make clear.

Forewarned, you can prepare yourself for potentially awkward encounters, like the visit Jennifer Huber takes to

Construction workers in Tokyo

a spa in Shizuoka. During a slimming body wrap, when the aesthetician giggles "big," Jennifer is suddenly self-conscious of her curvaceous figure. And Joyce Jemison must overcome her shyness more than once, when she soaks stark naked—as is the custom—at a hot spring in Nikko, and when she undresses down to her underwear for the rare opportunity to try on a traditional kimono with her host family in Iwanuma.

Lodging, too, can offer uncomfortable moments. Visiting Japan's notorious love hotels, Sugu Althomsons learns the etiquette of not making eye contact, while Steve Cooper practices thinking small within the confines of an Osaka capsule hotel. As for me, I discover that foreigners are not always given the warmest welcome, when nearly every innkeeper in the town of Aizu Wakamatsu refuses to take me in for the night.

From using Japanese toilets and riding in a Japanese taxi, to avoiding chopstick faux pas and learning to do your very best—even if that means eating a food you really don't like—these tales will help you overcome the occasional blunder. What I like most about them is the humility and humor with which they are told. No matter what the situation, the writers still love Japan. In fact, like me, they love Japan all the more for discovering that it's not all sake and cherry blossoms.

Fukushima Prefecture

Celeste Heiter experiences a lodging crisis in Aizu Wakamatsu

When you travel deep into the heart of Japan's main island of Honshu, the sophisticated trappings of Tokyo fall away with each passing kilometer, and the people of rural Japan emerge, many of whom are set in their provincial ways, unaffected by the cosmopolitan attitudes of their big-city neighbors. To a foreigner visiting the island's rustic Fukushima Prefecture, this can be both a blessing and a curse.

We arrived in the historic town of Aizu Wakamatsu late one afternoon during a particularly busy holiday season. Japan has an excellent network of tourist bureaus, and as was often our habit, we had waited until we reached our destination to arrange for our lodgings. We were met at the local bureau by Toshiko, a friendly and capable young woman who was eager to help us find a place to spend the night.

We were Toshiko's last customers of the day, and she gave us her undivided attention as she began making telephone calls to nearby inns. Meanwhile, we browsed around the tourist office, which was beautifully decorated with photographs, artifacts, and local crafts, until we began to realize that something was wrong. Toshiko was on her fifth or sixth phone call and still had found no lodgings for us.

The tension became increasingly audible in her voice as she made the eighth, ninth, and tenth attempts. Based on the half of the conversation that I could hear, and what little Japanese I could understand, it seemed that not one of the proprietors of the inns she contacted was willing to put up a couple of foreigners for the night.

I managed to infer from a comprehensible word here and there that they thought foreigners were too fussy. Foreigners didn't know that they were supposed to remove their shoes, they couldn't use chopsticks, they didn't know how to use Japanese toilets, and didn't like sleeping on the floor. Some innkeepers simply didn't allow *gaijin* to stay in their establishments.

Long after Toshiko should have closed up for the night and gone home, she was still on the phone, trying to find an inn that would take us. By now, that poor woman was so ashamed and humiliated by the refusals of all those innkeepers that she was on her knees on the *tatami* mat sobbing "*onegaishimasu*" into the telephone receiver, pleading with one after another to give us a room for the night. Meaning "Please do this for me," *onegaishimasu* can be used for anything from a small favor to, as in this case, a desperate plea. Still, no one was willing to take us in.

We were beginning to entertain the notion of sleeping at the train station or on a park bench, when at long last, after calls to no fewer than two dozen inns, Toshiko finally succeeded. Somewhere in the village of Aizu Wakamatsu, she had found the only innkeeper who would open her doors to a couple of weary *America-jin*. As if that weren't enough, Toshiko drove us there in her own car. I have no doubt that if she hadn't found lodgings for us, she would have put us up for the night in her home.

Having grown up in Alabama, amid the racial tensions of the Deep South, I witnessed firsthand the kind of insults and cruelty that people can inflict upon each other. I can honestly say that I have never engaged in racist epithets or exclusionary prejudice, but until that day in Aizu Wakamatsu, I had never been on the receiving end either.

The inn exceeded our now modest expectations. It was nicely kept, the evening meal was delicious and elegantly served, the futons were clean and comfortable, and to our added delight, the innkeeper and her daughters actually took a liking to us. After the dinner dishes were cleared away, we spent the rest of the evening chatting with them, and even took a group photo to commemorate the occasion.

It was an uplifting end to what had become a disappointing day, and although I had learned a painful lesson, Toshiko's kindness, and the gracious hospitality of our innkeeper, restored my faith in the people of rural Japan.

Aizu Wakamatsu

Samurai history, hot springs, signature catfish dishes, and the country's second largest national park are among the attractions around Aizu Wakamatsu. To find out more, visit the regional tourism website.

www.city.aizuwakamatsu.fukushima.jp/e/sight/index.html

Getting to Aizu Wakamatsu

A visit to Aizu Wakamatsu should be done as an overnight trip or longer from Tokyo. From Tokyo Station, take the Tohoku Shinkansen to Koriyama Station. Transfer to the Banetsu-Saisen Line to Aizu Wakamatsu Station.

Foreign relations

When preparing for your travels, you may read or hear about xenophobia in Japan, but in general, the people of Japan are warm, open, and hospitable toward foreigners, especially in cosmopolitan cities. However, there are a few who are either wary of or resentful toward visitors.

Japan has had a long history of political and cultural isolation, and in remote regions, there are people who have never met or even seen a foreigner, except perhaps on television, which doesn't always portray us in the most flattering light. Therefore, certain Japanese people don't know how to react, or what to expect when facing an encounter with a *gaijin*, as foreigners are called in Japan. Even the word itself carries with it a mildly negative connotation.

On one occasion, an old woman tending a sundries kiosk refused to take money from my hand, insisting instead that I put it down on the counter for her to pick up. Another time, in the access tunnels of Ikebukuro Station, an old veteran, accompanied by his nurse, blocked my path and refused to let me pass, even though it was he who was walking against the flow of pedestrian traffic. Why these particular individuals were openly hostile toward me is anybody's guess. However, since they were both elderly, I've speculated that perhaps they suffered a tragic loss in World War II; perhaps they'd had a bad experience; or maybe they were just raised with the kind of narrow-minded and antiquated prejudices that can be found in any society.

But negative encounters are rare in Japan, and for each of these reluctant or unfriendly individuals, there are countless others who look forward to the opportunity to get to know visitors from other countries, and even seek them out. Once, while traveling in Fukushima Prefecture, an old woman at Yunokami Onsen chased me for two blocks to present me with a souvenir cigarette lighter. In Tokyo, total strangers would stop me on the street and offer to buy me dinner or a drink, just for the chance to spend a few minutes chatting in English with me. Best of all, while staying at Chatani Ryokan in Ohara, the mother of a lovely family of five children invited us to visit them at their home, without even asking our names. That family eventually became lifelong friends, and my son Will recently spent the summer with them at their home in Kofu.

You never know who you might meet on your travels in Japan, but if you happen upon someone who is openly hostile, shrug it off and move on, knowing that the next person will probably greet you with a welcoming smile.

Shizuoka Prefecture

Jennifer Huber leaves her body fat in Shizuoka

Thinking my palate wouldn't tolerate raw fish and other strange foods, friends told me that I would lose weight in Japan. As I lay on a medical-style table with the lower half of my body snugly fit into a long nylon bag, I realized they were right ... but for the wrong reasons.

I was spending an afternoon in the city of Shizuoka, indulging in the slim-life experience at Art Beauty, an aesthetic salon. Prior to my getting into the bag, Yuki, the young technician, slathered my thighs and stomach with a clear, jelly-like substance. My legs, waist, and stomach were then tightly wrapped in plastic wrap before she zipped me into the "Comtheran." An air hose stuck out of each leg, and I wondered how in the world this would reduce my body fat.

She placed a towel over my breasts, patted them, giggled, and said, "Big."

Returning her smile, I hoped my chest remained the same size after the process.

She turned on the machine and asked, "Okay?"

"*Hai*," I nodded.

Once alone, I realized why she asked how I felt. The bag was constricting slowly, like a snake squeezing its prey. Feeling uncomfortable and finding it difficult to breathe, I attempted to maintain my composure and called out. "Help. Um. Help. Tight."

Apparently, neither Yuki nor the other staff members knew the meaning of these words, and no one came to my rescue. The tightness intensified, and just when I thought my eyeballs were going to pop out, the bag relaxed. A pattern of contracting and relaxing continued for fifteen minutes. This repeated process was massaging my body to promote blood circulation, which is supposed to reduce body fat. And maybe it did. As well as light headed, I felt trimmer after being released from the bag.

I was then led to an area where my body fat and metabolism were measured. Turned out my metabolic rate was higher than the average Japanese person, and my body fat was fifteen points above normal, so I was lectured on the importance of nutrition and exercise.

Next, Yuki led my curvaceous, nearly naked body to the "giggle machine." Face up on another medical-type table, I anxiously awaited the process. I heard the roar of a machine charging up, and before I knew it, Yuki was rubbing my body with what looked like a white plastic vacuum cleaner hose. Unlike a vacuum, the air blew out instead of in, and I could feel and see my fat ripple as she rubbed the hose over me, head to toe. The air tickled, and I couldn't help but laugh. Yuki laughed, too.

A purifying facial followed. My face was wrapped with gauze, followed by an application of a green tea mixture using Shizuoka brand tea. Green tea is rich in antioxidants and vitamins good for revitalizing the skin. While my face soaked in the benefits for fifteen minutes, my hands and feet were pampered with massages.

My hosts that night commented on how much my face radiated and how much slimmer I looked. Admittedly, my jeans fit a little looser, and when the time came, a little less of me returned to the United States.

Art Beauty

Art Beauty has many locations throughout Shizuoka Prefecture. Below is the address of the branch I visited. Using the Art Beauty website, you can also find other locations by clicking on the links next to the thumbnail photos halfway down the page. For each photo there is a pop-up of a map to that location; look for the location name listed in the URL.

1-2 Tenma-cho, 4F
Shizuoka
www.emuart.jp/beauty/art.html (Japanese)
(0120) 80-4436

Train: Tokaido Shinkansen or Tokaido Main Line from Tokyo to Shizuoka Station.

Directions: From the station, follow Tenma-cho Street north for two blocks. Turn right at the FS Building. Art Beauty is on the left at the first intersection.

Visiting Shizuoka

While you can do Art Beauty in Shizuoka as a day trip from Tokyo, you may want to stay for a few days, since the coastline of Shizuoka Prefecture is quite beautiful, and inland it borders Mt. Fuji.

www.shizuoka-guide.com/english/

Tochigi Prefecture

Joyce Jemison soaks in bliss at an onsen in Nikko

I am eighteen years old. I am thousands of kilometers from my home in the Napa Valley. And I am soaking stark naked in an *onsen* under the stars in Nikko, with two fifty-something women I just met a few days ago. How, you may ask, did I get here? Why ... on a group tour, of course.

The Napa-Iwanuma Sister Cities Thirty-Fifth Anniversary Tour had begun well-intentioned enough, with the coordinator hoping for a group of twenty travelers. What he ended up with was me, Betty, and Nancy, plus two older married couples. I was the only person under fifty years old. At first it felt a little weird being so much younger than everyone else. But even with such a big age difference, the others made me feel welcome and respected.

Both Betty and Nancy were kind and considerate. Betty, my roommate, was into photography, busily snapping away everywhere we went. Much of the time, I hung out with her, while she took pictures to her heart's content, and I stood in awe of everything around me. She was adventurous and open to trying new foods and experiences, while Nancy seemed more comfortable with things that were familiar to her. Ironically, because of that, it was Nancy who convinced Betty and me to join her for a soak in the *onsen*, since it was an experience she'd enjoyed in the past. Betty and I were concerned that we would be uncomfortable in the cold night air, but Nancy assured us that it would feel refreshing after our soak.

Nancy waited in the hall outside our hotel room, while Betty and I donned our special *onsen* ensemble: a white cotton *yukata* that was rather long for my small stature, a heavy brown shoulder wrap, and a pair of thin white slippers that were much too large for my feet. On our way out the door, we grabbed our washcloths, and headed down the hallway to the hot springs. Along the way, we passed two Japanese women coming back from the *onsen*, giggling at the sight of us. I was sure that I must have been the subject of their laughter, being noticeably too short for my *yukata*, shuffling along in the slippers, and most likely with the wrong side of my *yukata* on top. Unless you're a corpse, the left side is supposed to be wrapped over the right side.

At the end of the hallway, we had to cross several meters in the open air, which nipped at us through our robes as if to warn us that it was only going to be worse upon our return to our rooms. But Nancy promised us once again that after sitting in the hot water, we would feel like boiled lobsters, and the cold air would be welcome afterward. Having visited the hot springs back home in the Napa Valley, I wondered whether our *onsen* experience would be anything like going to the spas in Calistoga.

Once inside the *onsen* building, we found ourselves in a small wood-paneled anteroom outside the washroom. With my curiosity and excitement mounting, we undressed and put our garments into plastic hampers neatly stacked on shelves. There were instructions written in *kanji* on the hampers, but because none of us could read Japanese, we had to assume we were following proper *onsen* protocol. Once we were undressed, I felt suddenly awkward being naked with two women whom I barely knew. But if Betty and Nancy were nervous at all, they didn't show it. Nancy explained that being fully exposed around other people is just part of the *onsen* experience.

Through a sliding glass door, we arrived at the pre-*onsen* washroom. Betty and I stared blankly at the unfamiliar setup: low faucets, short wooden stools, plastic bowls, and a couple of bottles of colored liquids. Drawing upon her previous *onsen* experience, Nancy explained that we should sit on the low stools, wash our bodies with the red liquid and our hair with the white, and rinse by dumping water-filled bowls over ourselves. Sitting on the small wooden stool, washing my body and hair, rinsing with the bowl, with two other naked women, I was acutely aware that I wasn't in Calistoga anymore!

Having washed and rinsed, hoping we had cleansed ourselves adequately enough by Japanese standards, we passed through yet another sliding glass door, and making our way as if by Braille down a cobble-walled stairway, we waded through the natural overflow from the *onsen*. As I adjusted to the invitingly warm temperature of the spring, while peering to see the stairs through the deepening water, the gentle ripples and soothing flow were drawing me in, caressing my body, promising the bliss that would follow.

At the outer edge of the pool, we sat down on a smooth stone bench just below the water's surface. Slowly, the hot mineral water enveloped me, drowning my cares, relieving my tension. I was melting like butter in the sweet warmth of the spring. The fact that I was fully exposed escaped my mind, as I relaxed in the peace and comfort of the *onsen*. The stars above added their own touch of serenity, spreading their gentle light across the dark canvas of the night sky.

After a half-hour soak in the calming mineral water, we emerged, put on our *yukata*, and headed back to our rooms. Nancy was right, the chilly breeze didn't feel nearly as uncomfortable as we had feared. It was actually refreshing after poaching in the hot spring. Back in our hotel room at the end of a long day, Betty and I went right to sleep, satisfied that we had fully experienced one of Japan's finest pleasures.

Chuzenji Kanaya Hotel

From the outside, this hotel looks like a contemporary log cabin, while the inside offers a cozy and comfortable atmosphere. Some of the rooms have beautiful views of Lake Chuzenji.

2482 Chugushi
Nikko
(0288) 51-0001
www.kanayahotel.co.jp/english/chuzenji/
chuzenji@kanayahotel.co.jp

Sister cities

To find out more about Japan's sister cities around the world, visit the following website.

www.sister-cities.org

Hot spring etiquette

Contributor Elizabeth Sharpe offers the following:

- Even if you wear a bathing suit, don't be surprised that everyone else is naked. Hot springs in Japan are typically enjoyed in the buff, because the minerals in the water are meant to soak into the skin. Though naked is the norm, many Japanese understand that Western customs are different. If you're not comfortable bathing naked, ask the manager what the bathing rules are, since some baths do allow swimwear.
- Both men and women carry a "modesty towel," which is about the size of a small hand towel. After removing clothes and when standing up out of the

water, the towel is draped down over the front. In the water, both men and women will fold the towels and place them on their heads or lay the towels on the edge of the pool.

- Men and women remain separate, even if they are bathing in the same pool. They sit across from each other, and avert their eyes. They don't address or talk to people of the opposite sex while bathing.

Discovering Japan's onsen

There are numerous resources for finding *onsen* to enjoy during your trip. You might start with the photograph-laden book, *The Japanese Spa: A Guide to Japan's Finest Ryokan and Onsen*, by Elizabeth Heilman Brooke, or the website *Secret Japan.*

www.secret-japan.com/onsen/

Osaka Prefecture

Steve Cooper spends the night in a capsule hotel in Osaka

Before my Japanese friend Taro and I went out to eat blowfish in Osaka with a fake-Louis Vuitton dealer, there was one thing we had to do. We needed a hotel for the night. As luck would have it, we found a capsule hotel nearby, and since I had never stayed in one, I jumped at the opportunity.

Taro negotiated our stay with the hotel manager, at the remarkably cheap rate of about twenty dollars each. We left our bags with the man, who promised to look after them. While I said what I thought would be my final farewell to my luggage, he handed over our keys, explaining that they were for our lockers, which were available for storing clothes and other small personal belongings that we might need during our stay.

Osaka has a great nightlife ... a little too great, in fact. At about five in the morning we managed to find our way back to the hotel. The elevator took us to the fourth floor, where we located the lockers that fit our keys. After a quick change into my bathrobe, I headed back down to my "room." The capsule was exactly as one might imagine; a hole in the wall, measuring about one meter by one meter by two meters. I don't want to sound crude, but a capsule hotel is basically a morgue, with one distinct difference—signs of life from the residents.

Surprisingly, there was a television in my capsule, but at that hour I didn't have the energy to watch it. It took me a while to figure out that I was supposed to sleep with my head at the far end of the capsule, which I assume meant less likelihood of waking up to see a stranger changing in front of me, since the capsules don't have doors, but just shades to provide a bit of privacy and block the light.

When I awoke at nine, without thinking I sat up and banged my head on the ceiling. My first instinct was to assume that, like Gulliver, I had been abducted by very small people with a fetish for hard mattresses. But my memory soon came flooding back. And the sudden urge to get out of that tiny space alive, combined with the fact that in fifteen minutes I would be charged for an extra night, forced me out of bed.

Crawling out of the capsule, I found Taro asleep on the floor. Apparently, he had become even more disorientated than I had. Once I roused him, we hurriedly dressed and gathered our belongings for check out. On our way out the door, we passed a confused-looking backpacker. Taro and I exchanged wry looks, and then headed out into the bright morning sunshine.

Capsule Hotel Inn Osaka

This is said to be the first capsule hotel in Japan and is quite popular with foreign travelers.

9-5 Doyamamachi
Kita District
Osaka
(06) 6314-2100

Subway: Midosuji Line to Umeda Station.

Capsule Inn Akihabara

At least half the cost of an inexpensive hotel room, this is a great economical choice. The inn offers Wi-Fi on every floor, as well as a Japanese bath, just like at larger hotels. Because it's just a few minutes' walk from Akihabara Station, it's convenient no matter where you're headed in Tokyo.

6-9 Akihabara
Taito District
Tokyo
(03) 3251-0841
www.capsuleinn.com

Train: Yamanote Line to Akihabara Station.

Subway: Hibiya Line to Akihabara Station.

General Japan

Joyce Jemison plays dress-up, Japanese style

It's a chilly April evening in the small city of Iwanuma, the second night of my stay with my host family, the Dendos. After a full day of sightseeing and shopping in nearby Sendai with my fellow traveling companions and their hosts, I am back at the Dendo home for the night, and in for a uniquely Japanese experience: Mrs. Dendo has just informed me that she has invited her friend to come over and help dress her daughter Mari and me in kimono.

It's about nine, and although I'm tired after a busy day, the very thought of such a rare opportunity energizes me. It's not every day that a foreigner gets the chance to try on such elegant garments, and I'm thrilled.

Mrs. Dendo has already gotten out several bins, each containing what looks like hundreds of pieces of white cloth in all shapes and sizes, a length of silk cord in deep shades of crimson and flame-orange, and two large, grandly colored robes. Mrs. Dendo's robe is a light shade of green with hand-painted blossoms of pink, blue, yellow, purple, and red, dancing amid delicate leaves, ribbons of mauve, and patches of daisies. The other robe, which belongs to Mari, has a black background, decorated with red, green, and yellow circular fans floating among clouds of purple and green, entwined with threads of red, white, and yellow.

The doorbell rings. My host mother's friend has arrived, and it's time to play dress-up, Japanese style. Mrs. Dendo will tend to me, while her friend dresses Mari.

First, Mari asks me to undress down to my lingerie, and I feel a little bashful as Mrs. Dendo wraps me in the *susoyoke*, a simple white tunic. Next, she asks me what size shoes I wear. I tell her six, and by her confused expression, I realize they have a different sizing system. Hoping it will fit, she hands me a *tabi*, a special ankle-length sock made of plain white cotton, with clasps on the inner side, and a split between the toes for wearing the thong sandals. *Tabi* are measured the same way shoes are, and when Mari sees me struggling with it, trying to fasten the side clasps that don't want to reach around my foot, she hands me one that is slightly larger: a size twenty-three and a half. Perfect! The *tabi* feel soft as they hug my feet.

After fitting me with the *susoyoke* tunic, Mrs. Dendo wraps me in a long-sleeved *nagajuban* robe, followed by many long strips of cloth, some used to flatten my stomach like a corset, and others to drape over my whole body. As Mari and I act like dolls for the two women, Mari asks me every few minutes if I can still breathe. I answer yes, although it is a little harder now with so many layers constricting my ribs and stomach.

Throughout the process, I marvel at how wrong I was about kimono. Seeing pictures of them, and watching women wearing them on the streets of Tokyo, I assumed that they weren't that complicated, perhaps consisting of a few undergarments beneath the outer robe. But now that I'm being dressed in one myself, I realize that this is not so. I guess that's how you recognize a true work of art: when something complex appears deceptively simple.

After a half hour of being wrapped in one piece of cloth after another, it's finally time to slip into the elaborate outer robes. My host mother puts the green one on me, while Mari gets the black one. Next come the thin boards called *obi-ita*, which are placed on our stomachs to support the *obi* sash that will wrap around our midriffs.

My *obi* is white with a pink rope imprinted on it, made to appear as if it's tied in a bow on the right. Mari's *obi* is also white, decorated with orange semicircles on the top and bottom. Hers also includes the braided crimson and orange *datejime*, which is tied over her *obi*. To finish my *obi*, my host mother ties the ends into two fan-shaped bows in the back … and the ensemble is complete!

Standing there in this lovely outfit, I am honored, and even a little astonished. I feel special beyond my wildest imagination. While Mari and I exchange smiles and pose for photographs, I feel welcomed into the Japanese culture, and embraced with open arms. Losing myself in the moment, it's almost as if I too am Japanese. It's like a dream I never knew I had, and yet, it has come true this night.

Kimono around Japan

Ome Kimono Museum

Highlights at this museum, which is located in park-like surroundings, include imperial and period kimono.

4-629 Baigo
Ome Town
Tokyo
(0428) 76-2019
www3.kitanet.ne.jp/~kimono/oume/index.html

Train: Chuo Train Line from Tokyo's Shinjuku Station to Tachikawa Station. Transfer to the Ome Line and get off at Ome Station.

Nishijin Textile Center

This is the place for all things kimono. This fascinating facility features a museum, silk weaving and silk painting demonstrations, a kimono fashion show, kimono rentals, and even the opportunity to be dressed in a kimono and photographed by the staff. Reservations are required.

Horikawa-Imadegawa Minami-iru
Kamigyo District
Kyoto
(81-075) 451-9231
www.nishijin.or.jp/eng/brochure/

Subway: Karasuma Line from Kyoto Station to Imadegawa Station. From there, it's about a ten-minute walk. The textile center's website has a detailed map.

Kaga Yuzen Traditional Industry Center

For more on the silk kimono factory at this center in Kanazawa, go to Celeste Heiter's essay on page 105.

Celeste Heiter commits chopsticks taboo

On my first day teaching English, I went across the street to the basement level of My City department store during my break and bought some takeout tempura and a scoop of potato salad for lunch. I returned to the teachers' lounge to enjoy it in the company of my co-workers, and had just dived into the potato salad with a pair of chopsticks when I realized that I had no napkin. Not wanting to lay my chopsticks on the coffee table, I stuck them firmly into the potato salad and set the dish down to go in search of one. I heard a gasp of horror from several of the teachers.

"What?" I inquired, naively. "What'd I do?"

I was promptly informed by Judy, a rather intense young Australian woman, that offerings of food with chopsticks standing upright in them are presented to the spirits of the dead at funerals and gravesites, and to do so among the living is strictly taboo.

I had just committed the ultimate breach of etiquette. And that's not all. I soon learned that one should never point or otherwise gesticulate with chopsticks, that chopsticks should never be used to spear a morsel of food, that they should never be crossed in an X on a plate, and that the end of the chopstick that has been in your mouth should never be used to take food from a shared plate. It is also impolite to rub disposable chopsticks together to remove splinters, because it implies that they are cheap.

As if that weren't enough, food should also never be passed from one set of chopsticks to another because it is reminiscent of another ritual practiced at funerals. In this one, the charred remains of the deceased are transferred from the crematory chamber to the burial urn by passing them from person to person using chopsticks.

So, when it comes to chopsticks, if you want to stay out of trouble, the best rule of thumb is never to let them stray from the short and narrow path between your plate and your mouth.

Shopping for Chopsticks

Chopsticks make excellent souvenirs, both for yourself and for friends and family back home. Not only are they economical, readily available, and easy to transport in your luggage, your loved ones will remember you fondly each time they use them. This book features several essays with recommendations for places that carry a selection of chopsticks, including Oriental Bazaar (page 149), Tokyu Hands (page 195), hundred-yen stores (page 163), Kappabashi District (page 150), and Wajima lacquer shops (page 154).

B.Y.O.C.

Environmentally conscious travelers will be happy to know that there is a growing trend in Japan that encourages diners to carry their own chopsticks instead of using the disposable ones provided by restaurants. The Marche group in Osaka even offers a modest discount to those who bring their own chopsticks, and will wash them for you after your meal.

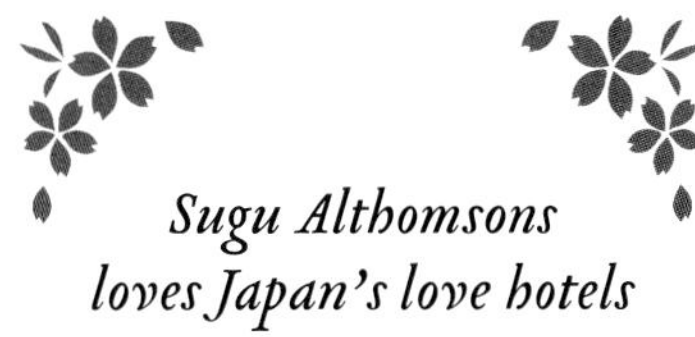

Sugu Althomsons loves Japan's love hotels

Japan's love hotels are havens for extramarital affairs, and for young Japanese who want privacy with their partners, since most live with their parents until they get married. That said, love hotels aren't just for locals. They also offer foreigners a fun, comfortable, and relatively cheap place to spend the night.

Be careful asking for a love hotel, though. As common as they are, few Japanese I've met felt comfortable giving directions to one. I usually identify them on my own, by their neon lights and gaudy décor. Sometimes they look like faux castles; sometimes they have flashing hearts or bursting neon fireworks. The names are usually random too: Hotel Yours, Hotel Image, or even the ultra-bizarre Gang Snowman.

Love hotels range from very tasteless to very classy, with everything in between. My companion and I stayed in a room that had an elegant (although fake) fireplace, but we also discovered one with tacky red velvet on everything, including the walls. Love hotels are typically designed for maximum comfort, with Western-style beds rather than typical Japanese futons, and many have evolved from fetish themed to romantic themed, geared more toward feminine tastes.

Love hotels offer almost total anonymity. I usually never see a staff member, even when it comes time to pay! The selection of available rooms is displayed in photographs that are lit up on a board on the wall in the lobby. Just pick the room that looks the most interesting to you. Each room is its own experience. One time, when we made our choice and paid, the path to our room was then lit, just like the Yellow Brick Road. Very rarely have I seen other guests making their way to the pay counter, but if I do, they usually avoid eye contact.

Amid all the glitter and bright lights of Japan, the first love hotel is difficult to spot, but once I knew what I was looking for, I could track one down in any city. Also, like birds of a feather, they tend to flock together. Good luck finding one, and enjoy your stay!

Love hotels in Tokyo

Located in the Shibuya District, a popular shopping and entertainment area, Love Hotel Hill is a good place to start, just to get a feel for what love hotels look like. Take the Yamanote Train Line or the Ginza Subway Line to Shibuya Station. Take the Hachiko exit toward the large intersection, and then venture into the side streets and alleyways off Dogenzaka Street.

Love hotel basics

Love hotels range from about $60 to $120, depending on what amenities, themes, and fetishes you prefer. Prices are for an overnight stay, but there are also "rest" plans for a few hours' stay, which run about half price. A love hotel is characterized by a sign out front that lists at least two prices: one for a "rest" and one for a "stay." The signs are usually written in English. Check-in for overnight stays start around 10 p.m., so you'll need to carry your luggage or put it in a coin locker for the day.

Catherine Tully is flush with advice for the ladies

After six months, living in Japan was killing my knees. Sitting on the floor much of the time was a big part of it, but, embarrassingly, using the Japanese bathroom is what really did it to me.

If you have never used a toilet in Japan, allow me to explain. Basically, it's like a urinal set into the floor. But this is hovering of a whole different kind, ladies. Believe me.

When you use a bathroom in Japan (sorry guys, I can only speak for females here), you need to get used to a number of things, and the toilet in the floor is just the beginning. Some establishments have plastic shoes by the bathroom that you slip your feet into after stepping out of your shoes. When finished, you return the plastic shoes to their original spot, and reclaim your own. I'm assuming that the shoes are a courtesy in case you miss.

During the time I lived in Japan, I began to understand many things about local bathroom customs. I was even able to accept the musical toilet paper rolls I encountered from time to time. Still, there was one thing that continued to baffle me—the location of the toilet paper. No matter which bathroom I used, inevitably the roll was behind me, a very awkward place to reach for it. This was especially true considering I was squatting and balancing in plastic shoes that were always much too small for my size nine feet. Quite an image, isn't it?

Finally, after three years of friendship, I decided I knew my Japanese friend Yuko well enough to ask her about this rather unusual problem. I approached the subject carefully, so I wouldn't offend her. "Yuko-san," I began tentatively. "Can I ask you a strange question?"

She smiled and nodded. By now she was used to my asking odd things.

I took a deep breath and explained my dilemma, telling her all about how I would reach behind me to grab at the roll of toilet paper, sometimes flailing about to keep my balance, once even stepping into the toilet with a loud splash.

Yuko was in hysterics, laughing so hard she actually snorted. When she finally regained her composure, she explained the mystery to me. I wanted to curl up and die of embarrassment. It was so simple ...

You see, for three whole years I had been using the toilet completely backward! Without the benefit of anyone to copy, I did what you would do in the States. I walked into the stall, turned around, and did my thing. In Japan, you merely walk in and face the back wall, no turning around. I marvel that in all that time, I didn't figure out the simple answer to this dilemma on my own, especially when it was right in front of me all along.

Words of wisdom

- Never wear shoes with laces when in Japan. You are always taking your shoes off—not just to go into the bathroom—but at homes, schools, and many other places. Slip-on shoes are the way to go.
- For the same reason, make sure you are wearing presentable socks at all times.
- Under no circumstances forget to change back into your own shoes after going to the bathroom. This can be quite embarrassing. I speak from personal experience.
- Carry a small packet of tissues with you at all times. Some public bathrooms don't have toilet paper.
- Be reassured: some places do have Western-style toilets.

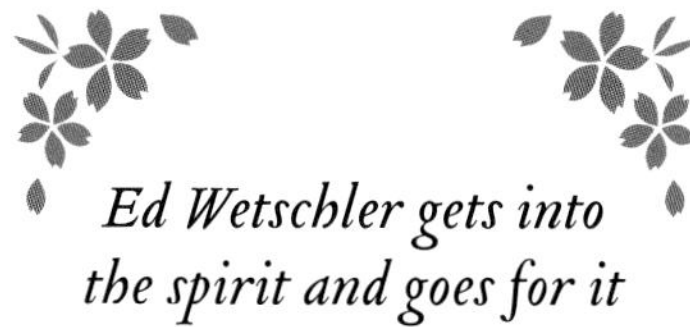

Ed Wetschler gets into the spirit and goes for it

Ganbatte! Persist! Do your best! Parents, teachers, coaches, and business managers in Japan exhort their charges to work hard, to be determined, to persevere. Friends encourage each other too, sometimes using "*ganbatte*" as a social greeting.

My wife Carol, who spent most of her childhood in Japan, feels that the "*ganbatte*" imperative does not just mean "Do your best," but rather "Do *better* than your best." And, she adds, "Don't even think about wimping out."

Carol is the daughter of a Japanese woman who could teach us all a thing or two about *gambari* (persistence). Her mother Mieko, lost her first husband, a member of the Imperial Armed Forces, during World War II. At the time, she and their baby son Kazumi, were living with her husband's parents, who owned farmland outside of Tokyo. When Mieko refused their order to wed their second son, they made her leave.

Struggling to survive in a country destroyed by war, Mieko eventually had to let her in-laws take Kazumi back so he would have a better life. She then soldiered on, eventually meeting a handsome American serving in the occupation. They got married, he managed to arrange military assignments that would keep them in Japan for much of the next twenty years, and she had five more children, including Carol, the one I was lucky enough to wed.

But Mieko never gave up the wish to reconnect with Kazumi, despite the fact that his paternal grandparents died in the 1940s, leaving no clue as to the boy's whereabouts. She made inquiries for years. After struggling so long just to survive, she was now spending her energy struggling to find her first son.

In 1975, more than twenty-five years since Mieko had last seen Kazumi, Meiko's sister finally helped her track him down. Kazumi promptly booked a flight to Seattle, where Mieko and her family were living, and thanks to never-say-die *gambari*, mother and son were reunited.

Fast-forward fifteen years to my initial visit to Japan. Carol and I spent the first week on our own, riding the trains, visiting Carol's old haunts, savoring Kyoto and Nara and Takayama, and loving everything we ate, with the notable exception of *uni* (sea urchin), one of the few foods that I simply cannot abide. We also looked forward to week two, because that's when Carol would visit Kazumi and his family, whom I would finally meet for the first time. Carol's parents were staying with Kazumi, so we would see them as well.

When Kazumi picked us up at Kawaguchi Station, he impressed me as a trim, charismatic man, a Japanese Paul Newman behind the wheel of his very fast car. He took us to his home, which is built on a suburban plot, and large by Japanese standards, thanks to an inheritance from his paternal grandparents. He and his wife Fumiko made us feel welcome, and it was good to see Carol's parents again, and to meet Mieko's sister, as well as Fumiko and Kazumi's grown children.

Later, when we were all sitting around the low dinner table, talking and nursing Asahi beers, the doorbell rang. A delivery man came in with three huge boxes of sushi and sashimi, an extravagant gesture on Kazumi's part. More beers materialized, we toasted the fact that we were all together, and we plunged our chopsticks into one of the boxes.

This nearsighted *gaijin*—me—wasn't paying attention to the selection, but when I brought my chopsticks closer to my face, I was truly puzzled. "Carol," I whispered, "this isn't a sushi I've ever eaten in Japan or New York. What kind is it?"

She hesitated, then whispered back, "It's *uni*."

I looked up at everyone. They were all looking back at me.

"What should I do?" I muttered under my breath, panic stricken at seeming ungracious in these circumstances.

But I knew what I should do. I remembered how Mieko had persevered to survive during and after World War II. And I understood how weak it would be for me to shrink from the "horrors" of *uni* in the presence of my mother-in-law, a woman who had triumphed over unimaginable struggles.

Carol turned to me, smiled, and said just what I knew she would say, "*Ganbatte*!"

Minding your manners

Roger J. Davies and Osamu Ikeno have divided their book, *The Japanese Mind: Understanding Contemporary Culture*, into chapters that each deal with a specific aspect of Japanese culture, such as rituals, role models, relationships, etc. It's perfect for travelers wanting a deeper understanding of Japan.

Home delivery

One of Japan's best kept secrets is its *demae*, restaurant delivery services. At lunch and dinner time, *demae* couriers on bicycles and motorbikes take to the streets with *bento* boxes stacked up over their rear wheels, or carrying trays with one hand while steering with the other, on their way to deliver meals to homes and offices. *Demae* is offered by thousands of restaurants all over Japan, and *demae* couriers deliver everything from steaming bowls of udon to lavish sushi dinners, often at no extra charge. Food is often provided on regular tableware rather than take-out containers, and includes all utensils and condiments. When delivery customers are finished with the meals, they leave the trays and dishes outside the front door for the courier to pick up later. If you would like to order in while staying at a Japanese hotel or inn that doesn't provide meals or room service, ask your concierge or innkeeper for *demae* recommendations.

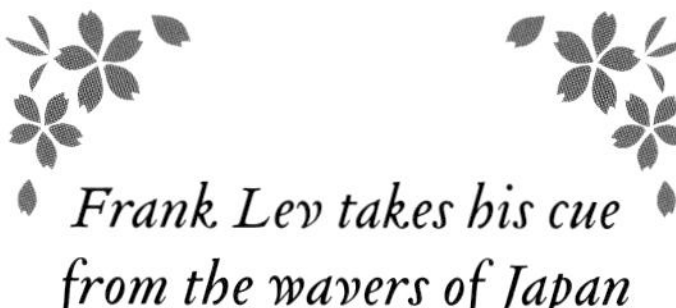

Frank Lev takes his cue from the wavers of Japan

In my hometown back in Ohio, there was an old man who everyone thought was crazy because he stood outside his house all day and waved to cars as they went by. I think most towns have a guy like this. He looks like he is having a great time. He seems to have found real peace. He is loony.

Many people recognize the guy as they drive by and honk their horns because it's fun to humor him. But he interprets it as a friendly sign and waves back, pleased. In his mind, he is doing his job. The real problem with a guy like this isn't that he is deluded, but that he was born in the wrong country.

In Japan, there is an army of workers whose job it is to wave. You see them wherever there is a construction site and the sidewalk must be blocked. Usually there is a waver at either end, and even in the heat of summer they are dressed in full uniform, complete with construction helmets, light-reflecting vests, and nifty flashlights with strobe flashers. When you approach the site, they give you the warmest, most gracious escort. Is there any lower, less-skilled job on earth than waving people around a blocked sidewalk? Yet these people give it 200 percent. I always wonder what is going on in their minds that allows them to do this with such dignity.

One of the most common expressions in Japan is "*Ganbatte*!" It means "Give it your best effort," and it is used anytime an event, a project, or even an ordinary workday is about to commence. The other day I was on my way to work, and I passed a construction site. The workers were, to my amusement, doing stretching exercises together. With the foreman leading them, they were shouting and stretching as if they were about to storm an enemy stronghold. As if to say, "This could be our last day on earth, let's do the best we can."

Walk into any convenience store and you will be greeted with "*Irasshaimase*!"—"Come on in!" If there are two people working, they will both greet you. If a third guy walks out of the back room as you walk through the store, he will greet you too. If someone has to go to the storeroom to get something, he will run. The staff will make every effort to serve you. That includes a big smile that most people reserve only for a long lost friend.

The Japanese people really take the concept of *ganbatte* to heart. In everything that they do, they give it their best effort in a way that only nerds and teachers' pets would in the States, where trying hard is definitely not cool. But in Japan even the cool people give it their best shot. So if you ever come to Japan, remember to go for it and be the very best tourist you can possibly be. Eat every food. Drink every beverage. Go to every temple, and celebrate every festival. And always remember: *ganbatte*!

Hand-painted antique sake bottles

Cotton yukata *drying in the sun*

Resources for the Road

Practical advice to help you prepare for your travels

In the winter of 1988, armed only with Boye De Mente's *Japan Almanac*, a set of alphabet primers called *Let's Learn Katakana* and *Let's Learn Hiragana*, and a tiny, well-thumbed pocket dictionary given to me by a friend, I took a leap of faith and moved to Japan. With plans for a lengthy stay, I had the luxury of time to discover Japan on my own, but it still presented a significant challenge.

In those days, the Internet was new, guidebooks I found in bookshops could be counted on the fingers of one hand, and video resources were limited to a few Kurosawa films and the television mini-series *Shogun*. When I look over the contents of this chapter, I have to wonder how different my trip would have been had these resources been available to me as I was planning my Japan adventure.

Booking a trip to Japan is easy. Preparing yourself for a meaningful journey requires considerably more effort. The best way to plan for any trip is by reading. Since you're holding *To Japan With Love* in your hands, you've obviously already discovered this little bijou as a source of inspiration. But you'll still need a basic guidebook. Since you'll rely on it for all your practical information, it's best not to order it sight unseen off the Internet. Before you make your choice, spend time in a bookstore familiarizing yourself with what's available, and picturing yourself using the book to make your way around Japan.

Literature, both classic and contemporary, still provides some of the best insights into the history and ideology of a culture. At the school where I worked in Tokyo, the teaching staff formed an informal book-swapping club centered around a table full of books in the break room, with the implicit policy: If you have a book, leave one; if you want a book, take one. It was in this marvelous little reading circle that I was first introduced to the classic works of Natsume Soseki, Yasunari Kawabata, and Yukio Mishima, three writers who profoundly influenced my

Traffic in Tokyo's Shinjuku District

Japan experience. In this chapter I share a few of my favorite works, with a few complementary selections by some of our writers, whose names are noted after their contributions.

Cinema is also an excellent way to gain insight. In selecting movies, I have deliberately left out such obvious choices as *Lost in Translation*, *Memoirs of a Geisha*, and the works of Japan's greatest filmmaker, Akira Kurosawa. Instead, I have included recommendations for lesser-known films that offer a more intimate and meaningful approach to the nuances of Japan.

Yet another indispensable resource, the Internet can often be overwhelming. A Google search for "Japan travel" yields more than seventy million results! With the help of my writers, I have winnowed the list to a few useful and creative websites, and even included an essay by my son Will Raus on taking advantage of wireless Internet while you're in Japan. In addition, for those dedicated travelers who want to learn the language, a list of resources—including warnings on the pitfalls of learning the language through film and TV—serves as your linguistic passport to Japan. Who knows? After all of your reading and movie watching, as well as Joeann Agarano's glimpse of a typical workday, you may even feel inspired to move to Japan.

Book Recomendations

FICTION

Black Rain
by Masuji Ibuse

A powerful pairing with John Hersey's 1946 non-fiction book *Hiroshima,* this poignant account of the bombing of Hiroshima and its impact on the lives of ordinary people is based upon true first-person accounts and interviews with survivors. Their stories have been interpreted for the novel as the post-traumatic flashbacks of a fictional character named Shigematsu Shizuma, and a collection of diary entries by his niece Yasuko. As the novel progresses, Shizuma recalls the horror of his experiences, and eventually receives the heartbreaking news that both he and his niece are suffering from radiation poisoning. *Black Rain* is a stern and stark reminder of the atrocities of nuclear war, yet somehow manages to remain life-affirming.

Kitchen
by Banana Yoshimoto

"The place I like best in this world is the kitchen. No matter where it is, no matter what kind, if it's a kitchen, if it's a place where they make food, it's fine with me." So begins *Kitchen,* award-winning author Banana Yoshimoto's culinary love story. The *chef du cuisine et amour* is Mikage Sakurai, a fetching young Japanese woman, barely more than a girl really, who suddenly finds herself all alone after the death of her grandmother, the last of her remaining relatives. Concerned that Mikage is depressed and in need of a surrogate family, a college classmate named Yuichi Tanabe, and his transsexual father-turned-mother Eriko, take her in. While preparing meals for Yuichi and Eriko as a means of justifying her existence and reciprocating their generosity, Mikage discovers that not only is cooking a therapeutic pastime, it is her raison d'etre. She nevertheless continues to grapple with repressed grief and existential angst, until an unexpected turn of events sets her heart on the path to love. Little over a hundred pages, *Kitchen* is a literary truffle composed of many subtle and delicate ingredients. Its light outer layer is a casual, straight-forward narrative, dusted with a sprinkle of self-deprecating humor. Yet at its core lies a delectable morsel of heartfelt pathos and insight into the depths of the human soul.

The Sailor Who Fell from Grace With the Sea
by Yukio Mishima

Set against the backdrop of post-WWII Japan, on the shores of Yokohama Harbor, Yukio Mishima's now classic work is a study in contrasts: summer and winter, land and sea, companionship and isolation, wanderlust and domestication, glory and nihilism. In this disturbing yet compelling novel, Mishima examines the futility of the human condition through the shifting perspective of three main characters: Ryuji Tsukazaki, a merchant marine; the widow Fusako Kuroda, an importer of European finery; and her misfit son Noboru, a boy poised on the tenuous cusp between childhood and adolescence. With a few deft strokes of his brush (all of his manuscripts were composed by hand with traditional Japanese brush-stroke writing), Mishima creates characters of depth and complexity: Noboru struggles with his desire to belong; Fusako fears compromising her independence; and Tsukazaki, adrift somewhere between shore and sea, grapples with the realization that he may never find glory sailing the ocean blue, nor true peace on terra firma.

NON-FICTION

The Chrysanthemum and the Sword
by Ruth Benedict

First published in 1946, *The Chrysanthemum and the Sword* began during WWII as an attempt to understand the Japanese people through an academic analysis of their history, culture, and ideologies. Its author, a cultural anthropologist, was commissioned by the US government's Office of War Information to research every aspect of Japan and analyze and report on her findings. Although the world is much changed, and American relations with Japan have come a long way since then, this historic work remains one of the most respected, albeit controversial texts, and one which has greatly influenced foreign policy toward Japan on a global level.

Dave Barry Does Japan
by Dave Barry

The eccentricities of the Japanese people and their culture are lampooned as only Dave Barry can. With his unique flair for humor and hyperbole, Barry imbues his observations on every aspect of travel in Japan with keen and unbridled wit, including the seemingly insurmountable language barriers, embarrassing etiquette blunders, exorbitant prices, bizarre foods, white-knuckle driving experiences, and the absurdities of Japanese pop culture. This is a side-splitting send-up, especially for anyone who has already traveled to Japan.

The Inland Sea
by Donald Richie

Donald Richie's chronicle of his escape from Tokyo to the simple beauty of the small island communities in the sea that separates Shikoku and Honshu offers a master class in Japanese appreciation. Never banal, *The Inland Sea* is the story of a nation that is changing before the eyes of a man who himself is undergoing a massive transition. Although a foreigner, Richie writes with the honesty and gentle touch of an insider, one who speaks the language and who understands the people. This 1971 classic still lives and breathes, and thus is timeless travel literature in the truest sense. (Nolan Webb)

JAPROCKSAMPLER: How the Post-War Japanese Blew Their Minds on Rock 'N' Roll
by Julian Cope

In spite of the decidedly non-PC title, this book is a respectful and detailed discussion of Japanese pop music in the 1960s and '70s. Important movements in Japanese music including Eleki and Group Sounds are covered, and the history of this twenty-year musical journey also includes guest appearances by Karlheinz Stockhausen, John Cage, Yoko Ono, John Lennon, The Ventures, and many other Western artists. Today's Japanese groups known in the West, including The Boredoms, Pizzicato Five, Yellow Magic Orchestra, and Shonen Knife, exist because of the pioneers of the modern music movement in Japan, and are all finally given their due in English, thanks to Julian Cope. This book is a must for anyone fascinated by Japan's musical landscape. (Joe Wallace)

www.japrocksampler.com

Passport's Japan Almanac
by Boye De Mente

This vintage volume by Boye De Mente, a veteran of Japanese business and culture, is still one of the best travel and cultural guides to Japan. Organized from A to Z, this fascinating and informative primer highlights not only the most important tourist sites, but also offers insight into Japanese culture and customs. Although it's a little dated, and currently out of print, it's well worth tracking down a used copy online. (FYI: At age eighty, Boye de Mente is still going strong.)

www.boyedemente.com

The Roads to Sata: A 2000-Mile Walk Through Japan
by Alan Booth

A relatively unknown classic, this book documents Alan Booth's epic walk along the back roads of Japan from the northern tip of Hokkaido to the southernmost cape in Kyushu. Booth uses rich descriptions and gentle humor to reveal a Japan that few foreigners see—the places in between places, often well off the beaten track. He allows you to not only experience Japan with sensitivity and respect, but also to share the experience of what it is like to be viewed by the Japanese, as you tag along for two thousand miles and immerse yourself in the beauty of the country. (Nolan Webb)

Something Like an Autobiography
by Akira Kurosawa

As Japan's preeminent post-war filmmaker, Kurosawa left behind an amazing body of work. His films speak as much to the human condition as to the unique character of Japanese culture after WWII. Movies like *Seven Samurai, Stray Dog, Yojimbo*, and *The Bad Sleep Well* are credited with helping to invent modern cinema. In *Something Like an Autobiography*, Kurosawa muses on his formative experiences, his motivations on becoming a filmmaker, and his take on living in the years following the MacArthur-led occupation of Japan. This filmmaker provided the inspiration for such cinematic luminaries as George Lucas and Sergio Leone. Even American moviegoers who have never seen a frame of Kurosawa's films owe him for their enjoyment of favorites like *Star Wars*, *Last Man Standing*, and *A Fistful of Dollars*. I highly recommend this book as a gateway to the incredible world of Kurosawa's films, and as a way for Western travelers to better understand the nuances of Japanese culture. (Joe Wallace)

Wrong About Japan
by Peter Carey

When many people think about travel in Japan, temples, gardens, and castles come to mind. But that's not all there is. Not by a long shot. Peter Carey's *Wrong About Japan* details a quest with his teenage son Charley to see the "real Japan." Fueled by Charley's newfound love of *anime*, their trip takes father and son to various *anime* meccas, including the Ghibli Museum (see page 201) to explore the work of director Hayao Miyazaki; Akihabara Electric Town, whose shops are shrines for lovers of *anime*; and Sunrise Studios, the birthplace of the *anime* television series *Mobile Suit Gundam*. Along the way, Carey shows the reader that there's so much more to Japan than what is found in most travel guides. (Will Raus)

You Gotta Have *Wa*
by Robert Whiting

Using baseball as metaphor, Robert Whiting illuminates one of Japan's most important cultural concepts: *wa*. Although typically translated simply as "harmony," *wa* is so much more than that. Contained within this tiny two-letter word is the pervasive Japanese ideology that the needs of the group always supersede the desires of the individual, implying a spirit of cooperation and a selfless willingness to put the needs of society ahead of one's own ambitions. Japanese baseball is a wildly popular sport, and as Whiting shows through his examination of its rituals and history, it serves as the perfect venue for demonstrating the concept of *wa*.

RECOMMENDED SOURCES

Boston Book Company
www.rarebook.com/

With around thirty thousand titles in stock, this bookstore boasts a collection that it describes as "one of the largest and finest inventories of books relating to Japan and East Asia in the country." It contains thousands of rare books, some of which are first editions dating from the nineteenth century. There is an emphasis on art and design books. As well, you will find valuable old prints, photographs, and woodcuts—all with prices to reflect their scarcity.

Infinity Books Japan
www.infinitybooksjapan.com

This online bookseller has an impressive inventory of secondhand books in English. On the left-hand side of the website's main page, under "Browse by Category," click on "Japan." This will take you to a selection of Japanese books and books about Japan, arranged by topic, and all in English. From typical travel guides to arcane human behavioral texts, this is an amazing and far-reaching selection.

Kinokuniya
www.kinokuniya.co.jp/english/contents/network04.html

You can get lost for hours in a branch of Kinokuniya, with its fascinating inventory of Japanese books, *manga*, and magazines, some of which are in English. Japan's most famous bookstore has locations all over the world (see website), as well as an online source, which is mostly in Japanese.

Stone Bridge Press
www.stonebridge.com
http://stonebridgepress.blogspot.com

This publisher, based in Berkeley, California, specializes in books about Asia, and has an irresistible array of Japan-related titles that includes travel, business, culture and design, language, literature, *anime*, and reference. No matter what your interest, you're sure to find a book or two that you simply must have. And make sure to check out the press blog, covering current literature, arts, and pop culture.

Used book websites
www.abebooks.com
www.alibris.com

For tracking down used copies of many titles mentioned in this chapter, *AbeBooks* and *Alibris* are reliable starting points.

Paul Sharp reviews two of his favorite Japanese authors

During my five years in Japan, the authors Eiji Yoshikawa and Haruki Murakami deepened my understanding of the country's rich culture. Their works helped me better appreciate Japan's past and present, and since many Japanese people are familiar with them, I was also able to initiate some interesting conversations.

What might read as dry history in a textbook is transformed into a rich literary work by Yoshikawa. Immersing his complex characters in actual events, he was famous for his meticulous research, and was so highly regarded in Japan that a literary award for historic fiction was created in his name. Be prepared to dedicate yourself to Yoshikawa's world, as his novels are epic. Among translations in English are *The Heike Story,* which focuses on the clash between nobility and commoners in Kyoto during the Heian period (AD 794-1185), and both *Taiko* and *Musashi*, each of which follows young men pursuing the samurai tradition at the end of the later feudal war era.

In contrast, Murakami's works explore modern Japan, representing it in a way that travelers who have visited Tokyo will recognize. Although they are surrounded by millions of people, his characters inhabit a lonely and contemplative world. With his unique descriptions of ordinary (and not so ordinary) events, Murakami makes magic seem probable. Many young Japanese feel that they can relate to his characters.

My favorite Murakami novel is *Wind-up Bird Chronicle*. Through the seemingly simple story of a man searching for his missing wife and cat, the reader gets a taste of history, magic realism, romance, humor, and the emotional issues which have made Murakami famous. At six-hundred-plus pages, this book is pretty long. If you'd like an easier place to start, then I recommend *Norwegian Wood*, the book that turned Murakami into a literary superstar in Japan.

In a quiet way, through the story of a man looking back on his relationships in the late 1960s, *Norwegian Wood* deals with issues of loss and sexuality. Murakami's characters internalize their experiences so well that I felt I was personally undergoing them with each page. Although I've mentioned only two, all of his books are amazing, uniquely coloring the way you will experience Japan.

Celeste Heiter recommends three Japanese classics

So beloved is the writer Natsume Soseki that his face appeared for many years on Japan's thousand-yen bill. But his mass popularity isn't the only reason his three most well-known novels are an excellent place to begin enjoying the Japanese classics. Not only do they offer a nostalgic glimpse into old Japan, but also their characters are timeless archetypes of Japanese literature.

Published in 1906, *Botchan* is the *Huckleberry Finn* of Japan—a novel that captures a cultural moment in time, and that is now required reading for all Japanese students. It follows an idealistic young college graduate who is assigned to work as a math teacher at a rural middle school on the island of Shikoku. He is puzzled by the archaic customs of the locals and vexed by the ridicule of his mischievous students, and as a man of strong morals, he is disillusioned by the treachery of his co-workers. In the end—representing the values that the Japanese hold so dear—he must rely on his own sense of integrity to rise above the moral decay and find peace within his heart.

I Am a Cat is known in Japanese as *Wagahai wa neko de aru,* a title that promises the book's nonpareil humor. While *neko* simply means "cat," the

Japanese language contains more than one hundred words for the pronoun *I*, and *Wagahai wa ... de aru* is the most formal, self-aggrandizing, and presumptuous of them all, since it would never be used to refer to anyone except the highest royalty. The story is told from the perspective of the cat in the title, who thinks of himself in such arrogant terms. He eavesdrops at the neighbors' windows, and spies on their comings and goings, while passing judgment upon them with a level of wit befitting the most evolved literary minds. *I Am a Cat* is a terrific introduction to Japanese humor, and an especially entertaining read for cat lovers.

Kokoro, meaning "heart" or "feeling," is a three-part novel, beginning with *Sensei and I*, which focuses on a young college student who befriends a reclusive elderly man known only as Sensei. While the narrator learns much about himself as their friendship grows, Sensei remains a mystery. Eventually, in part two, *My Parents and I*, the young man graduates and returns to the bedside of his dying father, where he continues his friendship with Sensei through an exchange of letters. In *Sensei and His Testament*, Sensei's last letter serves as the novel's conclusion and explains Sensei's enigmatic behavior for so many years, revealing finally his tragic past. With its thoughtful exploration of relationships, subtle metaphors, and mindfully crafted characters, *Kokoro* lives up to its title: a Japanese classic with a lot of heart.

Website and Blog Recommendations

Anime News Network

www.animenewsnetwork.com/

If it's *anime* you're looking for, *Anime News Network* has it. At this website you will find an extensive encyclopedia of *anime* and *manga* series, as well as reviews of new releases, the latest in *anime* news, and a collection of columns, including the entertaining *Chicks on Anime* (the female perspective), *Buried Treasure* (vintage *anime*), and *The X-Button* (related video games). If you want to know where the next *anime* convention will be held around the world, check here first.

Expat Blog

www.expat-blog.com/en/destination/asia/japan/

Looking to see who's blogging in your favorite Japanese city? Check out this gateway to dozens of Japan-based bloggers. From India to the Caribbean, bloggers come from around the globe, offering their culturally unique perspectives. Browse the categories, which are organized by prefecture, and make sure to bookmark your favorites, so that you can keep up with *Loco in Yokohama*, *Life with Hubby*, *New Worlds to Conquer*, or whichever blogger captures your interest.

Kids Web Japan

http://web-jpn.org/kidsweb/index.html

With sections like "Spooky Japan" and "Virtual Culture," this website for ages ten to fourteen is a wonderful way for kids to learn about Japan. They can take a basic language lesson, learn all about sushi, explore Tokyo's "cool" attractions, and take fun quizzes about daily life in Japan. Want to know how the Japanese use bathwater or if Hello Kitty has any siblings? This is the place to start.

J-Box

www.jbox.com

This is a great website selling all manner of cool Japanese wares. Categories include magazines, music, *manga*, and our favorite, "Wacky Things." This is the place to go for your Miku Hatsune (Leek Girl) action figure or Cinnamoroll cartoon character mold for your boiled eggs. As for more conventional products, there's an entire section devoted to *bento* box accessories, as well as one for traditional items such as incense, *happi* coats, and—yes, it's actually listed under "traditional"—an R2-D2 Soy Sauce Bottle.

Japan-Guide.com

www.japan-guide.com

This is a well-organized resource for both travelers and those living in Japan. It contains information on every topic imaginable, beginning with basics like sightseeing and finding a job. From discovering Japan's Chinatowns to learning how to pay your taxes while working in Japan, its scope is comprehensive. There is even a network for meeting people around the world who share your interest in Japan.

Japan National Tourism Organization (JNTO)

www.jnto.go.jp

This website is the quintessential guide to Japan. You can browse through a variety of subjects. "Area of Interest" includes historical sites, shrines, and hot springs; "Seasons" proves that there's more to Japan than just cherry blossoms; and "Festivals & Events" makes it clear that you'll be hard-pressed to visit Japan at a time when there isn't a festival occurring somewhere in the country. Along with featuring a vast collection of well-written travel articles and photos, this site provides trustworthy information on transportation, accommodations, and other travel essentials.

Jorudan

www.jorudan.co.jp/english/

Contributor Nick Hall writes: "For British train passengers like myself, the efficiency of Japan's railways is nothing short of awe-inspiring. Being used to regular delays and cancellations back home, it's such a novelty traveling in a country like Japan where public transport generally runs on time. This punctuality is particularly evident when using Jorudan's invaluable Train Route Finder to plan journeys. Simply type in the station you're leaving from and your destination, and the website will give you a number of highly detailed choices based on speed and cost. It's such an accurate website that you can even plan journeys across the entire length of the country involving several trains. And no matter where you want to go in Japan, it's almost certain your trains will be on time, so chances are you'll arrive exactly when Jorudan says you will."

Metropolis

http://metropolis.co.jp/default.asp

Shopping, dining, and clubbing. Sports, theater, and pop culture. You'll find it all at this online English language weekly. The travel section is a particular gem, providing insider tips in the spirit of *To Japan With Love.* Articles run the gamut from locals offering advice on where to find a date in Tokyo, to profiles on Japanese fashion designers, to tips on where you can get behind the wheel at a Tokyo racetrack.

Of Rice and Zen

www.ofriceandzen.org

This Kyoto-based online magazine features reviews and recommendations for an array of all things Japanese. Consider an entire essay on Pocky, the ubiquitous Japanese snack food, or one about Fushimi Inari Taisha, the Shinto shrine with the famous and fantastic thousand *torii* gates. You can find *kanji* writing software for learning to do brush-stroke calligraphy, as well as a review of a café where the servers dress like sexy French maids. Ranging from the traditional to the off-the-wall, this website's eclecticism offers the ultimate in cool.

Will Raus roams freely on Japan's wireless networks

When I spent the summer traveling around Japan, the availability of wireless Internet (Wi-Fi), was definitely a great enhancement to my trip. Even in remote areas, with a little determination, and sometimes a little luck, I was able to get online and keep in touch with family and friends back home.

Staying connected via Wi-Fi was especially easy with my own laptop computer, since the standard laptop adapts to both standard US current (110 volts) and the less powerful Japanese electrical current (100 volts). Also, both use the same plug, meaning you won't need to bring a plug adaptor with you. Still, believe it or not, using laptops in public doesn't appear to be very popular. In the seven weeks I was in Japan—one of the most technologically advanced countries in the world—I don't recall seeing a single laptop in use, except at the home where I stayed in Kofu. For travelers, the best bet for finding an Internet connection is a lodging where most guests are foreigners with laptops in tow.

One place where I wasn't at all surprised to see Wi-Fi was the Capsule Inn Akihabara, which is popular with tourists. Not only did it have wireless, it also had a router for each floor, just to ensure that the signal was as strong as it could be for each sleeping unit. And at a modern, urban *ryokan* in Kanazawa, the proprietor not only had a wireless network, but also provided a USB wireless adapter for guests to use, just in case their laptops didn't have built-in Wi-Fi.

You might also find Wi-Fi in the most unexpected places. One striking example was on a road trip that took my dad and me from Hokkaido down through the remote countryside of northern Honshu. To break up the long journey ahead of us, we booked a small boarding house between Aomori and Kanazawa. However, we ran into a few problems, shall we say, with the GPS system, which sent us so far off course that what should have been a scenic three-hundred-kilometer drive ended up being closer to six hundred kilometers.

When we arrived at our destination, the place looked like something out of a Stephen King novel. It was a rustic, two-story farmhouse in a desolate warehouse area at the top of a hill, with the front lawn badly overgrown, and only a couple of lights on. Of course, the innkeepers were perfectly fine people, and they even had dinner waiting for us, despite the fact that we were nearly two hours late. And not only did they have Wi-Fi, they also had little hand-out cards with the network connection information for their guests. It was a welcome surprise at the end of a long, technologically misguided day.

I chose some inns on my trip because they had Wi-Fi. For example, Ryokan Kangetsu, a traditional-style inn in Chidori-cho, a quiet yet conveniently located district of Tokyo. But innkeepers don't always expect guests to bring laptops or to use wireless Internet. Therefore, you may need to ask if the inn has Wi-Fi, and if they will let you log on. Although some inns may not offer it as a standard amenity, many are quite willing to allow their guests to use it. At an *onsen* I stayed at in Ohara, the owners let me to use their Wi-Fi in a guest room that happened to be empty, which was close enough to their office for me to log on to their network.

Being able to keep in touch while in Japan, no matter where I was, made the trip special in many ways. Not only did it let me share my trip along the way, it let me bring a little piece of home with me wherever I went.

"Chatting" around the world

Many of the large Internet portals and search engines have their own instant messenger programs, which are programs that allow two people to send messages back and forth instantly. They are simple to use, and you can download them for free. The most commonly used versions are AOL Instant Messenger (AIM), Yahoo!

Messenger, Windows Live Messenger, and GoogleTalk. When choosing an instant message program for your trip, keep in mind that users who want to chat via instant message both need to have the same program. To coordinate times for chatting with others around the globe, the website *Time and Date* is a good resource. It lists the current times for major world cities; you can also set up a personal world clock with just the cities you need.

www.aim.com
http://messenger.yahoo.com/
http://get.live.com/messenger/
www.google.com/talk/
www.timeanddate.com

Tokyo lodging gem

Located in Tokyo's Chidori-cho, the most striking feature of the Ryokan Kangetsu is that the lobby is actually an open-air garden, complete with a small stream running through it. The accommodations are traditional Japanese *tatami* rooms ranging from small annex rooms, perfect for one or two people, to huge deluxe suites, complete with painted wall screens and multiple rooms. There is also a beautiful open-air bath, and the inn provides *yukata* robes, which you can purchase and take home with you at the end of your trip. To top it off, Ryokan Kangetsu is located only two minutes from the Chidori-cho Train Station, making it convenient for excursions to downtown Tokyo.

1-2-20 Chidori
Ota District
Tokyo
(03) 3751-0007
www.kangetsu.com/sub7.htm

Train: Tokyu Ikegami Line to Chidori-cho Station.

Movie Recommendations

Firefly Dreams
(*Ichiban Utsukushi Natsu*)

This engaging film tells the tale of Naomi, a misguided Japanese teenager who routinely ditches school for shopping and goes nightclubbing to escape her troubled home life. When Naomi's adulterous mother runs off to live with her lover, her father packs her off to the town of Horaicho, where his sister runs a small country inn. There, Naomi is reacquainted with the elderly Mrs. Koide, who was once her nanny and who now suffers from Alzheimer's. Naomi is assigned to the task of being Mrs. Koide's companion and caregiver, and over the course of the summer, a rare friendship blossoms between them. As Naomi acquires a sense of acceptance and belonging, she learns not only humility and grace, but also to sit still, to endure the passage of time. And for the first time in her life, she learns what it means to love.

Hiroshima Mon Amour
(*Ni-ju-yon Jikan no Joji*)

The subject of much comment and controversy, *Hiroshima Mon Amour* is the vintage brainchild of French director Alain Resnais and novelist-turned-screenwriter Marguerite Duras. Filmed in black and white, this pensive and self-conscious elegy tells the story of a one-night *affaire du coeur* between a French actress, known only as Elle (She), and a married Japanese architect, known only as Lui (He). Historical footage of horrific human suffering in Hiroshima is punctuated by the occasional frame of Elle's hand clenching and kneading the flesh of Lui's naked shoulder as she speaks. *Hiroshima Mon Amour* is a film of pairings and paradoxes—of macrocosm and microcosm, of re-membering and forgetting, of ecstasy and despair, of intimacy and exposure, of love and war, of death and rebirth, of the temporal and the infinite. It is undeniably one of the most important films of the twentieth century.

Japanese Story

Set against the brilliant backdrop of Australia's Pilbara desert region, this cross-cultural drama unfolds between tomboyish Australian geologist Sandy (Toni Collette) and reticent Japanese steel industry representative Hiromitsu (Gotaro Tsunashima). The two are thrust together when Sandy's boss gives her the task of playing tour guide, which involves a five-hour drive to outlying mining facilities and babysitting Hiromitsu through a night of drunken karaoke. As if that weren't enough, Hiromitsu coerces Sandy into driving him to see the world's largest open strip mine. As one might expect, what began as an odious corporate obligation is transformed into a romantic fantasy as the two become sexually involved. They also begin to bridge the cultural gap toward a genuine friendship. That is, until things go terribly wrong. *Japanese Story* is beautifully scripted and artfully imbued with subtle irony in its pairing of genders, cultures, and values.

The Last Samurai

The year is 1876, and on opposite sides of the globe, two nations are recovering from civil wars: the United States after the war between North and South, and Japan after the fall of the last shogun, which brought the end of militaristic feudalism and the restoration of imperial rule under Emperor Meiji. Although more than half a century would pass before the United States and Japan faced off in military conflict, in this epic film, the destiny of the two nations intersects in the life of one man: American Civil War veteran Nathan Algren (Tom Cruise). Within the context of the Meiji Restoration, *The Last Samurai* represents the end of an era. Much like the antebellum world of America's Old South, the world of feudal Japan was doomed by civil rebellion and the relentless march of progress.

My Neighbor Totoro
(*Tonari no Totoro*)

In this engaging tale, young Mei and her older sister Satsuki discover the hidden world of the *Totoro* when they move to the countryside to be near their mother, who is recuperating from an illness. Just what is a *Totoro*? Elusive woodland creatures that can only be seen by children and young-at-heart grownups, the whimsical apparitions sprang from the imagination of Hayao Miyazaki, Japan's favorite animation filmmaker. For viewers accustomed to the typical American animated film, with its talking critters, objects come to life, and hero-vanquishes-villain storyline, *My Neighbor Totoro* may seem a little tame. But what it lacks in laugh-a-minute action, it more than makes up for with its enchanting characters and quaint depiction of everyday life in rural Japan. Whether it's a close-up of hollyhocks before a gathering storm, raindrops rippling the surface of a rice paddy, or the microcosmic world of a snail inching its way along a blade of grass, not even the smallest detail has been left unattended.

The Twilight Samurai
(*Tasogare Seibei*)

In this understated samurai drama, the recently widowed Seibei Iguchi is left to care for his two young daughters and ailing mother. But as a minor samurai serving as a provisions officer, Iguchi must sacrifice his family life to obey the orders of the ruling *daimyo*. Based on the novel by Shuhei Fujisawa, *The Twilight Samurai* is an elegant and even-handed work that pays homage to the ancient samurai tradition without glorifying its brutality. The subtleties and implications of honor and allegiance are revealed in artfully crafted dialogue, punctuated by silence that says it all. No crescendos, no swaggering heroism, just a simple story of one humble samurai accepting his duty.

Woman in the Dunes
(*Suna no Onna*)

Vast sand dunes on the Sea of Japan provide the setting for this Hiroshi Teshigahara classic. Adapted from the novel by Kobo Abe, the film opens with Jumpei, an amateur entomologist from Tokyo, in search of an elusive beetle. When he misses the last bus back to town, locals offer him lodging at the home of a young widow. Jumpei is surprised when they instruct him to use a rope ladder to climb down into a sand pit, where he finds the widow's rustic beach house. In the middle of the night, he is awakened by the widow shoveling sand into large metal bins. She explains that she must toil away like Sisyphus at this nocturnal task, lest the sand engulf her house. Although Jumpei intends to depart in the morning, the rope ladder disappears. So begins months of captivity. For all its stark simplicity, *Woman in the Dunes* is an existential masterpiece. The search for meaning within the archetypal struggles of Man versus Man, Man versus Nature, and Man versus

Himself is illuminated by transcendent black-and-white cinematography that captures in micro-detail the textures and contours of this strangely sandy and forbidding world.

Midnight Eye

Film buff Johannes Schönherr writes: "This is the most comprehensive site for Japanese cinema in the English language that I know of. Interviews with directors, features on all kinds of movie-related subjects, film reviews, film book reviews—you name it, it's all there. If you want to learn more about Japanese cinema, this is the place to begin your explorations."

www.midnighteye.com

On the small screen

Television, as well as movies, can be a good way of learning more about Japanese culture, but as Will Raus writes: "It's sometimes hard for newcomers to understand the world of *anime*. Most of the shows on TV are the same cliché junk that gives *anime* a bad name. However, the one that defines the genre and everything terrific that it can be is *Cowboy Bebop (Kauboi Bibappu)*. Each episode is a stand-alone work of art. Some are serious, some are action-packed, and some are just fall-down funny, with a masterful jazz-inspired soundtrack all the way through. From start to finish, *Cowboy Bebop* is the perfect way to venture into anime."

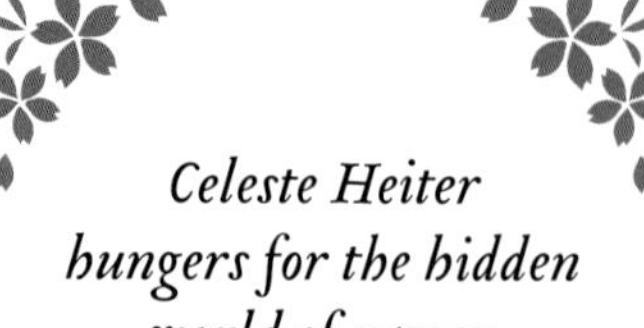

Celeste Heiter hungers for the hidden world of ramen

The thousand ways that food ignites the human spirit—from a decadent culinary orgy to a humble-yet-perfect bowl of steaming-hot *ramen*—is the stuff of which director Juzo Itami's *Tampopo* is made. This bacchanalian, Japanese take on the "spaghetti western" romp features Itami's real-life wife Nobuko Miyamoto in the title role of Tampopo, a noodle shop owner struggling to make a go of it after her husband's death. She is paired with Tsutomu Yamazaki, who plays Goro, a rakish trucker whose character is best described as "Shane-meets-Henry Higgins."

One rainy night, after too many hours on the road, Goro pulls over for a bowl of *ramen* at Tampopo's shabby little roadside restaurant. When an intoxicated diner insults Tampopo's artless cooking skills and lack of business acumen, Goro chivalrously intercedes on her behalf, only to wake up the following morning, bruised and battered from the night's brawl, but in the blissful care of Tampopo.

Over breakfast, Goro reluctantly but candidly critiques Tampopo's noodles. "They've got sincerity," he says. "But they lack guts." Goro gives her a crash course on the fundamentals of restaurant counter service, and just before he can exit stage left, Tampopo hornswoggles him into becoming her teacher and mentor.

With that, Tampopo and Goro embark on a quest for the perfect *ramen* recipe: the silkiest noodles, the most savory broth, and just the right combination of precisely prepared toppings. As they prowl the outskirts of Tokyo, slyly querying noodle cooks, spying through cracks in kitchen walls, and snooping in restaurant garbage cans for the secrets they seek, the story takes brief excursions into the lives of miscellaneous onlookers and passersby. These wry vignettes infuse the film with a sense of humor and sometimes even erotica as food becomes a motif and a metaphor for life's more profound elements.

Back at the ranch, Tampopo and her noodle shop get a makeover. In a metamorphosis oddly reminiscent of both *Rocky* and *My Fair Lady,* Tampopo the noodle chef, and Tampopo the noodle shop, make their debut with sparkling panache and spit-shine polish. Every scene in *Tampopo* is flavored with a hint of irony, and Itami uses his filmmaking craft to lampoon the absurdities of the Japanese way, while holding up a mirror to the foibles of human nature. *Tampopo's* scenes of bon vivant vagabonds sitting around an open campfire, critiquing the gastronomic merits of the table scraps they've purloined from the dumpsters of gourmet restaurants, are at once both boldly hilarious and touchingly sardonic.

Alas, the comedic genius of the ill-fated Itami was lost to the world the day he leapt to his death over tabloid allegations that he was having an affair. But he bequeathed a legacy of buoyant humor and unique satire to fans and film lovers around the world, and *Tampopo* is unequivocally his best work. The next time you find yourself in the supermarket, staring at those ten-for-a-dollar packages of instant *ramen*, get hold of yourself and go rent *Tampopo* instead. Treat your soul and your senses to the real thing.

In search of ramen

For our writers' recommendation on where to find the best *ramen*, go to page 24 and page 33.

Learning Japanese

Designing with Kanji: Japanese Character Motifs for Surface, Skin & Spirit
by Shogo Oketani and Leza Lowitz

This is an original way to learn the history and etymology of *kanji* script basics. It will also ensure that your tattoo for "Wind God" (*fujin* with a long u) doesn't come out as "wife" (*fujin* with a short u)! Although the concept behind this book is learning to use *kanji* for various design projects, including your own body, its basic principles and range of fun facts make it an entertaining primer.

Genki: An Integrated Course in Elementary Japanese
by *The Japan Times*

While I lived in Japan, I took an intensive two-week language course which used volumes I (dialogue and grammar) and II (reading and writing) of this series. Not for the dabbler, these books are rigorous enough to give a student the necessary grounding to prepare for the Japanese Language Proficiency Test. Supplementary materials, such as flash cards and listening quizzes, can be found on the *Genki* website. (Elizabeth Sharpe)

http://genki.japantimes.co.jp

Let's Learn Hiragana, Let's Learn Katakana, and Let's Learn Kanji
by Yasuko Kosaka Mitamura

These are excellent texts for beginners learning the three alphabets of the Japanese language. I bought the books before moving to Japan to teach English and studied them faithfully every night after work. The mnemonics used to enforce character recognition are so well done that even twenty years later, I still recall and rely on them when I translate Japanese text.

Japanese in 10 Minutes a Day
by Kristine K. Kershul

Regardless of how busy you might be, you surely have ten minutes a day to spare for learning Japanese. Containing a CD, this highly effective program allows you to grasp language basics, which will serve you well when you first arrive in Japan.

Making Out in Japanese
by Todd and Erica Geers

This cheeky little phrasebook contains everyday expressions that you won't find in dictionaries and textbooks: phrases to help with casual conversation, handling conflicts, and even the language of romance. The book is out of print, but the effort to track it down is well worth it.

Online language learning

With its interactive capabilities, the web can be a great resource for online lessons. At *Yookoso!* you can sign up for "*Kanji* a Day," learn Japanese through song lyrics, study notes from various Japanese courses, and discover numerous links to other language learning sites. *JapanesePod101* uses podcasts to guide students through self-study courses, as well as introduces listeners to interesting facets of Japanese culture. (Scott Nesbitt)

www.yookoso.com
http://japanesepod101.com/

The Original "Point-and-Speak" Phrasebook JAPAN (English edition)
by Toshiya Enomoto

This book was given to me while in Japan, and I found it extremely useful. With English, *romaji*, and *kanji* captions, cartoon-like pictures illustrate everything from expressions and feelings to food and emergencies. An introduction in *kanji* and

English explains to the Japanese why a *gaijin* is handing them the book. Along with being full of practical tips on learning the language, it also offers advice on understanding the culture, a Tokyo train map, a list of holidays, tips on how to count, and a glossary with more than two thousand useful words. The back of the book even has an area for writing questions and answers with an erasable marker. (Jennifer Huber)

Conversational Japanese
by Pimsleur

With this set of CDs, sixteen thirty-minute lessons teach you the basics, such as greeting people, asking the time, and making dinner or lunch plans with a friend. Conversations rather than drills reflect the natural language learning process. While the lessons are not nearly comprehensive enough to enable fluency in Japanese, they are a good way to begin learning the language. (Joyce Jemison)

Webster's New World Compact Japanese Dictionary

For a good, all-around portable dictionary, this is the best of the bunch. It's sturdy and compact, with easy-to-read English/Japanese and Japanese/English entries. This is the dictionary I used while living and traveling in Japan, and although it's practically indestructible, I somehow managed to go through three of them! My original copy is a wonderful keepsake, as its once blank pages and inside covers are filled with rubber-stamped images from places I visited and little handwritten notes on special words and phrases that I learned along the way.

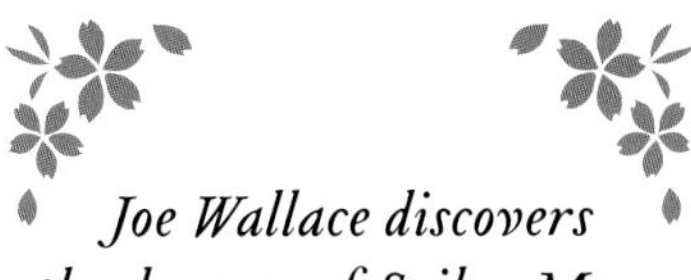

Joe Wallace discovers the dangers of Sailor Moon

A co-worker of mine recently experienced a moment of pure embarrassment while working with a Japanese television crew. He was trying to impress everyone with his language skills, and said hello to a dog using the Japanese he learned from watching *anime* DVDs.

The crew stifled their laughter, and the reporter somehow managed to tell my poor co-worker that he was speaking Japanese like a little girl. Turns out he had developed most of his language skills by watching the *anime* program *Sailor Moon*, absorbing vocabulary from its schoolgirl characters, not realizing the importance of context in Asian languages.

Imagine discovering that some of the phrases you memorized from classic samurai movies are the equivalent of saying, "Git along, little doggies" or "Aw, shucks, pardner! T'weren't nothin'." It's the same effect as a non-Western speaker learning English from John Wayne films.

Wanting to improve my own limited grasp of the language, I have also watched movies, but I concentrated on films set in the present. There are many great Japanese directors who deal with contemporary themes: Takeshi "Beat" Kitano, Takashi Shimizu, and Hirokazu Koreeda, just to name a few. I picked up some good slang and regional expressions, without having to decipher the Japanese equivalent of "thee and thou." Even so, I sometimes struggled to use what I learned in the proper social context.

It's also important to keep in mind that learning Japanese from films requires some patience, but there are plenty of movies you can watch to pick up a few common phrases and expressions. Believe it or not, watching some of the most famous (to Americans) Japanese movies in the original Japanese is a great place to start. For silly fun for the whole family, check out the 1990s Godzilla films, *Godzilla vs. Destroyah* (no, that's not a typo!) and *Godzilla vs. King Ghidorah.*

Fans of *anime* should view *Cowboy Bebop* (see page 244), but with the understanding that this television show offers colloquial "guy talk." It's sort of like watching Spike TV to learn English—not the kind of language you'll use in everyday tourist conversation, but entertaining. You can also pick up a lot of tough gangster talk and slang from watching the amazing series by Kinji Fukasaku, sold in America in a boxed set called *The Yakuza Papers: Battles Without Honor & Humanity.*

While Japanese films can help foreigners understand aspects of the culture, there are dangers in relying on them as your sole source of education. I learned basics about politeness and the use of honorifics in this way, but in Japan, there are layers of subtle behavior depending on the situation. One of the first things I found out about being polite in Japan is to use the suffix *san* after someone's name. It's rarely explained why this is so important, and observing uses of *san* and the more familiar *chan* at the movies doesn't make things any clearer. The best advice for honorifics? *San* is easy and polite, and you never have to wonder if you're being accidentally rude.

While I still believe you can learn a lot about any country by watching its movies, Japanese society is complicated. A good basic language class is essential. And of course the best way to learn about any culture is to experience it in person. When I finally switched off the television and got out into the streets of Tokyo, only then did I truly learn how to navigate the culture—and put what I learned from the movies into context.

It's true, some of us try to get by on our own, but the culture gap will inevitably rear its ugly head. Just ask my co-worker, who now learns his Japanese the old-fashioned way, using a textbook. He still watches *Sailor Moon*—which is, after all, part of Japanese culture—but now he knows better than to talk like its schoolgirl characters.

Living in Japan

Joeann Agarano relives a gaijin girl's workday

The Shinkansen (bullet train) reverberates through my fifth-floor apartment in the Namamugi neighborhood, waking me without fail as it does each day. I rise at half past seven, and open the window to let in the frigid morning air, wet and lush. I tie up the green butterfly curtains and watch this clear-eyed city of middle-rise residential buildings and quaint, pointed Japanese roofs yawn to life. I check the television for the weather before leaving. Yokohama is a temperamental brat in autumn. Most days are cold and dry, but one needs to watch out for these rainy, strong-winded exceptions.

I walk the three minutes to the train station. My street is filled with tiny shops inserted among the residential buildings: a neighborhood salon with a dreadlocked lad for its logo, small pubs tucked away in unexpected spaces, and ubiquitous, twenty-four hour *pachinko* parlors.

It is Tuesday, Namamugi's garbage day, and so along the designated pick-up points on street corners are bulky, transparent plastic bags awaiting the city truck. I pass by the neighborhood grocery store, where shop workers are busily arranging the fresh produce for display. As I pass they utter a polite, "*Ohaiyo gozaimasu*" ("Good morning"). I nod back with a smile, and walk onward to the station entrance, using the stairs up to the train platform instead of the escalator. I have five minutes to spare before the local train arrives.

This is a routine I will miss someday, and the punctuality that pervades this country—the synchronized time, the big public clocks, accurate to the minute. I look around, lazily watching people as I stand at my usual waiting place, near a vending machine selling Kirin drinks. As always, an express train buzzes through the station, right on time, blowing its cold gale. A minute more and my train arrives. I enter and sit among people who seem to take their country's efficiency for granted.

There are days when I want to slack off and work at my job as a process design engineer at a less precise and harried pace. But then the fervent energy in my office buoys me with the drive and work ethic for which the Japanese people are known. When I look around at my disciplined co-workers—the managers striving just as hard as the company's young engineers—I cannot help but be challenged to keep pace, adapting to the long hours that are punctuated only by five-minute coffee breaks.

I leave at seven thirty each evening, often tired and hungry. For the most part, I brown bag my lunch and cook dinner at my apartment. But on days such as this, when the hunger becomes unbearable before I reach home, I always choose between *gyudon* (beef over rice) at Matsuya, the less popular yet more delicious and cheaper alternative to Yoshinoya, or *tendon* (tempura over rice) at Tenya Express. I love them both, these two fast food outlets, with franchises scattered all over Japan, offering filling and inexpensive meals for the working class.

After supper, I browse around the Book Off store to check for new stocks of used and inexpensive music CDs. Or I buy myself a green tea ice cream at a *hyaku-en* (hundred-yen) shop near the office to cleanse my palate on a windy autumn night.

Finally, I walk toward home, the train trailing my thoughts, and marvel at the Japan that I live in. My quiet Yokohama suburb, the little stunted trees heavy with the yellow ripeness of peaches, the simple-yet-good-enough life I have. This is so unlike the fast and frenzied Japan I imagined before I came here. I love how these bits of ordinariness have come together—fragile trees, dying leaves, *gyudon*, *tendon*, tiny apartments, trains ... and me, the *gaijin* girl living among it.

Living in Japan

If the essays in this book inspire you to take your trip one step further and move to Japan, the following resources will be helpful. They are obviously selective, and if you search around on the Internet, you will find numerous other websites, books, and magazines for foreigners living in Japan.

Career Cross Japan

www.careercross.com/en/

One of the best sites on the Internet for Japan job seekers. With listings in both English and Japanese, it is searchable by industry, region, experience level, and English/Japanese language fluency. It also has a Career Advice section with information on composing cover letters and resumes, completing applications, and interview advice. A sleek, well-designed, and organized resource for job seekers.

Gaijinpot.com

www.gaijinpot.com

Along with job postings, this website has plenty of practical information, including apartment listings, book recommendations, and a classified section—need a baby walker or laptop? Check here.

Ganbatte Means Go For It! or ... How to Become an English Teacher in Japan

by Celeste Heiter

Written by the editor of *To Japan With Love*, this book will get you started on your life as an English teacher in Japan.

Japan Helpline

www.jhelp.com

Everyone needs assistance from time to time, and the *Japan Helpline* has all the essentials for getting the information you need, including emergency services, counseling agencies, links to government and professional services, and cultural assimilation resources.

Jim Breen's Japanese Page

www.csse.monash.edu.au/~jwb/japanese.html

A virtual emporium of links to Japanese resources from Japanese culture and history to esoteric Japanese software programs, and everything imaginable in between. With his lengthy residence in Japan, along with his background in computing and telecommunications, Jim Breen has assembled a mind-boggling and ever-growing collection of information on all things Japanese.

Kimi Information Center

www.kimiwillbe.com/index.html

An excellent resource for everything you need to make your move to Japan, including job listings, living accommodations, "sayonara" sales for furnishings, sightseeing guides, help links to information on immigration, getting a driver's license, problem solving, medical services, etc. Established in 1987, Kimi Information Center also has an actual office in the Tokyo.

Oscar Building, 8F
2-42-3 Ikebukuro
Toshima District
Tokyo
(03) 3986-1604

Train: Ikebukuro Station on the Yamanote Line.

Subway: Ikebukuro Station on the Marunouchi or Yurakucho Subway Line.

Epilogue

One writer treasures the opportunity to rediscover Japan

Will Raus rediscovers his homeland

I was born in Tokyo in 1989, went home to California with my parents when I was an infant, and finally had the chance to return to Japan when I was nine. It was my first time traveling outside the States, and because my father and I stayed in Kofu with his Japanese friends, Masaki and Yuko Shimizu and their five children, we enjoyed extraordinary hospitality and a much more in-depth experience than most tourists.

The Shimizu family knew all the best places to go, and throughout our seven-week stay, everything we did was unforgettable. At a Venetian glass exhibit at Lake Hakone, I got to make a blue glass pendant for my mom. At a hillside picnic feast in Kofu, I was as fascinated by the fireworks display as a group of teenage Japanese girls was of me. And on a trout fishing trip in the foothills of Mt. Fuji, we kept our catch, and Yuko cooked it up for dinner that night. It was amazing to see *taiko* drummers reenacting history on the beach at Wajima with their ferocious, pounding rhythms. And a highlight for any kid my age, especially since we had fast passes and got to skip to the head of the lines, we spent our last day at Tokyo Disneyland.

Ever since I landed back in the States, I dreamed of the day that I would be able to return to Japan and experience it all again. Nearly ten years later, my dad announced that this would be the summer it finally happened. He started researching airfare, contacted the Shimizu family, updated our passports, and that was that. Of course, the excitement of making travel plans conjured up fond memories of my first trip to Japan, but it also made me aware that it had been a long time since I was there, and that I was a very different person at nine than I was at eighteen. I had aged in both mind and body, as had our friends in Japan, and I knew that this would probably be a very different trip from my last one.

Sumo wrestler wearing a yukata *in Tokyo's Ryogoku neighborhood*

My first realization happened at the Shimizu home. Sure, it was the same house in Kofu that I knew so well, but where it had once been filled with the activity of the Shimizu children, it was now quieter and less crowded, since they had all grown up and moved away to college. Dinner conversations were about mature subjects, such as American politics, a hot topic at the time. Masaki and Yuko speak excellent English, and as they talked to my dad, I was now able to participate, which made me feel like one of the adults instead of just another kid in the room.

Another major moment happened during my visit to the Kamakura Daibutsu. This Buddha has a special significance in my life, because it is my mother's favorite place in the world, and she went down into the belly of the great statue while she was pregnant with me. When I visited the Daibutsu at age nine, I was absolutely astounded at and dwarfed by its majestic thirteen-and-a-half meter height. Knowing that it meant so much to my mother made it all the more impressive. On my most recent visit, I was again completely enthralled by it, but in a different way this time. As I entered the hollow statue, I marveled at how this gargantuan structure is constructed with eight ring-shaped bronze pieces, which are stacked atop one another and fused together. At eighteen, I had gone beyond simply being impressed by its size and beauty; I was able to appreciate it in a detailed and analytical way.

Most telling of all, however, was the road trip of over sixteen hundred kilometers that my dad and I took. The Shimizu handed us the keys to their brand new silver Peugeot convertible, and set us free to drive from Kofu to the remote island of Hokkaido. The result was an epic journey through the wilds of northern Japan. An excursion of this magnitude would never have been possible when I was nine. The trip involved hundreds of kilometers of driving per day, and there is only so much countryside a kid can take before boredom sets in.

At eighteen, though, I was old enough to have a driver's license, which meant that I could spell my dad from time to time, while relishing the freedom of the open road in a snazzy French sports car. Since I don't do much recreational driving in America, other than traveling back and forth to college classes, this was a highlight. The Japanese countryside is pretty incredible, especially when you're high above the ground on the elevated expressways. Then there was the car itself. It had all kinds of cool features, like automatic headlights that were activated when it got dark or we entered a tunnel (there were plenty of tunnels due to the mountainous terrain), and automatic windshield wipers that turned on when it started to rain. Once, when it was raining heavily, I actually hydroplaned the car, but I managed to keep calm enough to remain in control.

As we drove from Aomori to Ojiya to Kanazawa and back to Kofu, we saw things the average tourist rarely sees, and this includes many Japanese tourists: the parts of Japan that aren't all shiny and new, nor are they historic or cultural. This was a Japan where even rice doesn't grow, the signs don't bear a word of English, and where, in some places, the streets were completely deserted ... but oddly enough, were lined with well-stocked vending machines. On our first night we stayed in Aomori, near Lake Towada at the Oirase Green Hotel. Aomori is a rather small town, and we saw only three people while we were there. The streets were completely barren, and the only people we met were the owner of the inn and the couple who owned the restaurant where we ate that night. Given the generally crowded atmosphere of Japanese cities, it was amazing to be in this place where there was absolutely nobody around.

At our journey's end, I plunged headlong back into shiny Japan by way of an overnight trip from Kofu to Akihabara, Tokyo's "Electric Town." Since my first trip to Japan, I'd developed a growing fascination for Japanese *anime*, and now that I was in the motherland, I had my sights firmly fixed on a visit to this

anime mecca. In Japan's modern pop culture, Akihabara is *the* gathering place for the Japanese video game, electronics, and *anime* culture. It is where everything I love comes together, and was the only place I truly had my heart set on seeing, so I had to make it happen.

From Kofu, I hopped on an overnight bus headed to Tokyo, and rode the Yamanote Line to Akihabara. When I arrived, I stared up at the huge buildings adorned with billboards advertising the latest cell phones, the newest *anime* series, and the hottest video games. In shop after shop, there were wall-to-wall display cabinets filled with anime figurines, *manga* stores with bewildering arrays of Japanese comic books, and DVD shops with any *anime* title you could possibly want. My goal, though, was the figurine shops.

I really wanted a bunch of *anime* figurines to sit on my desktop back home. And without giving a moment's thought to my travel budget, I ended up spending four thousand yen on a set of figurines from one of my favorite video games. I also threw down fifty-eight hundred yen on the *Melty Blood: Act Cadenza* videogame, and was especially happy when I found out that it came with the game's soundtrack, which is top notch. It's a miracle I made it out of there for under ten thousand yen. Akihabara was everything I'd dreamed that it would be. I guess some things you just never outgrow.

Looking back, it's amazing how much I learned about myself on that trip. It was more than just a vacation, and my deeper interest in politics and Japanese culture made me finally feel like an adult. Japan will always be an integral part of my life, and once again, I find myself counting the days until I return, knowing that no matter how much I age, Japan will always be there, waiting for me to rediscover it.

Shinjuku District in Tokyo

Sunset on Tokyo Bay

Contributor Biographies, Credits, and Inde

Joeann Agarano
(Pg. 249)

Joeann Agarano is a twenty-eight-year-old Filipina who works as a process engineer. She is very thankful that her job has brought her to so many places. She has lived and worked in Japan, South Korea, Malaysia, and has traveled around Bangkok, Hong Kong, and the Philippines. Traveling has always been her one indulgence, enabling her to learn about the world and to grow from her experiences. Travel is what grounds her in the belief that there are many kinds of beauty in this world. Joeann is currently based in London.

http://ahundredaday.blogspot.com

Ali Al Saeed
(Pg. 57)

Ali Al Saeed is a best-selling, award-winning author from Bahrain. His debut novel, *QuixotiQ*, was published in 2004. For the past eight years, he has been writing for and contributing to several newspapers and magazines, including *Gulf Daily News*, *Bahrain Tribune*, *Bahrain This Month*, and *Clientele*.

ali.alsaeed@gmail.com

Sugu Althomsons
(Pg. 126, 169, 221)

Since 2006, Sugu Althomsons has worked in Hamamatsu, Japan, as a language teacher. He graduated from the University of Iowa with a degree in English, and is an aspiring writer, web developer, and English teacher. If you would like to read more stories and see more pictures, please visit his website.

www.gurusugu.com

Billy Applebaum
(Pg. 20)

He may have called New York, Atlanta, and Tokyo home, but Billy Applebaum—an adventurer at heart—knows that home can be wherever you lay your head. His adventures have taken him from the summit of Mt. Fuji to the picturesque beaches of Thailand, and his culinary experiences have been just as adventurous. He has eaten fish sperm, camel, and even man's best friend. Currently living in Tokyo, Billy felt an immediate connection to this unique part of the world. He believes people should always try to live outside their comfort zones, and not be afraid of things that make them a little nervous. To learn more about Billy's life in Japan, visit his blog.

www.tokyobilly.com

Philip Blazdell
(Pg. 55, 72)

Philip Blazdell has been traveling for the last fifteen years and would like to stop now, thank you very much. His travels began when he followed a girl in purple pajamas to Istanbul. He currently divides his time between his home in Middle England and San Francisco International Airport. When not bouncing around the world at eleven thousand

Brass ladles for cleansing and purifying at a temple fountain

meters, he can be contacted at the following email address.

nihon_news@yahoo.com

Chris Carlier
(Pg. 116)

Chris Carlier is a British bloke who loves living in Tokyo. His website is full of drinking stories, bar reviews, and booze news from Japan. Under the pen name, Rex Chesney, Chris wrote the humor book *Senseitional: Confessions of English Teachers in Japan.*

www.gaijintonic.com

Robert Carmack
(Pg. 22)

Robert "The Globetrotting Gourmet" Carmack grew up in America's Pacific Northwest and has lived abroad for some thirty-five years. With equal aplomb, he can arrange a rare tour of the Japanese emperor's private soy sauce brewery or prepare a Shan-style curry with the hill tribes of Thailand. Robert has written numerous cookbooks, including *Vietnamese Cooking* and *Thai Cooking*, and with his partner Morrison Polkinghorne co-hosts the blog *Quisine*. He holds the coveted Grand Diplôme from La Varenne, the prestigious cooking school in France, and has worked closely with preeminent food authority James Beard in New York. He offers gastronomic tours of Asia through his popular culinary websites.

www.globetrottinggourmet.com
www.asianfoodtours.com

Hauquan Chau
(Pg. 120)

Hauquan Chau lived and taught for over ten years in Japan. More of his Japan-related essays may be found on the websites *ThingsAsian, Glimpse Abroad, Verbsap*, and *Eclectica*. His essay, "Teaching the F-word," was featured in *The Best Creative Nonfiction, Vol. 2,* published by W.W. Norton.

Stefan Chiarantano
(Pg. 51, 98, 160)

A native of Toronto, Stefan Chiarantano has taught English as a second language in Taiwan and Japan. Japan inspired him to pen his travel experiences. His passions include making experimental films, black-and-white photography, traveling, books, and music.

Steve Cooper
(Pg. 24, 39, 216)

An Irishman living in Argentina, Steve Cooper was lucky enough to work for a year in Tokyo. Weekdays and nights were filled with food and karaoke; weekends with trips around the country. Japan rekindled his love for travel and, in no small part, is probably the reason that he has been traveling ever since.

Shane Cowlishaw
(Pg. 109)

Shane Cowlishaw is a Kiwi who spent the past five years lost overseas after heading away for a one-year OE in Korea. Since then he has lived in Japan and traveled extensively around Asia, and has resided in beautiful Vancouver, British Columbia, and the Canadian Rockies. He is now back in New Zealand, studying journalism post-grad in Wellington, and is looking forward to escaping again to new parts of the globe.

Mary Cook
(Pg. 96)

Mary Cook is a Nichiren Shoshu Buddhist and a UK-based writer and former newspaper reporter whose articles, poems, and short stories have appeared in numerous publications, both in print and online. She has worked as an overseas correspondent for the Tokyo-based publication *Hiragana Times*, and has also been a columnist for *InkSpotter News*.

Chloe Dalby
(Pg. 201)

Chloe Dalby is a student at Oberlin College in Ohio. She spent a summer studying calligraphy in Nara, and plans to spend her junior year back in Japan.

Liza Dalby
(Pg. 79)

Liza Dalby is a cultural anthropologist and author of *Geisha*, *Kimono: Fashioning Culture*, *The Tale of Murasaki*, and *East Wind Melts the Ice: A Memoir Through the Seasons*.

www.lizadalby.com
www.hiddenbuddhas.com

Annie Donwerth Chikamatsu
(Pg. 200)

Annie Donwerth Chikamatsu holds a master's degree in Applied Linguistics and has taught English university courses in the United States, Malaysia, and Japan. She also studied in France. She now spends time writing stories for children and adults, and writing about life in Japan for *Here and There Japan*.

www.hereandtherejapan.org

Sara Francis-Fujimura
(Pg. 56, 155, 163, 203)

Sara Francis-Fujimura is a freelance writer from Arizona who travels to Japan every summer to visit family with her husband Toshi, and Katie and Andy, their children. She writes regularly for *Raising Arizona Kids*, as well as many other local and national publications.

www.sarafujimura.com
http://momszone.org/blog_talk/

Landon Fry
(Pg. 59, 136)

Landon Fry is a freelance writer and student from Missouri. He is currently working on a series of short stories about his experiences as an exchange student in Japan. While in Japan he attended Kansai Gaidai University in Osaka.

landon.fry@gmail.com

Kimberly Fujioka
(Pg. 75, 102)

Kimberly Fujioka lived for six years in Japan's Gunma Prefecture. She has written children's stories and a book about the small mountain villages of central Japan. Kimberly founded a writing business, English Writing Help, which helps international scholars and researchers publish their academic and scientific writing. She currently lives with her husband and son in northern California.

www.englishwritinghelp.com

Kate Glynn
(Pg. 196)

Kate Glynn moved to Japan in 1980, and spent her childhood running around the streets of Yokohama and Tokyo. She returned to the United States for college, and trained as a helicopter pilot in the US Navy. She now manages to visit Yokohama between deployments. Kate currently lives in Texas with her husband Pat, a Marine Corps pilot, her son Keegan, and two Great Danes.

Arin Greenwood
(Pg. 61, 184, 190)

Arin Greenwood is a writer and lawyer who until recently was living in Saipan, a tropical island near Guam. She is currently between homes—if you can recommend anywhere great she should try living for a while, drop her a note! Arin writes about all kinds of interesting subjects: Japanese cowboys, Micronesian traditional canoers, people who keep chickens as pets, and more.

www.aringreenwood.com

Michael John Grist
(Pg. 166, 174)

Michael John Grist is a freelance fiction and non-fiction writer living in Tokyo. His website contains a wealth of information on the ruins (*haikyo*) of Japan, as well as links to his dark and weird short fiction.

www.bigreddot.net

Nick Hall
(Pg. 33, 39, 238)

Nick Hall lived in Japan for five years and now lives in London, where he works as a web producer. He still contributes articles on Japanese travel, food, and culture to publications including *Kansai Time Out*, *Kansai Scene*, and *Japanzine*, and has his own Japan-themed website *Big On Japan*.

www.bigonjapan.com

Jennifer Huber
(Pg. 118, 172, 211, 246)

Jennifer Huber spent a month in Japan's Shizuoka and Yamanashi Prefectures as part of Rotary Foundation International's Group Study Exchange

Program, a cultural and homestay program for young professionals. She lives in Florida, works in the tourism industry, and writes to support her traveling habit. Her musings about life are blogged at *Quirky Kitsch Girl's View.*

www.quirkykitschgirl.com

Rie Imanaka
(Pg. 50)

Rie Imanaka is a writer from Shinagawa District in Tokyo. Her dream is to become a translator and writer of teen books. She likes reading, dancing, singing, and music. Rie is also a musician who plays the piano, and sings and dances when she thinks no one is around.

Alice Jackson
(Pg. 149)

Alice Jackson grew up in Sidney, Ohio, where she began writing to pen pals in Japan, England, and India, which sparked her interest in travel. While teaching in Tokyo, she met her husband John, and together they have three grown children. A former teacher and school principal, Alice works for the Napa Valley Unified School District as a videographer and producer of programs for Napa's public access TV station. She has traveled to Mexico, Canada, Fiji, Jamaica, Guam, Russia, China, Thailand, Egypt, Eastern Europe, Scandinavia, and Vietnam, and has been back to Japan six times since 1960.

Joyce Jemison
(Pg. 213, 217, 247)

A college student majoring in English, Joyce Jemison hopes to minor in Japanese. She is in love with Japan and is eagerly awaiting the opportunity to visit again. Her hobbies include reading and watching *anime.* She currently lives with her parents in Napa, California.

Tim Kaiser
(Pg. 53)

Timothy Kaiser grew up in western Canada. Drawn to Asia in 1989, he now makes Hong Kong his home. He has won writing awards in several countries, and in 2003, Chameleon Press published *Food Court,* a collection of his poetry.

Josh Krist
(Pg. 63)

Josh Krist worked for a research center just outside of Kyoto, and is now a freelance travel, technology, and alcohol writer who lives in San Francisco. He co-authored *San Francisco: The Unknown City,* a guidebook from Arsenal Pulp Press, and has written about Vietnam, the French Caribbean, Arizona, Mexico, and Thailand for the Lonely Planet guidebooks and website.

Dwayne Lawler
(Pg. 74)

Australian actor Dwayne Lawler was born in Sydney. His most recent roles include *Tokyo Vampire* at the Riant Theatre in New York and *Macbeth* at the New National Theatre in Tokyo. He is the founder of Rising Sun Theatre and the Director of the Tokyo Fringe Festival.

www.TokyoVampire.com

Diana Lee
(Pg. 176)

Originally from San Francisco, Diana Lee enjoys traveling around the world. She has lived and worked in China and Cameroon as a high school and university instructor. Now residing in Japan, she runs a cram school and works as a writer for Mathaba News Network. Diana also operates a website which features her writings on world travel and current trends focusing on Japan as the main exporter of Asian culture. Her other works have appeared in anthologies, magazines, and e-zines. As a pet lover, nature admirer, and a free thinker, she embraces life with honesty and enthusiasm.

http://uniorb.com/
www.mathaba.net/authors/lee/

Frank Lev
(Pg. 105, 124, 134, 158, 225)

Frank Lev has been teaching English around the world since 1993. He is currently living in Seoul, South Korea. He has also lived and taught in Japan, Taiwan, Ecuador, and the San Francisco Bay Area. When he isn't teaching, he can be found playing street jazz, writing, meditating, or hanging out in museums.

Leza Lowitz
(Pg. 100)

Leza Lowitz is an award-winning poet, translator, and author of over fifteen books, many about Japan. Her travel writing has appeared in *An Inn Near Kyoto, Expat, They Only Laughed Later*, and many other anthologies. She currently owns and operates Sun & Moon Yoga in Tokyo, where she lives with her Japanese husband, young son, and wild *ninja* dog.

www.lezalowitz.com
http://sunandmoon.jp/

Karryn Miller
(Pg. 95)

Karryn Miller is a freelance writer, yoga teacher, and photographer. She has lived in both South Korea and Japan and traveled extensively throughout Southeast Asia. Her stories and photos have appeared in a number of magazines and books including *Condé Nast Traveler*, *Yoga Journal*, and *The Japan Times*.

Barbara Mori
(Pg. 80)

Barbara Mori is a professor of sociology at Cal Poly in San Luis Obispo, California. She lived in Ohara for two years while doing her dissertation research, taking the bus into Kyoto every day.

http://cla.calpoly.edu/~bmori

Scott Nesbitt
(Pg. 85, 246)

Scott Nesbitt, a writer based in Toronto, Canada, spends a good chunk of his day penning various pieces for corporate clients. While he also blogs and contributes to a variety of print and online publications, he has yet to snag that elusive book contract.

Jennifer O'Bryan
(Pg. 40, 150, 194, 199)

During her time in Japan, Jennifer O'Bryan found herself drawn to the country's eclectic food scene, from rooftop beer gardens to an Amish café. She was also fascinated by Japan's eccentricities, as she shopped for fake sushi and visited a shop where customers come to pet and feed cats.

Tim Patterson
(Pg. 141, 188)

Tim Patterson is an editor at *Matador Network*, an online community for passionate travelers. He lived for two years in Hokkaido, and now splits his time between Vermont and Cambodia.

www.matadornetwork.com/

Heather Poppink
(Pg. 198)

A lifelong Japanophile, Heather Poppink taught English for one year at a high school in Shiga Prefecture, and was a stay-at-home mother in Tokyo for two years. She has a BA in psychology and currently leads the contract negotiation team at a Fortune 500 financial services company. She lives in Farmington Hills, Michigan, with her husband, three children, and miniature dachshund.

Will Raus
(Pg. 71, 131, 234, 239, 244, 253)

Will Raus was born in Tokyo and now lives in California's Napa Valley. He returned for a six-week visit to Japan at age nine, and again at age eighteen. He is a black belt in taekwondo, and as a student at Sonoma State University, he is majoring in Computer Science with a minor in Voice. One of his great interests is Japanese animation, and he writes a weblog called *ThingsAnime* for *ThingsAsian*.

www.thingsasian.com/blogs

Geoff Reid
(Pg. 128)

Geoff Reid lived and worked in Asia as a participant on The Japan Exchange and Teaching Program (JET). After returning to Canada, he completed a graduate degree and served as Senior JET Program Coordinator at the Embassy of Japan. He is currently working as a policy analyst for the Canadian government.

Jessica Renslow
(Pg. 89)

Jessica Renslow is from Gary, Indiana. In 2003, she received a BA in Japanese. Then she ran away to Pippu on Japan's Hokkaido Island for three years. She is the author of *The Guerilla Guide: Surviving Japanese*

Primary Schools. Currently, she lives in Hollywood, California, where *anime* pays her bills. She recently finished translating *Digimon Data Squad*, and has been the production coordinator for *Bleach, Naruto, Blue Dragon*, and more.

www.hajet.org/publications/
www.almostfairytalesfilms.com/EN.html

Mark Schilling
(Pg. 151)

Born in Zanesville, Ohio, in 1949, Mark Schilling has been living in Tokyo since 1975. He is currently Japan correspondent for *Variety* and senior film critic for *The Japan Times*. Book publications include *The Encyclopedia of Japanese Pop Culture, The Yakuza Movie Book: A Guide to Japanese Gangster Films*, and *No Borders, No Limits: Nikkatsu Action Cinema.*

http://japanesemovies.homestead.com/

Johannes Schönherr
(Pg. 87, 244)

Johannes Schönherr is a German freelance writer and film show organizer who has been living in Japan since 2003. His publications include *Trashfilm Roadshows*, from Headpress, as well as many articles in publications and websites such as *Kansai Time Out, Japan Visitor*, and *Midnight Eye.*

Paul Sharp
(Pg. 139, 235)

Paul Sharp spent five years making road trips around Japan. Now living in Canada, he survives as an artist and T-shirt designer. You can see his work at the website *SemiQuestion.*

www.semiquestion.com

Elizabeth Sharpe
(Pg. 178, 215, 246)

Elizabeth Sharpe lives in Seattle, Washington, where she works as a writer and writing teacher. Still, her heart remains in Asia, where she lived for four years teaching English to students in Nepal and Japan.

http://elizabethsharpe.blogspot.com/

Sarah Skilton
(Pg. 41)

Sarah Skilton currently lives in Los Angeles with her husband Joe, and blogs for a Japanese-American business company, Japanizmo.

www.japanizmo.com

Kena Sosa
(Pg. 65, 143)

The very first time Kena Sosa set foot on a plane, she was on her way to Japan as an exchange student at the age of nineteen. She never imagined that this trip would be a defining moment for her future. From her adventures in teaching English to sleeping under a *kotatsu*, years later she still has so many stories to tell. Her adventures have been read in *Appleseeds*, *ESL*, and *Multicultural Review*, as well as the guidebook *The V!VA List Latin America*. She is currently collaborating with *ChildArt*, a quarterly magazine.

www.kenasosa.com

Renée Suen
(Pg. 18, 41)

Renée Suen is a native of Canada. Having traveled abroad to various Asian countries, she has had the opportunity for numerous gastronomic explorations. Of her many trips, Japan is always a highlight. Currently finishing her graduate studies in Cardiovascular Sciences at the University of Toronto, Renée loves the science behind the food she eats, and enjoys experimenting with both traditional and nouveau culinary movements. She hopes to return to Tokyo for further sensory overload.

www.tasteto.com
www.flickr.com/photos/sifu_renka/

Jacqueline Taylor
(Pg. 30)

Jacqueline Taylor is an Australian travel television producer and freelance travel print journalist. Despite brushes with severe Indian cholera and knife-wielding Japanese *fugu* chefs, she is nevertheless devoted to traveling, eager to eat and experience whatever the world next sends her way.

www.jactaylor.com

Catherine Tully
(Pg. 35, 222)

Catherine Tully is a writer, photographer, and educator who lived and worked in Japan for three years. She writes about travel, the arts, and numerous other subjects.

www.catherinetully.com
www.freelance-zone.com

Cobus van Staden
(Pg. 28)

Cobus van Staden is from South Africa. He has lived in Japan for six years and is busy with a PhD about *anime* and how movies are understood. He has recently finished his own movie, the feature film *Fluorescent*. He lives in Nagoya.

Joe Wallace
(Pg. 233, 247)

Joe Wallace is a freelance writer based in Chicago. He lived in Japan for three years and has been hooked on Japanese culture ever since. Wallace writes travel pieces about a variety of destinations, including Iceland, Korea, and Norway. He is editor and webmaster of *Freelance-Zone*, his blog about the freelance life.

www.freelance-zone.com

Nolan Webb
(Pg. 186, 232, 233)

In their letters from pre-Tiananmen Beijing, the Canadian writer Wayne Edmonstone, along with his wife

Mary Jane, sparked Nolan Webb's fascination with Asia. After many years abroad in Japan and Ecuador, Nolan now lives in Vancouver, British Columbia, with his wife Mizuho.

nolanwebb@yahoo.com

Ed Wetschler
(Pg. 223)

Associate editor of *Caribbean Escapes* and associate editor and columnist at *Everett Potter's Travel Report*, Ed Wetschler has written for *The New York Times*, *Brides.com*, *Delta Sky*, and other publications. When he resigned as an editor-in-chief at one of the Hearst magazines, he and his wife bought a house and decorated it with artworks from Japan, where his wife spent much of her childhood.

www.everettpotter.com

Merry White
(Pg. 32)

Merry White is professor of anthropology at Boston University, and a specialist in modern Japan, food studies, and social change in East Asia. She has published books on teenagers and popular culture in Japan and on families and social policy, as well as other works on women and globalization. She is also the author of two cookbooks. She is currently writing a book on the social history of coffee and the café in Japan.

Quintin Winks
(Pg. 181)

Quintin Winks is a freelance writer, photographer, and contradiction. His need to write is constantly threatened by his inability to sit still, making him the fidgety subject of librarians' disapproval. He resolves this struggle with long stints traveling overseas, punctuated by tufts of gray hair on deadline.

http://westcoastwindow.blogspot.com

Alan Wiren
(Pg. 82, 137)

Alan Wiren has been living and working as a freelance writer in the Far East for the past twenty years. He is a regular contributor to *Kansai Time Out* and *Kansai Scene* magazines, and the website *Japan Visitor*. He and his wife currently make their home in Osaka.

http://www2.gol.com/users/miandal/

Alice Yamada
(Pg. 26, 27, 42, 77)

Alice was born and raised in Japan under the close supervision of her food-loving grandparents. Every year since moving to the States, she travels back to Japan in February for *fugu* season, and upon joining the coolest biotech company in California, she recently added an annual November trip to enjoy *matsutake* season. Alice combines her molecular biology expertise with her love of cooking. To compensate for her gastronomical debauchery, she fights in judo tournaments and runs marathons.

www.epicureandebauchery.blogspot.com/

Helen Yee
(Pg. 15, 37)

Helen Yee is a freelance writer who loves to eat. She has feasted her way through over twenty different countries, but still considers Japan her favorite. When she's not eating, she's probably planning her next meal—sometimes both at once. A keen photographer, Helen shares all her delicious epicurean adventures on her blog, *Grab Your Fork.* She still doesn't like *natto.*

http://grabyourfork.blogspot.com

Jasmin Young
(Pg. 123, 157)

Jasmin Young is a freelance writer and illustrator who has lived in Japan since 1997. She obtained her Doctorate of Psychology from Southern California University's long distance learning program. Jasmin lives outside the bustle of the big city of Tokyo, in a quaint beach town, where the ocean inspires the themes in her artwork. She is the English coordinator and columnist for the *Sotobou Shimbun* newspaper. Recently married to a Japanese citizen, Jasmin has made the amazing culture that is Japan her permanent home away from home.

www.JasminDesigns.com
www.DrJasminsEnglish.com

CREDITS

"Alice Yamada eats *unagi* on memory lane in Nagoya" reprinted in an edited and updated form from "Horai: The Origins of Hitsumabushi," originally published at *My Epicurean Debauchery* (http://epicureandebauchery.blogspot.com/). Reprinted by permission of the author. Copyright © 2005 by Alice Yamada.

"Alice Yamada follows her bliss in Kyoto" reprinted in an edited and updated form from "Spa and Kaiseki: The Ultimate Japanese Luxury," originally published at *My Epicurean Debauchery* (http://epicureandebauchery.blogspot.com/). Reprinted by permission of the author. Copyright © 2005 by Alice Yamada.

"Alice Yamada loves being a tempura bar fly in Nagoya" reprinted in an edited and updated form from "Bar Fly in Japan: Yaegaki, Part 1," originally published at *My Epicurean Debauchery* (http://epicureandebauchery.blogspot.com/). Reprinted by permission of the author. Copyright © 2005 by Alice Yamada.

Credits

"Arin Greenwood wanders among old farmhouses in Osaka" reprinted in an edited and updated form from "Though the Autumn Days Were Short, the Memories Will Be Lifelong," originally published in *The Christian Science Monitor*. Reprinted by permission of the author. Copyright © 2006 by Arin Greenwood.

"Celeste Heiter commits chopsticks taboo" reprinted in an edited and updated form from "Chopsticks Taboo," originally published in *Vignettes of Japan* (ThingsAsian Press). Reprinted by permission of the author. Copyright © 2003 by Celeste Heiter.

"Celeste Heiter experiences a lodging crisis in Aizu Wakamatsu" reprinted in an edited and updated form from "Onegaishimasu," originally published in *Vignettes of Japan* (ThingsAsian Press). Reprinted by permission of the author. Copyright © 2003 by Celeste Heiter.

"Celeste Heiter hungers for the hidden world of *ramen*" reprinted in an edited and updated form from "Film Review: *Tampopo*," originally published at *ThingsAsian* (www.thingsasian.com). Reprinted by permission of the author. Copyright © 2002 by Celeste Heiter.

"Celeste Heiter is dazzled by fire flowers in Tokyo" reprinted in an edited and updated form from "Hanabi," originally published in *Vignettes of Japan* (ThingsAsian Press). Reprinted by permission of the author. Copyright © 2003 by Celeste Heiter.

"Celeste Heiter pictures herself trading places in Wajima" reprinted in an edited and updated form from "Wajima," originally published in *Vignettes of Japan* (ThingsAsian Press). Reprinted by permission of the author. Copyright © 2003 by Celeste Heiter.

"Celeste Heiter sees everything and nothing in Kyoto" reprinted in an edited and updated form from "Ryoanji," originally published in *Vignettes of Japan* (ThingsAsian Press). Reprinted by permission of the author. Copyright © 2003 by Celeste Heiter.

"Celeste Heiter walks away from a Buddhist temple in Kanazawa" reprinted in an edited and updated form from "Kanazawa," originally published in *Vignettes of Japan* (ThingsAsian Press). Reprinted by permission of the author. Copyright © 2003 by Celeste Heiter.

"Frank Lev comes face to face with a sumo wrestler in Osaka" reprinted in an edited and updated form from "Sumo," originally published at *ThingsAsian* (www.thingsasian.com). Reprinted by permission of the author. Copyright © 2001 by Frank Lev.

"Frank Lev commits petty larceny on Mikimoto Island" reprinted in an edited and updated form from "Mikimoto Island," originally published at *ThingsAsian* (www.thingsasian.com). Reprinted by permission of the author. Copyright © 2001 by Frank Lev.

"Frank Lev takes his cue from the wavers of Japan" reprinted in an edited and updated form from "Wavers," originally published at *ThingsAsian* (www.thingsasian.com). Reprinted by permission of the author. Copyright © 2001 by Frank Lev.

"Frank Lev takes a whack at Zen meditation in Kyoto" reprinted in an edited and updated form from "Zen," originally published at *ThingsAsian* (www.thingsasian.com/). Reprinted by permission of the author. Copyright © 2001 by Frank Lev.

"Frank Lev takes you out to the ballgame in Nagoya" reprinted in an edited and updated form from "Baseball," originally published at *ThingsAsian* (www.thingsasian.com). Reprinted by permission of the author. Copyright © 2001 by Frank Lev.

"Hauquan Chau braves Wajima's 'Night of the Mikoshi'" reprinted in an edited and updated form from "The Night of the Mikoshis," originally published at *ThingsAsian* (www.thingsasian.com). Reprinted by permission of the author. Copyright © 2004 by Hauquan Chau.

"Liza Dalby fictionalizes her favorite garden in Kyoto" reprinted from *Hidden Buddhas* (Stone Bridge Press). Reprinted by permission of the author. Copyright © 2009 by Liza Dalby.

"Michael John Grist trespasses in Izu-Nagaoka" reprinted in an edited and updated form from "Sports World Haikyo, Izu," originally published at *Michael John Grist: A Writer in Tokyo* (www.michaeljohngrist.com). Reprinted by permission of the author. Copyright © 2008 by Michael John Grist.

"Nolan Webb follows the road less traveled in the Kyushu Highlands" reprinted in an edited and updated form from "Roads Not Taken," originally published at *ThingsAsian* (www.thingsasian.com). Reprinted by permission of the author. Copyright © 2003 by Nolan Webb.

"Philip Blazdell perches on the roof of Japan in Nagano" reprinted in an edited and updated form from "Nagano, Japan: The Spiritual Tourist," originally published at *ThingsAsian* (www.thingsasian.com). Reprinted by permission of the author. Copyright © 2002 by Philip Blazdell.

"Philip Blazdell chooses his favorite temples in Kamakura" reprinted in an edited and updated form from "Kamakura," originally published at *ThingsAsian* (www.thingsasian.com. Reprinted by permission of the author. Copyright © 2002 by Philip Blazdell.

"Rie Imanaka drifts through Tokyo's floating world" reprinted in an edited and updated form from "Yakatabune: A Summer Evening Aboard a Japanese Pleasure Boat," originally published at *ThingsAsian* (www.thingsasian.com). Reprinted by permission of the author. Copyright © 2002 by Rie Imanaka.

"Steve Cooper revels in *ramen* in Toyama" reprinted in an edited and updated form from "Maratakaya," originally published at *Zarzamora* (http://zarzamora.blogspot.com). Reprinted by permission of the author. Copyright © 2005 by Steve Cooper.

"Will Raus discovers the green that never ends on a train out of Tokyo" reprinted in an edited and updated form from "Japan: The Green That Never Ends," originally published at *ThingsAsian* (www.thingsasian.com). Reprinted by permission of the author. Copyright © 2002 by Will Raus.

ACKNOWLEDGMENTS

Looking back at how Japan has shaped my life, I couldn't have been more honored and excited when Albert Wen, the publisher at ThingsAsian Press, asked me to edit *To Japan With Love.* I would like to express my sincere appreciation for this amazing opportunity and for his faith in my ability to make it happen. In addition, I would like to convey my heartfelt gratitude to Kim Fay, the editor of the To Asia With Love guidebook series, for her unflagging dedication to excellence. I would also like to thank the many contributors for their generosity of time and talent, especially my son Will, and my friends Robert George, Dwayne Lawler, and Alice Jackson for taking time out of their busy lives to indulge my wish to include them in this guide. Finally, I express my thanks to the people of Japan for being the inspiring people that they are.

INDEX

Editor and Photographer Biographies

Celeste Heiter

With her lifelong love of Japan, its people and its culture, Celeste Heiter believes that she may have been Japanese in a previous incarnation. In this lifetime, however, Celeste was born in Mobile, Alabama, where she earned a bachelor's degree in Art and English from the University of South Alabama. Inspired by an enduring dream to visit the Great Buddha at Kamakura, she moved to Tokyo in 1988, and spent two years teaching English conversation. Celeste now makes her home in California's beautiful Napa Valley, with the most treasured souvenir of her life in Japan: her son Will, who was born during her stay in Tokyo. She is the author of *Vignettes of Japan*, *Ganbatte Means Go For It*, *Five Seven Five*, and *The Sushi Book*. Please visit *Chopstick Cinema*, Celeste's daily blog about her adventures in Asian food and film.

www.chopstickcinema.com

Robert George

During his eighteen-year residence in Japan, Robert George worked in film and video production while traveling extensively throughout Asia honing his craft as an international travel photographer. Robert returned to the States in 1999 and now lives in Sacramento with his wife Mayumi and his son Alex, but continues to travel to Asia for his work.

To Asia With Love Series

To Vietnam With Love
A Travel Guide for the Connoisseur
Edited & with contributions by Kim Fay
Photographs by Julie Fay Ashborn

To Thailand With Love
A Travel Guide for the Connoisseur
Edited & with contributions by Joe Cummings
Photographs by Marc Schultz

To Cambodia With Love
A Travel Guide for the Connoisseur
Edited & with contributions by Andy Brouwer
Photographs by Tewfic El-Sawy

To Myanmar With Love
A Travel Guide for the Connoisseur
Edited & with contributions by Morgan Edwardson
Photographs by Steve Goodman

To Shanghai With Love
A Travel Guide for the Connoisseur
Edited & with contributions by Crystyl Mo
Photographs by Coca Dai

To North India With Love
A Travel Guide for the Connoisseur
Edited & with contributions by Nabanita Dutt
Photographs by Nana Chen

To Japan With Love
A Travel Guide for the Connoisseur
Edited & with contributions by Celeste Heiter
Photographs by Robert George

To Nepal With Love
A Travel Guide for the Connoisseur
Edited & with contributions by Cristi Hegranes
Photographs by Kraig Lieb

For more information, visit www.toasiawithlove.com